Magadan

Sea of Okhotsk

• Noril'sk

E D S O C I A L I S T R E P U B L I C

R. Lena

R. Yenisey

Khabarovsk

Irkutsk •

Vladivostok

1 – ESTONIAN SSR

2 – LATVIAN SSR

3 – LITHUANIAN SSR

4 – BELORUSSIAN SSR

5 – UKRAINIAN SSR

6 – MOLDAVIAN SSR

7 – GEORGIAN SSR

8 – AZERBAIDJAN SSR

9 – ARMENIAN SSR

10 – TADJIK SSR

11 – KIRGHIZ SSR

Also by Alec Nove

The Soviet Economic System
The Soviet Middle East (with J. A. Newth)
Was Stalin Really Necessary?
Economic History of the USSR

Stalinism and After

Alec Nove

Professor of Economics and Director of the Institute of Soviet and
East European Studies, University of Glasgow

London
GEORGE ALLEN & UNWIN
Boston   Sydney

George Allen & Unwin (Publishers) Ltd,
40 Museum Street, London WC1A 1LU, UK

George Allen & Unwin (Publishers) Ltd,
Park Lane, Hemel Hempstead, Herts HP2 4TE, UK

Allen & Unwin Inc.,
9 Winchester Terrace, Winchester, Mass 01890, USA

George Allen & Unwin Australia Pty Ltd,
8 Napier Street, North Sydney, NSW 2060, Australia

First published in 1975
Third impression 1979
Second edition 1981

British Library Cataloguing in Publication Data

Nove, Alec
    Stalinism and after. – 2nd ed.
1. Russia – History – 1917–   2. Russia –
Politics and government – 1917–
I. Title
947.084   DK266

ISBN 0–04–320144–X

Library of Congress Cataloging in Publication Data

Nove, Alec
    Stalinism and after.
Bibliography: p.
Includes index.
1. Communism—Soviet Union—History. I. Title.
HX313.N65 1981   947.084′2   81–8058
ISBN 0–04–320144–X (pbk.)   AACR2

Printed in Great Britain
in 10 pt Baskerville type
by Biddles Ltd, Guildford, Surrey

Preface

The object of this book is to explain how Stalinism came to be, what was its nature, how it was modified after the despot's death and what kind of system is now presided over by Leonid Brezhnev. To this end I concentrate on causes and trends rather than on detail. If you wish to know the date at which Stalin arrived at Tsaritsyn, the text of any paragraph of the Constitution or the output of steel in 1970, this is not the book for you. I do not wish to imply that these things are unimportant, and you will find in the list of recommended reading a number of books which deal with them. In fact, it is my hope that you will be sufficiently interested in this dramatic and eventful period to wish to read much more about it.

This is not a biography of Stalin, of Khrushchev or of Brezhnev. We are concerned with them, of course, but as political men. We are concerned also with another and vital question: what difference did their personalities make? A great revolution, carried out in the name of equality, freedom and justice, turned into Stalin-despotism. Why? How? Is this explicable primarily in terms of Russia's historical heritage, or the Russian revolution and its isolation in a hostile environment, or was it the result of the logic of Leninism, the seizure of power by a Marxist party in a backward peasant country? These are impersonal explanations. Do they miss out the vital factor of Stalin's peculiar personality? Similarly, we may ask ourselves whether the attempt by Khrushchev to demolish the Stalin myth and to alter course was a personal aberration; we should note the scope of 'destalinisation', and also of the partial return to more repressive methods under Brezhnev. These have been combined with a vigorous and flexible search for better relations with the West, while exchanging angry polemics with Russia's erstwhile Chinese allies. What do Brezhnev and his comrades think they are doing, what aims are they pursuing? These seem to me to be questions of importance and interest.

The book is almost without statistical tables and wholly without footnotes. The reader may be assured that statements of fact or citations are accurate, to the best of my ability. Hypotheses and interpretations are clearly indicated as such. In some degree the interpretation is personal, being influenced not only by the author's family background and reading but also by observations and conversations on numerous visits to the Soviet Union. I realise that academic histories are usually written in the third person. None the less, the occasional injection of personal reminiscences and opinions seem to me to do more good than harm. In the Soviet Union in particular, documentary and written evidence is sometimes hard to come by and can be misleading, and evidence based on personal experience may be usefully cited to highlight certain events and to justify interpretations. To take one example, not a single Soviet source has ever mentioned that there were riots in Tbilisi in the summer of 1956, yet these riots certainly occurred, and I know this because of what I heard and saw in Tbilisi shortly afterwards.

Needless to say, there is scope for a variety of different views. Some regard the USSR as a socialist society, with flaws no doubt, but socialist. The Chinese in describing the USSR use such words as 'revisionist social-imperialist' (indeed, in a radio transcript I see the words 'diabolical social-imperialists'), and the leaders as 'fascists' and 'new tsars'. Some old cold-warriors see the USSR as pursuing world revolution and world conquest in the name of Marxism-Leninism. Another school of thought emphasises the nationalist and great-power aspect of Soviet policy, and considers the ideological pretensions to be mere verbiage. Even among groups calling themselves Trotskyists there are disputes about the nature of the Soviet Union. I hope that this book will help you, the readers, to pick your way among these various interpretations. It is not my task to ram any one of them down your throats, though you will observe that I do have my own views. We may be confident that historians and socialist thinkers will be discussing the fate of the Russian revolution for a hundred years or more, if the human race survives that long.

It is customary to express thanks in the preface for the advice of colleagues, and I usually do so gratefully. This work, however, was largely written on a Hebridean island where I had no advice, which may be my bad luck or not, as the case may be. I must, however, thank Mita Kanerova for checking dates and quotations, and Maisie Wotherspoon and Elizabeth Hunter for deciphering my handwriting.

Contents

Chapter 1

Genesis

The Russian Political Tradition

Stalin was born in Gori, Georgia, in 1879, and his name was Djugashvili. The pseudonym Stalin was adopted to suggest 'steel', and proved to be well chosen. His early education was in a religious seminary. No doubt these facts are an important element in Stalin's personal psychology, and no doubt this personal psychology played its role in Russia's and the world's twentieth-century history. Yet it is perhaps even more useful to see him as a *Russian* leader, heir to a Russian tradition and meeting Russian needs in ways which had deep Russian roots. This is not the only such case in European history. One has only to remember Napoleon, a very French emperor who was nevertheless a Corsican.

In fact it is part of the Russian tradition that she is ruled by foreigners. *The legend of the foundation of the Russian state* in the tenth century is as follows. After a period of chaos, the notables met and decided to write to a Varangian (Viking) prince, saying: 'Our lands are vast and bountiful, but there is no order in them. Come and rule over us.' Then came Rurik, the founder of the dynasty, and so Russia (or Rus') was born. No doubt it can be argued that this did not happen so, that Vikings needed no invitation to come and plunder and colonise. But the existence and durability of the legend is significant. In my young days it was known by every Russian schoolboy.

Absolute rule by one called in to establish order in a disorderly land, was one element of the tradition. The absolutist tradition was doubtless reinforced by Russia's adherence to the Orthodox Church, and therefore Byzantine influence prevailed, while links with the Catholic western Slavs were weakened. Another element was provided by the *Tartar conquest*, which brought Russians into close touch with an initially successful Oriental despotism, and underlined the vulnerability of the Russian lands (by then again disunited). The frontiers to the east, west and south were open, there were no natural barriers, Russia was backward and relatively weak. Despotic and ruthless Muscovite princes succeeded in the end in overthrowing the Tartar yoke, and gradually absorbed or conquered rival princes. They also subdued the westward-looking trading city-states of Novgorod and Pskov, which had close links with the German Hanseatic league towns. Muscovy, the easternmost and most Tartar-influenced of the principalities, became the focus-point of Russian unity. For a long time Muscovy remained weak and vulnerable, and in 1571 Tartar slave-raiders burnt most of Moscow, and Polish armies occupied the Kremlin itself in 1610–12.

In other European countries, unity was disrupted by struggles between the powerful feudal nobility and the king. In Russia such a struggle was nipped in the bud by Ivan the Terrible, who destroyed much of the nobility and separated the rest from what might have become territorial power-bases. It is not for nothing that Stalin declared this bloodthirsty monarch to have been a great statesman, remarking in an unpublished aside that he (Ivan) should have spent less time praying and more in destroying the enemies of the state, a mistake Stalin himself never committed. The survivors of the old aristocracy became gradually merged in a class of *service gentry* (*dvoryanstvo*), who owed their entire position and status to the Tsar. Peter the Great, moderniser of Russia, made the gentry families serve the state (i.e. himself) for life, in a civil and military service of fourteen ranks. True, the compulsion to serve was dropped in 1762, but the gentry had little else they could do, except vegetate on their estates. The great Russian nineteenth-century poet, Pushkin, remarked that by west European standards Russia had no aristocracy, since all depended on rank and rank depended on the monarch, who could and did promote men from the lower orders. This, he pointed out, led to 'cowardly slavishness' towards authority.

Slavishness of a different kind was developed among the bulk of the people, the peasants, by the institution of *serfdom*. Its principal purpose was to compel the peasants to serve the servants of the Tsar. This is why Peter the Great, uneasily aware of the abuses of serfdom, found it necessary to strengthen it. It was part of the pattern of the *universal service state*, believed by Peter to be necessary for Russia to raise itself to great-power status. This dominance of state and state-defined purposes over society was a major feature of Russian history.

Of course it is to be found in some degree elsewhere too: Frederick's Prussia and Louis xiv's France are but two examples. But nowhere else was the state's dominance so complete, nowhere did it last so long. In a very real sense, Stalin's Russia is a continuance of this long tradition.

Chekhov, another great writer, once said: 'We [i.e. the Russians] must squeeze the slave out of ourselves drop by drop'. The readiness of many to accept Stalinist despotism is to be explained among other reasons by this deeply-rooted national characteristic.

The Renaissance passed Russia by. Until the nineteenth century Russian culture was as backward as the way of life of the bulk of her people. Hardly anything was written which can be read with pleasure today. Then, with dramatic suddenness came the flowering of Russian literature, which made it one of the world's finest: Pushkin, Lermontov, Gogol, Tolstoy, Dostoevsky, Turgenev, Chekhov. With them there came on the scene that most Russian of phenomena, the *intelligentsia*. Some of them were of the gentry, conscience-stricken at the sight of serfdom, privilege, oppression. Some rose from below, were sons of village priests, merchants, even ex-serfs. Indeed Lenin's grandfather had been a serf, while his father became an educational official and rose in the civil service to reach the status of hereditary gentleman. The *intelligentsia* combined in themselves a number of features: they were opposed to the Tsarist system, but this did not lead most of them to harbour any sympathy for Western liberalism. On the contrary, they disliked the 'merchant' culture of western Europe, and dreamt of finding some new Russian road. Some believed that the old Russian peasant communal traditions pointed the way, others like Lenin thought that Russian capitalism was destroying the old institutions, though he hoped to move rapidly to socialism. Some were deeply conservative, idealising the era before Peter the Great's enforced 'Europeanisation' of Russia. Others were revolutionaries of many hues. They had no responsibility for doing anything, so they formed factions and argued endlessly. Among them there were some who believed that conspiracy and terrorism were the best weapons to use, since the inert and ignorant people would not listen to propaganda. Tsar Alexander ii was assassinated by these terrorists in 1881, and his successor, Alexander iii, was to have been assassinated too, but the conspirators were arrested and executed, Lenin's elder brother among them. These *intelligentsia*-terrorists were a remarkable breed, men devoted to raising up the people, ready to die for their beliefs, yet singularly lacking in either political effectiveness or any appeal to the people on whose behalf they fought and suffered.

No wonder Lenin, in his own doctrine, emphasised organisation and conspiracy, had little illusion about or use for spontaneous mass action. It is said, though with little evidence, that he reacted to his brother's death with the words: 'We will go another way'. Individual terrorism, the blowing up of tsars and ministers, was not his road. We will be discussing in some detail very soon the road he did take.

Lenin, though himself a man with a distinguished university record, had little patience with the Russian *intelligentsia*. They were ineffective, they talked too much, they did not understand power and politics, they had namby-pamby scruples. Yet many of his own comrades were precisely such men. Indeed, the Bolshevik party in 1917 could be said to have been dominated by the ultra-radical wing of the *intelligentsia*. The rise of a Stalin, who was so very different, is partly to be explained by Lenin's search for tough organisers who did not possess the typical *intelligentsia* defects. It was late in the day when Lenin observed that Stalin had other defects, perhaps more formidable ones. And later on Stalin himself took a terrible revenge on his educated comrades.

There were other elements in what can be called the Russian tradition. There were the *rebels*, men like Stenka Razin and Pugachev, Cossack freebooters, peasant bandits. In the national consciousness there was the danger of anarchy, disorder, of chaos, in which life would be nasty, brutish and short, and from which Authority and Autocracy could be the only salvation. It is not just a matter of the historical memories of past centuries. In 1919 large areas were controlled by peasant bands of so-called 'greens', neither White nor Red, some of whom kept tame anarchist philosophers in their baggage train. Against this, too, the Stalin system came into being.

Then there was the old Russian mixture of indolence, drunkenness inefficiency and generosity. The indolent appeared in Russian literature under the name of 'Oblomov', the idle gentleman. Lenin took the disease of *Oblomovism* seriously enough to fulminate against it at party meetings after his victory. He knew that the Russians needed organising, that they had to learn the ways of the west, of businesslike behaviour, of thrift, and he said so. He was very conscious, too, of the lack of educated people. For far too long the Tsars had held back education, had sought to prevent its spread to the 'lower classes'. After 1900 progress was rapid, in this as in so much else. Russian universities were good, the best scientists and doctors were excellent, many school teachers were skilled and devoted. But by the time of the revolution there were still few qualified people, and the World War, civil war and emigration were to deprive Russia of most of them by the time the Bolsheviks finally triumphed. The human material was coarse and ill-qualified. No one knew this better than Lenin. He hoped that revolution in more advanced countries would come to the rescue of backward Russia.

Finally, on this list of traditional attitudes there was a kind of nationalist exclusiveness. This took many forms. There was the religious idea of Moscow as the 'third Rome', taking over from Byzantium after its conquest by the Turks. Russia was the home of the true religion, Orthodoxy, *Pravoslavie*, a Church as national and nationalist as any in Christendom. Foreigners were almost always 'heathens' as well as dangerous or subversive. Anti-religious revolutionaries took over the notion of Russia as the country in which light and truth can be found, and eventually Stalin was to link together the internationalist communist creed with the glorification of the past and present of a Russian state. With these ideas there went, for many centuries, restrictions on the movement of foreigners, suspicion, passports, visas. Restrictions applied also to Russians. The poet Pushkin appealed in vain to Tsar Nicholas I to let him visit the West, and was reprimanded by the chief of the gendarmes for visiting the Caucasus without permission.

Indeed, many of the rules and regulations under which Soviet citizens live today have simply been taken over from the Tsars. They may seem shocking to us, but we have a different historical experience. Peasants could not move to town without having to obtain a passport; even a Russian could not move into Moscow or St Petersburg (Leningrad) without a residence permit. This was so under Nicholas II, it became so under Stalin. The habits of centuries assert themselves in two ways: they affect what the rulers consider right and proper to do, and also what the ruled are accustomed to regard as normal and tolerable in the behaviour of Authority.

Of course many individual Russians did not and do not fit these generalisations. In any case, the old ways of life and thought were dissolving under the impact of the industrial and commercial developments which began in the 1860s and gathered rapid momentum in the 1890s. None the less, just as Tsardom remained little changed (despite the parliament or *Duma* decreed in 1905) until its fall, so some deeply Russian features survived, greatly to influence events after the revolution. Indeed, the revolution itself had the

effect of expelling many of the liberal-European features which had
begun to influence the body politic in the reign of the last Tsars, and
so to strengthen traditional attitudes, even while adopting the most
advanced and extreme revolutionary programmes.

The Circumstances of Revolution

The Russian Empire at the turn of the century was a backward
European country, but none the less a great power. Her industrial
production was approaching that of France, though of course her
population was five times greater. A working class was forming, some
of it based in large modern factories erected with the help of foreign
capital and foreign specialists, the rest in old-fashioned workshops.
But most of it was of recent peasant origin, and the bulk of the
population still consisted of peasants. Life was hard in the new
industrial settlements, the workers discontented and ready to listen
to socialist propagandists. The country was still ruled by the Tsar
and by a bureaucracy responsible only to him.

In 1904 the government blundered into a war with Japan which
ended in ignominious failure. This touched off a revolution in the
cities and peasant riots in the villages. The Tsar was obliged to grant
a constitution, but the Duma was found too radical and the stern
suppression of the rebels was followed in 1907 by an electoral law
ensuring a safe majority for the propertied classes. Industrial
development was resumed, and 1913 was the culminating year of a
boom period in agriculture and industry alike.

The government, shaken by the peasant riots of 1905, introduced
far-reaching changes in the villages: the so-called Stolypin reforms
tried to break up the village commune to encourage better-off
peasants to consolidate their holdings, to buy land, to become richer,
and so more loyal to the throne. Two million households had become
peasant-proprietors of the Western type by the time the war broke
out in 1914. Who knows, perhaps Stolypin, the then Prime Minister,
was right when he claimed that political stability under Tsardom
would come given time. But he was assassinated in 1911, and war
was soon to engulf Europe.

Stalin at this period was still a minor party functionary in the
Caucasus. He attracted notice as a political bank robber, 'expropriat-
ing the expropriators' in aid of party funds. His political activities
also attracted the attention of the police, and he was arrested and
exiled. By the standards he later imposed, his treatment was mild: he

was free to live as he pleased in a remote Siberian village, he was not in a prison or camp. He was, however, effectively isolated from political life.

What were Lenin and other revolutionaries hoping for before 1917? What were their programmes, what were the nature of their disagreements? These are not questions of abstract theory, they deeply affect our understanding of what the revolution was about, and many of the later events.

Marxist ideas played a very important role, and found a ready audience among Russian intellectuals. *Das Kapital* was translated first into Russian. Some revolutionaries disapproved. Heirs of the radical wing of the Slavophils, they believed in a solution based on peasant communal traditions. They did not care for the dictatorship of the proletariat and disliked industrial civilisation. They attracted support, though of a rather passive kind, among the peasants. The Socialist-Revolutionary Party, founded in 1904, became the chief protagonist of these ideas.

The principal Marxist party was the Social-Democratic party, founded in 1898. This split in 1903 into the so-called Bolsheviks (or majority-men) and Mensheviks (minority-men), nicknames which were the result of one vote at one conference, but which stuck. Their chief bone of contention was apparently organisational: whether or not the party should be based upon a select group of revolutionary conspirators, or have a broader base. On to this difference were grafted others. Lenin's Bolsheviks came to attract the more ruthless and extreme elements and they became identified with a more revolutionary approach, though of course the Mensheviks too desired the overthrow of Tsardom. But before 1917 there was no strong distinction between the two factions, and many members in Russia were impatient of their leaders' quarrels, which seemed to them to be splitting hairs.

Brief mention must be made of another Marxist-inspired party, the Jewish Bund, which defended specifically Jewish working-class interests. There were Jews in high positions in all the other revolutionary parties, including the Bolsheviks. This was because they were literate, able, and frustrated by the discriminatory restrictions imposed on them by the Tsarist regime.

A full account of Marxist theories and of their various interpretations would require another book. Karl Marx believed that capitalism, with the private ownership of the means of production, had enabled the owners of capital to exploit the working class, or proletariat, who sold their labour power to the capitalists. The workers created value, but the capitalists appropriated part of the product for themselves. This system was a great advance on the feudalism that preceded it, liberating productive forces and greatly expanding the output and productive capacity of society. However, as Marx saw it, capitalism was bound to generate contradictions which would ultimately destroy it. As capitalism developed, so there would be ever greater concentration of capital in fewer hands, in great monopolistic corporations. The mass of the workers would remain poor. The small business men would be driven by the monopoly-capitalists out of business and into the ranks of the workers. The class struggle would become more acute. Workers would feel increasingly discontented and 'alienated' from the process of production and from society. There would also be deepening crises and slumps. A highly developed capitalism would then run into grave difficulties, and the way out would be socialism, ultimately communism, a form of society in which the means of production would belong to the people, and in which the 'anarchy' of the market would be replaced by planning. Marx foresaw a future ideal society in which goods would be abundant, everyone would be fully educated, jobs would be interchangeable, money and acquisitiveness would disappear, production would be for use and not for sale, all would be equal, freely contributing to social work to the best of their ability, and drawing whatever they needed from the abundant stocks of goods and services. There would then be no state, since the state is an organ of the exploiting and dominant class, no army, no police. Communism would be world-wide. This happy future was, of course, not seen as an immediate prospect. At first there would be civil strife, revolution, and the mass of the people, the working class, would exercise the 'dictatorship of the proletariat' over the handful of capitalist exploiters. Then there would be a transition period of unknown length, after which socialism would come into existence.

Marx himself described his ideas as scientific, comparing them with so-called Utopian socialists, who merely dreamed of a future just society. Some elements of Marx's vision of the future state may seem Utopian, unreal, to most readers of this book, as they do to its author. However, Marx did have a powerful theory of history, based upon class struggle and material interest (though he did not deny that ideas affect events too), and he is regarded as one of the founders of modern sociological analysis. His attacks on the existing order were strong and effective, at a time when workers were indeed extremely poor and the gap between classes extremely wide. Although he himself made it clear that under capitalism production expanded mightily, his doctrines could be and were used to explain poverty in terms of exploitation, and his vision of a future just society inspired generations of socialists to strive for change through revolution, which would liberate mankind from oppression.

Marx did occasionally refer to the 'Asian mode of production', in which a despot assisted by courtiers and bureaucrats ruled over society (this rule being reinforced and explained by control over water for irrigation), but the bulk of his analysis related to developed capitalism and the contradictions of its maturity, out of which socialism would come.

Marxism was all very well, but what would its doctrines mean in peasant Russia? Did not Marx foretell proletarian revolution in developed Western countries? His doctrines envisaged the concentration of capital in few hands in advanced capitalist countries, the squeezing out of peasants, small traders, petty farmers, so that the mass of the people were proletarianised. Russia was not like that. The mass of the peasants were only beginning to emerge from the medieval forms of communal tenure into the consciousness of the virtues of private ownership. Indeed, as we shall see, most of them had still not made the mental transformation when the revolution broke out. Yet the communal institutions were decaying, were permeated by market relations; Lenin in his first major work had asserted this, arguing against those who would base a future Russian revolution on peasant communalism.

What was the way out for a Marxist socialist? The moderate wing, i.e. most of the Mensheviks, argued that Russia was becoming ripe for a bourgeois revolution to overthrow the Tsar. Thereafter capitalism could develop in a democratic republic, and then only gradually would conditions ripen for socialism.

Lenin and most of his Bolshevik colleagues reasoned otherwise. Lenin's own thoughts underwent changes, and the following is only a brief summary of his ideas.

Firstly, the peasants may be backward and confused, but they wanted the lands still owned by the great landlords and the church. In this respect they were potentially revolutionary. True, once their land-hunger was assuaged, the better-off peasants would cease to be radical, and would oppose socialism, but Lenin hoped that the poorer peasants would make common cause with the working-class. The essential point, tactically, was that the peasants could play a vital part in the overthrow of the existing order. The moderates feared the brutality and ignorance of the dark masses; Lenin was prepared to ride the storm.

Secondly, he envisaged the Russian revolution as part of a world revolution. Backward Russia might be the weak link in the world imperialist chain. Then the chain must be broken at its weakest link, and the long-forecast revolutions in advanced Western economies would follow, and these countries would come to the aid of their fellow-socialists in Russia, and thereby resolve the contradictions inherent in trying to build socialism in a largely peasant country.

Thirdly, Lenin (unlike the Mensheviks) was temperamentally unwilling to wait for conditions to ripen. Marxism is at once a revolutionary and an evolutionary doctrine. History is made by men who take advantage of opportunities. Without favourable circumstances, the revolutionary will be crying in the wilderness, a mere Utopian rebel. But for Lenin it did not follow that one had to wait for social-economic circumstances to 'ripen'. One might seize power and *then* change society. To Mensheviks and other moderate Marxists this was heresy. This was standing Marxism on its head. But for him – and for such activist comrades as Stalin – the evolutionary and long-term view was the negation of what they stood for. They wanted power, they wanted a socialist transformation that would begin in their lifetime, whereas to wait for a proletarian majority was to wait for many decades at least. However, the logical consequence of this approach was a prolonged period of rule by a minority party, while society was being altered from above.

But if this were the task of a conspiratorial and disciplined party, argued Trotsky (not then a Bolshevik), the party would substitute itself for the proletariat and in due course a dictator would substitute himself for the party. The danger of this kind of bureaucratic despotism existed indeed, and we shall see that the history of the revolution bore out this tendency, which was perhaps inherent in the Leninist concept of change organised and imposed from above in a predominantly peasant country.

Before 1917, the chances of a Bolshevik takeover seemed remote. Tsarism was being challenged, it is true, but Lenin and his comrades were not the most effective-looking of the challengers. The outbreak of war in 1914, and the severe defeats and privations suffered by Russia in 1915 and after, shook the regime. The weakness of Tsar Nicholas II, the power exercised by Rasputin, the corruption and inefficiency of the war machine, might have seemed to offer revolutionary opportunities, but even at the end of 1916 Lenin, in his Swiss exile, expressed the view that he might never see the revolution.

In the end, Tsardom fell almost of its own accord, without organised action by any of the revolutionary parties. A provisional government was set up in March 1917, and one of its first actions was to release political prisoners. Back from Siberia came Stalin and other exiles. A month later, Lenin returned from Switzerland through Germany in the famous 'sealed train'. General Ludendorff hoped that Lenin would help to weaken the Russian war effort. This proved to be the case, but in another way it was one of history's major miscalculations: Lenin in no way pursued German interests, and after his victory he and his cause challenged all that Ludendorff and his German fellow-conservatives stood for.

This is no place for yet another description of the events of 1917. At first Stalin and his comrades did not see the opportunities ahead. It needed Lenin in his famous April theses, to rally the party to a policy aimed at the overthrow of the Provisional Government and the seizure of power. The party adopted the slogans of 'peace' and 'land', and war-weary soldiers began mass desertions to return to their villages to participate in land seizures. Authority was breaking down. Trotsky joined the Bolsheviks in July, and Kerensky, who emerged as leader of the Provisional Government, used his eloquence in vain to steady the situation. The Provisional Government adopted some progressive social legislation, but was unable to cope with the mounting chaos, to which the Bolsheviks made their contribution but which was only partially due to their activities. The government had no popular mandate. It shared power with the Soviets, rough-and-ready assemblies of workers', peasants', and soldiers' deputies, which were to give their name to the 'Soviet' system of government, but which until October 1917, were controlled by the Mensheviks and Social-Revolutionaries. They were divided on the vital issue of how and whether to end the war, and felt unable to tackle the complex issue of land reform without a mandate from the people, expressed in a free vote for a Constituent Assembly. (Lenin, indeed, accused them of delaying elections to this Assembly, but when they were held and produced an anti-Bolshevik majority, he had no hesitation in closing it down.) The Provisional Government faced an impossible task, made no easier by its own disunity and inexperience, and by the fact that it lacked the semi-divine attributes of the Tsar without being able to acquire any other kind of legitimacy in the eyes of the masses. It steadily lost support among the workers and soldiers, while its socialist pretensions alienated the middle classes and most of the officers who began to seek a solution in military dictatorship. Lenin, by contrast, pursued single-mindedly the overthrow of the government, by whatever means were to hand. When he had majorities in the Soviets, he put forward the slogan 'All power to the Soviets'. Kerensky did not dare to call upon the forces of the Right, since as the confused plot around General Kornilov showed, they might well dispose of Kerensky himself. He drifted helplessly until he had to flee, leaving his ministers to be arrested in the Winter Palace (7 November 1917; this was 25 October by the old Julian calendar, then still in use, hence the 'October' revolution).

We need not say that the Bolshevik triumph was either inevitable or predestined, since the circumstances which brought it about (the war, the weakness of Tsar Nicholas II, the tactical genius of Lenin, and so on) would then have to be regarded as 'inevitable' too. What is surely true is that the Bolsheviks were able to seize power with relatively small forces, while the army and the bulk of the citizens looked on indifferently; the Provisional Government was defended at the end by a handful of unenthusiastic soldiers, of which the largest unit was a women's battalion.

'We will now build socialism,' announced Lenin to a wildly cheering crowd. What was it he thought he was building? What construction materials were to hand?

Lenin's political and economic ideas were said later to underlie Stalin's policies and actions. Stalin's future enemies – Trotsky, Bukharin and others – did not fail to claim that *they* were the true Leninists. It is therefore only right to devote a little space to his ideas.

Revolution? Yes. But what was to be done with power once it was won? Nowhere in Lenin's works, up to and including 1917, is he on record as favouring a one-party state. He seems to have sincerely believed that the state would wither away, and that until that time, while suppressing bourgeois counter-revolutionaries, the state would become the organ of the masses, without a professional bureaucracy, with every citizen taking his or her turn to run the government. Economic problems he saw mainly as problems of technique and of accountancy, workers' control over the economic apparatus being made possible (in his view) by industrial concentration and monopolistic cartels. By workers' control he did *not* mean that factories must be run by their workers: 'nothing so silly as railways to the railwaymen and tanneries to the tanners'. He envisaged the 'workers' controlling the whole economy collectively, in some way he never defined.

As for the peasants, at this stage Lenin found it tactically right to adopt the programme of which the peasant masses approved: legalisation of land seizures, toleration of the traditional peasant community's control over the land, and therefore cultivation based on the family, with land divided into strips within the age-old three-field system. Far from encouraging the extension of the Stolypin reform, the Bolsheviks treated the richer peasants who benefited from it as 'kulaks' ('fists', exploiters) and encouraged a class war against them. This may have done them some political good, but in terms of agricultural productivity this was a reactionary solution, which caused great complications later. Of course, collective cultivation was seen as the way out, but it was obvious that the peasants would oppose so radical a change in their lives and expectations, and it made little progress until it was imposed much later.

Lenin's ideas underwent changes as the bitter experience of government under conditions of civil war taught him and his comrades some unforgettable lessons. The influence of the dramatic years 1917–21 on the whole course of subsequent history, and on Stalinism, cannot possibly be overestimated. It was in the civil war that Stalin and men like Stalin emerged as leaders, while others became accustomed to harshness, cruelty, terror, which at this period were indeed essential for survival. At first, the leadership was overweighted with intellectuals, men of action indeed, but men with scruples, often with a European education: such were Bukharin, Lunacharsky, Kamenev, Krestinsky. Even when they approved of terror, it worried them. Lunacharsky was, indeed, so concerned about architecture that he resigned when the Kremlin, held at that moment by anti-Bolsheviks, was bombarded.

The tough men inevitably came to the fore. Many of the old devoted Bolsheviks perished in the fighting in the civil war. Many workers fled from the cold and hungry cities as industry ground to a halt and transport was disrupted. Anarcho-syndicalist and libertarian ideas were plainly inconsistent with the necessities of the time. Harsh discipline alone would serve the regime. The miseries of the war-communism period caused widespread discontent, and it soon became clear to the leadership that organised opposition was too dangerous to be tolerated. Indeed, opposition factions inside the Bolshevik party itself came to be looked upon as an impermissible luxury, and were formally banned in 1921. Lenin himself, as his articles and especially his letters bear evidence, played a notable role in imposing terror and eliminating dissent. No doubt this brilliant and ruthless political leader saw that the alternative was loss of power, and this would carry with it a high risk of being hanged, amid the bitterness and hatred of fratricidal strife. It is quite wrong to imagine that he was a gentle or tolerant man, though he certainly was not personally brutal. Similarly Trotsky could express such ideas as 'in defence of terrorism'.

Revolutionary terror was the task of the Cheka, a name made up of the Russian initial letters of Extraordinary Commission. Originally set up to deal with an admittedly desperate emergency, it killed and imprisoned the enemies of the revolution in the name of the freedom of mankind. Dzerzhinsky, its first chief, was said to suffer acutely every time he signed a death sentence. (He had much occasion for suffering.) Unfortunately, this secret police became part of the Soviet system, and under various names – OGPU, NKVD, and now KGB – it played a role very different to that originally envisaged by those who made the revolution.

Civil war was accompanied by 'war communism'. This was an attempt at total mobilisation of the exhausted and ruined country, central control over production, accompanied by a ban on private manufacture and private trade, and, most important, the imposition on the peasants of compulsory delivery of produce to the state. Money rapidly lost all value. Virtue was made of necessity, and all this was said (and was believed by many) to be the first stage of a direct transition to Communism. The peasants detested having to deliver food in exchange for 'worthless pieces of paper', and requisition squads scoured the countryside. Black markets flourished, illegal traders were seized and often shot. Party officials, lacking any experience of planning, made a hash of the task of running industry, a task made very hard for them by the demands and destruction of civil war. In this setting ruthless commissars fought, improvised, confiscated, executed. In this terrible school Stalin and most of his future henchmen learned their lessons about the art of government. They applied these lessons only too thoroughly.

'NEP' and the Rise of the Secretariat

By the end of 1920 the civil war was over. The country was bled white, starving, ruined, much of industry was closed down, transport at a standstill, most townspeople had fled to stay with relatives in the country. The attempt to continue the policies of war communism, (an attempt which was made) threatened disaster. Revolts broke out. World Revolution was clearly not around the corner. The attempt in 1920 to advance into Poland, after defeating a Polish invasion, was a bitter experience: far from welcoming the Red Army as class brothers, Polish workers and peasants drove them back. Stalin was then the political chief of the Southern Army group; with Voroshilov, he ignored orders to advance northwards, thereby contributing to the success of the Polish attack in front of Warsaw. The Commander-in-Chief, Tukhachevsky, criticised them publicly for this, and this quite possibly contributed to his being shot in 1937, since Stalin had a long and vengeful memory.

How, then, was Russia to survive under Bolshevik rule, isolated in a largely hostile world? Lenin's answer was: to adopt a so-called New Economic Policy (NEP), thereby conciliating the peasant majority and making it possible to restore quickly the ruined economy. NEP was a compromise. The peasants, after paying tax, were left to dispose of their surpluses as they saw fit. Private trade was again permitted. Small-scale private manufacture, and petty craftsmen, were given the go-ahead. The state kept a firm grip on the 'commanding heights' of the economy: large-scale industry, large shops, most wholesale trade, banking, foreign trade. But state industry was told to produce for the market, state trusts and combines behaved commercially. There was little central planning. Though Lenin looked forward to the gradual spread of agricultural co-operatives, there was no attempt to herd the peasants into collectives.

Reconstruction was rapid and successful. But it was accompanied by a vice-like grip of the Bolshevik Party at all levels of political power. Economic liberalisation was not accompanied by political liberalisation. On the contrary, the economic rights given to private enterprise necessitated, in Lenin's eyes, the tightening of political controls. For he realised that spontaneous political and social forces in a predominantly peasant ('petty-bourgeois') country would give expression to interests inimical to socialism. So the advance would only be resumed if the Party kept power in its hands, and then only if the Party itself prevented the development of internal factions, which might express within its ranks the heretical opinions banned outside. Such, then, became the logic of the one-party state, the Party itself requiring to be kept pure by periodic cleansings. The snuffing out of democratic dissent outside required the elimination of freedom in the Party itself.

At first this logic was not clearly perceived, certainly not by Trotsky and most other future victims of totalitarianism. They only became alarmed when they saw how skilfully Stalin used the situation to further his own ambitions.

All this had some organisational consequences. The levers of power required an operational headquarters, which must also allocate the Party cadres to key posts throughout the country. The Party had been organised on a narrow, conspiratorial basis before the revolution. Many members were recruited in 1917, many more when it became clear that it was and would remain the ruling party. The experienced, literate and reliable kernel was not large. These were the 'cadres', the full-time party men who were available to be rushed wherever they were needed, to take responsibility for the complex and daunting task of civil war, reconstruction, police and repression. They had to be used to supervise the trained but politically unreliable specialists, or the loyal but ignorant comrades fresh from factory, mine and Red-army battalion. One can see how vital it must have seemed to distribute these cadres among the various key posts to be filled, tasks to be performed. Who but the Secretariat of the Party could carry out this necessary task? Election, within or outside the Party, became increasingly insignificant. Appointment of disciplined strong-minded men, capable of forcing through Party policy in the given locality or sector, became the essential feature of the system. The criterion of success of those appointed became the way in which they carried out Party policy. The old catchphrase 'democratic centralism' expressed the idea that the Party members had to obey instructions issued by a freely elected leadership. Conspiratorial necessity limited the possibilities of election in pre-revolutionary times. Civil war and the struggle for survival made democratic forms within the party unworkable after the seizure of power. Though in the first years there was still, by later standards, free discussion and examples of real choice between Party candidates (for instance for central committee membership), centralisation and discipline came increasingly to dominate all party procedures.

The Secretariat, however, was at first ill-adapted to carry out its task. Intellectuals like Krestinsky and Preobrazhensky came and went. At a Party congress a delegate complained: 'Papers are all in confusion, there is not even a registry of incoming and outgoing correspondence'. To this Trotsky retorted: 'There is no bureaucracy!' The delegate replied: 'Indeed there is no bureaucracy, but there is chaos'.

In 1922, Stalin was brought in to run the Secretariat. Up to that date it was not considered to be a top leader's post. Lenin was still dominant in the Party, and the public at large, including Party members, knew far more about men like Trotsky, Bukharin, Zinoviev, Rykov, than they did about Stalin. He had spent most of the civil war as a commissar with an army group and held the post of Commissar for Nationalities and also head of a 'workers' and peasants' inspection'. Lenin saw that a tough organiser was essential and appointed Stalin to the job in the knowledge that these qualities were accompanied by certain defects. No doubt he hoped that he could keep these defects within bounds.

At this point accident, or rather the logic of medicine rather than of politics, takes over. Lenin was struck down by disease. By 1923 he was scarcely capable of work, and he was finished as a politically active figure well before he died in January 1924. In his last conscious months he became increasingly alarmed about the way things were going. He saw the growth of bureaucratisation, and within it the growth of the power of the Party Secretariat and particularly of Stalin. The Secretariat's power to shift Party members around could be and was being used to pack key committees, to send off to remote provinces anyone who spoke out of turn or who threatened Stalin's grip on Party organs. Of course at this period Stalin's personal power was still limited, he had to form alliances, manoeuvre, speak with tact to still-powerful comrades. Thus, with Lenin ill, he skilfully aligned himself with Zinoviev and others who disliked Trotsky's arrogance and mass appeal. Trotsky's supporters were shifted away from politically influential posts, and these came to be more and more in the hands of Stalin's associates. It became known that open support for Trotsky would cause harm to career prospects. Even in Trotsky's own People's Commissariat (War) men loyal to him were being shifted and replaced. Already then the Party's decisions were due less to debate or discussion than to pre-congress organisational manoeuvres, of which Stalin was a master. By the end of 1923 he had virtually destroyed Trotsky's entire political base. Yet his allies – who were nearly all later to become his victims – had no notion as to the consequences of their acts.

But the sick Lenin saw what might happen. It was a tragic scene: the founder of Bolshevism and of the Soviet State lying in his sickbed, seeing what was going wrong, appreciating in particular the role Stalin might play, but already powerless to stop it. He sent letters, messages. He tried to encourage the victims of some particularly unpleasant ploy of Stalin's in his native Georgia. He dictated a testament, warning the Party. About Stalin this is what he wrote: 'Comrade Stalin having become the General Secretary has accumulated enormous powers in his hands and I am not sure whether he will be able to use this power with due care'. Shortly afterwards he added a much sharper postscript. 'Stalin is too rude, and this defect . . . is intolerable in the person of a general secretary.' Stalin should therefore be replaced by one 'more tolerant, more loyal, less capricious . . .'

At his last gasp, outraged by insults proferred by Stalin to his wife, Krupskaya, Lenin went further, trying to break off all relations with Stalin. Conceivably he might yet have toppled him if he could have recovered sufficiently to address the Party as a whole, or its central committee. But this was not to be. Would history then have been different? Would another man have played Stalin's role? Or did Stalin dare to defy Lenin only because he knew that the old man would soon die? We will never know the answers to such questions. But we can clearly see that the rise of such as Stalin, and the power of the Secretariat, were not accidental.

Stalin brought to the Secretariat men personally loyal to him, who were to make their career alongside him. Among them, Molotov played a particularly significant role. Molotov served Stalin faithfully, using his considerable organisational gifts to effective purpose. But perhaps more important than individuals like Molotov was Stalin's appeal to middle-grade Party officials who had emerged in the civil war, after having served in minor capacities in the illegal pre-revolutionary Party in Russia. They were in the main semi-literate simple people, who understood little of the subtleties of the cosmopolitan intellectuals, of whom they were jealous. They were all for discipline, were pleased to be told what to do, were even more pleased if no one was allowed to argue with them when they did it. We shall see how important the mentality of these men was in explaining the growth and evolution of Stalinism.

The rise of Stalin and the Secretariat took place while the Soviet economy was being rapidly restored under the beneficent influence of NEP. He consolidated and extended his power in the course of a great debate, which was in one sense independent of the power struggle, since it reflected the basic dilemmas of a Marxist party in power in a peasant country. But of course the manoeuvres and counter-plots of politicians were intertwined with genuine perplexities. Where, they all said, do we go from here?

The Great Debate: Socialism in One Country

'Oh ye, whose task it is
To put between high banks of concrete
Our country's stormy and anarchic waters,
More severe, even more grim than he,
You follow Lenin's road.'

In these words the poet Esenin addressed Lenin's heirs. Esenin himself loved old peasant Russia, and was shortly to commit suicide. Yet he felt instinctively what was to be done, and the coercive logic of the situation.

Let us look at the problems faced by Stalin, or by any other Bolshevik who happened to be in power. If, even in the briefest sketch, things look complicated, the reason is that they *were* exceedingly complicated. Yet to understand what Stalinism was all about, it is necessary to dwell on the problems of the twenties. To see him merely as a power-hungry despot is to see only one aspect of the truth.

There was the problem of *industrialisation*, begun under the Tsars, and disrupted by war and revolution. New and large investments were necessary to carry Russia forward, beyond reconstructing the industries which already existed in 1913. How were the necessary resources to be obtained? There were now no landlords, no large capitalists. Foreign capital was unlikely to be forthcoming, since the Bolsheviks had repudiated past debts. Accumulation and sacrifice would be at the expense of the people, and the bulk of the people were peasants.

Industrialisation had two other aspects. One was military: Russia had a feeble war industry and lacked steel and machinery-making capacity. Yet there she was, isolated in a hostile world. Security considerations provided a sense of urgency. The other aspect was political. Bolshevism rested on the idea of a working-class dictatorship. The working class was small. The survival of the regime in the long run, i.e. its political security, required a much larger proletariat, a large industry. Lenin once put the point vividly: 'Either the political conquests of Soviet power will perish, or we will place them upon an economic foundation. This does not now exist.'

The *peasant problem* was intimately linked with these considerations. The peasants, having seized the landlords' land in 1917–18, were now a conservative or at least non-socialist force, interested in higher prices for food and not in the least interested in financing industrial development. The land was being cultivated in fragmented small-holdings, many of them divided into strips in medieval style, and by antique methods. The traditional peasant communal institution, known as the *mir* or the *obshchina*, controlled the use of the land and in effect ran the villages, rendering the local Soviets largely power-less, especially as the Party had few members in rural areas. Again this raised the issue of political security. But perhaps more important still was the contradiction between peasant agriculture and the needs of industrialisation. The peasants ate better, but sold less of their produce. This was a consequence of the elimination of land-lords and of most large peasant ('*kulak*') holdings by the revolution, as these had specialised on production for the market instead of their own subsistence.

True, the more enterprising peasants were once again consolidat-ing their holdings, leasing their poorer neighbours' land, setting up as mini-capitalists. This more commercial attitude was economically desirable, no doubt, but appeared politically dangerous to the regime. Tons of ink were devoted to earnest argument about the *kulak* menace. Might it not lead to the domination of the countryside by men whose class interests were anti-Soviet? (It was hoped that the poorer peasants would show more sympathy for Soviet power.) But industrialisation requires more marketings of farm produce, to feed the growing towns and for export. How was it to be obtained?

These problems and dilemmas were an inescapable consequence of the seizure of power by the Bolsheviks in a predominantly peasant country, under conditions of international isolation. Less clear was the choice of a way out.

At first all the leaders, including Trotsky, accepted NEP and its logic; Trotsky's criticisms were aimed at the 'regime in the party', its bureaucratisation. But after he was thrust out of the seats of power Trotsky criticised the party majority for being soft on *kulaks*, urged a speed-up in industrial investment and also attacked the record of the Communist International in Germany, China and elsewhere. His ally Preobrazhensky publicly advocated 'primitive socialist accumulation' at the peasants' expense, and argued that the effort to 'build socialism' in Russia would fail without the help of revolution in advanced countries.

The other wing of the Party was most clearly represented by Bukharin, with whom Stalin chose at that time to ally himself. Bukharin believed in NEP, and in an alliance with the bulk of the peasantry. He was conciliatory to the better-off peasants, whom he wished to encourage to grow more produce for the market. This logically called for increased production (and imports) of industrial goods which the peasants wanted. In the long run he expected socialism to be built. 'Socialism in one country' was possible, he asserted, but by cautious stages, 'at the speed of the peasant nag'. To go faster was to endanger the alliance with the peasants and thereby to threaten the stability of the whole Soviet regime. He denounced Trotsky's policy as adventurist, and as lacking faith in Russia.

Trotsky's career has been the subject of a good biography in three volumes by Isaac Deutscher. He was a man of brilliant intellect and eloquence, who rose to prominence as chairman of the St Petersburg Soviet during the disorders of 1905, and subsequently took an independent line, disagreeing with Lenin on many issues. He helped devise the so-called theory of 'permanent revolution', in which the process of revolution not only spreads over the world but must occur continuously within each country. During the First World War, in exile, he took a position similar to Lenin's, and soon after his return to Russia in 1917 he joined the Bolshevik Party and was a leading co-worker of Lenin's during the seizure of power, becoming first Commissar of Foreign Affairs and then Commissar for War. In the latter capacity he played a major role in organising the Red Army in the civil war. Despite his eminence, or because of it, he was never 'accepted' by other Bolshevik leaders, and his somewhat arrogant manner did not help. As soon as Lenin's health failed, they tried by every means to discredit Trotsky. His past disagreements with Lenin were magnified, his doctrine of 'permanent revolution' presented as a threat to a hard-won respite; the masses had had enough of revolution.

Stalin accepted the principle of *socialism in one country*, and used Bukharin in the fight to destroy Trotsky and Zinoviev (who, when it was too late, joined Trotsky in defying his ex-ally Stalin). He never went as far as Bukharin in enunciating a pro-peasant policy, but preferred to bide his time, creating meanwhile a politically impregnable position, so that when the clash with Bukharin came the latter had no choice but meek surrender.

Stalin's doctrine had a ready appeal to Party members. Revolution in the West was unlikely for many years to come. What business had the Bolsheviks to rule Russia unless they at least claimed to be building socialism? It was all very well for Trotsky to quote Lenin's words about world revolution and Russia's backwardness. The difficulties faced by an isolated backward Russia were a fact. Yet what was the ruling party to make of its power? The Mensheviks and the Western Social-Democrats had criticised them for seizing power 'prematurely', in a situation 'unripe' for socialism. Most Party members must have yearned for a leadership which would confirm their belief that their efforts were not in vain, that success, though difficult, was possible. Stalin could appeal also to a latent nationalism: Russia would show the world a new way of living. This theme too had deep roots: poets like Blok and Voloshin during the revolution, and in past centuries the religious ideologists of 'Moscow the Third Rome'. Truth and righteousness would come to the world from Soviet (or Holy) Russia.

Against such an appeal to political self-preservation, national tradition and harsh realities, Trotsky was powerless. Even without the clever manipulation by Stalin of the party machine, he had lost and he knew it. He saw himself the victim of the self-interest of the party-state bureaucracy, and of the weariness of the people, who had suffered much and were unwilling to listen to prophets of still more (indeed 'permanent') revolution. Stalin also proved himself to be a master of intrigue and political manoeuvring, arts in which Trotsky proved to be incompetent. So we must see his defeat as due to a combination of adverse circumstances and personal qualities and deficiencies, with the circumstances as the decisive factor.

By 1926, Trotsky, Zinoviev and the so-called 'left-opposition' were helpless and isolated in the Party. They persisted in playing to the rules, keeping disagreements within the Party which was now controlled by their enemies. For them the Party was all that mattered. Or maybe they understood too well that the mass of the people were hostile to all Bolsheviks, and so an appeal to the (peasant) majority against the ruling caucus made no sense. Anyway, it was not until November 1927 that a few desperate oppositionists went out into the streets to demonstrate, to appeal at least to the city 'proletariat', to their Party comrades. They were speedily silenced, many were exiled, Trotsky was sent to Alma Ata, in distant Central Asia, and was then exiled from the USSR to Turkey, whence he wandered helplessly until a Stalinist assassin finished him with an ice-pick in distant Mexico in 1940.

Up to 1927, Stalin was in alliance with Bukharin. Bukharin had succeeded Zinoviev as the head of the Communist International, which in these days still seemed to matter, at least to the faithful.

Rykov, an ally of Bukharin, was prime minister. Tomsky, also of the Bukharinist persuasion, was boss of the trade unions. Through cronies such as Molotov, Stalin controlled the Party Secretariat, but his control was not yet absolute. The supreme body at the top of the party, the Politbureau, could decide against him. Lenin's testament was known to them. They – or rather the Stalin-Bukharin majority – had decided to keep it secret, but it could be revived, and Stalin still could not afford to offend his allies, certainly not until Trotsky, Zinoviev and their friends were totally destroyed politically, and even then he had to tread warily. We must surmise that he deeply resented these limitations on his power and bided his time; later he would create and seize opportunities to rid himself of men on whose loyalty he could not rely, and who were intellectually his superiors. Bukharin was a man of undoubted brilliance, charm, eloquence, held in great affection and esteem by many party members (as Lenin had said). He was, however, no match for Stalin in political in-fighting.

While on one level Stalin could be seen as wanting the Bukharin group out of the way in order that he should achieve supreme power, it is true and perhaps more important to see that they clashed over policy. So we must return to the 'great debate', and go on looking at the very real dilemmas which faced the Bolsheviks in the mid-twenties.

NEP seemed to be a great economic success. By 1926 Soviet industry had reached the production levels of 1913. So now they had to move on, to plan the future economic development of Russia. Discussions raged about how best to proceed, at many levels, including the economic-technical one. How fast? In what direction? Should investments be channelled to agriculture, so as to buy modern machinery from the West, paying for it with farm exports? Or should Russia aim to make her own machinery at the earliest possible moment? Should industrial investment concentrate primarily on consumer goods industries or on heavy industry? Since there was much unemployment, might it not be wiser to invest in industries using a great deal of labour? What kind of planning should there be? What role should be reserved for prices and market forces, which were of major importance under NEP? In trying to cope with these and other questions, Soviet economists can be said virtually to have invented development economics, anticipating many arguments which were first heard in the West when development and growth became fashionable, i.e. after the Second World War.

Economics as such is not our concern, but it is easy to see that many of the above questions had political aspects of the very highest importance. 'How fast' meant: 'how hard is it desirable or feasible to squeeze the peasants?' Bukharin, as has already been pointed out, wanted to avoid conflict with the peasants, which meant being content with a modest rate of capital accumulation and thereby slow growth. Priority for heavy industry not only meant the creation within Russia of the sinews of future growth, and of the basis of a modern arms industry, but also multiplied the sacrifices (no one can eat or wear steel or machine-tools) and once again brought the peasant question to the fore. A decision in favour of centralised planning and against market forces would – and did – change the political as well as the economic scene, impelling it towards what came to be called totalitarianism. So political issues, the personal power struggle and economic difficulties were all of great significance, and interpenetrated each other. This had some tragic results. Thus a non-Party 'technical' economist who advised that more should be invested in consumer goods industries could be labelled an ally of the Bukharinist faction and, when repression grew, he might be arrested and never seen again.

But this is to run ahead. Mass terror was still in the future. Party leaders who spoke their minds in 1926 did not expect to be jailed, and Stalin still had not the power to jail them.

Stalin was a secretive man, and his published works and speeches give us less insight into his real thoughts than is usual with politicians. Indeed he lied on a prodigious scale. Consequently we do not know when he made up his mind to part company with Bukharin and steal the policy clothes of the Trotskyist opposition. The most likely explanation is that he always regarded NEP as a forced, temporary compromise, that he preferred ruthless strong-arm methods to accommodation, that he wished to launch a major industrialisation drive as soon as it was practicable; therefore he had misgivings about Bukharin's line. We do know that when Bukharin went so far as to launch the slogan 'get rich' (i.e. encouraging the *kulaks* to produce more for the market), Stalin said: 'This is not our policy'. However, tactical exigencies, and the country's weakness and vulnerability, inclined him to play along with the Bukharin group until Trotsky was eliminated. In 1927 he became strong enough to act on his own, though he still had to play his cards with caution. The party congresses in 1925 and 1927 had gone on formal record in favour of industrialisation and also of the growth of collectives in agriculture.

But these resolutions were not controversial. Questions of tempos and coercion were.

Already in 1926-7 a speed-up in investment began, and grain prices were kept low. Very quickly this caused trouble, and Stalin's reactions to the resultant crisis showed how his mind was working.

The Great Turning-Point

People first became aware of a crisis in connection with grain procurements. Grain in Russia was then, and still is to some extent, 'the staff of life', and also a major export. In the winter of 1927-28 it became apparent that the peasants were not willing to sell enough grain at the official price. Many hoarded it to await higher prices, or fed their livestock better. In doing so, they behaved as economic men. It is absurd to 'blame' them though Stalin treated them as conspirators.

At the same time investments were increasing, some major construction projects were begun, ambitious versions of a five-year plan, the first in history, were being drafted. The impact of this on the economy was to create goods shortages. The reason for these shortages was that the new investments diverted resources into major construction projects, increasing at the same time the incomes of those working on them, while the supply of consumer goods could not match the increases in purchasing power. This, in a free-market economy, would have been reflected by inflationary price rises, but the state tried to keep prices low by strict controls, and this led to an imbalance between supply and demand. The NEP traders and petty manufacturers could cash in, by selling scarce goods at high prices. Increasingly they were treated by Party officials as black-marketeers; they were taxed arbitrarily, refused licences, denied materials and transport. This took time, but NEP was beginning to break up in the winter of 1927-28, with Stalin's evident approval, even though in all official speeches the principles of NEP continued to be exalted. Bukharin had every cause to be worried.

Then came the flashpoint. Defying the Party's own rules, ignoring the Politbureau, acting directly through his cronies in the Party machine, Stalin dealt with the grain procurement problem by violence. Disregarding the law, the police set up road-blocks, seized peasant produce en route to the (legal) markets, confiscated 'surplus' and 'hoarded' grain. Stalin himself went to the Urals and Siberia to

supervise the operation in these areas, and called this extortion
technique 'the Urals-Siberian method'. In the light of subsequent
arbitrariness and brutality, this might seem to us to be 'normal'
behaviour. But in terms of NEP it was an outrage. Local officials
were taken aback. Many thought that laws should be observed.
Stalin reprimanded them: 'Suppose this is an emergency measure.
What of it? . . . As for your prosecuting and judicial officials, they
should be dismissed!'

Force, not economic means, not persuasion, had been used against
the peasants. Not just against 'kulaks' or other real or imagined class
enemies, but also against millions of so-called 'middle peasants',
ordinary smallholders. NEP was doomed. A new coercive era was
beginning.

Bukharin was horrified. A row blew up in the Politbureau. Stalin
admitted excesses, retreated in words, allowed the publication of a
resolution which apparently censured over-zealous application of
policies designed to meet an emergency. But he kept his grip firmly
on the apparatus of power, began a campaign to isolate and discredit the so-called 'right-wing deviationists', the name given by
Stalin to anyone who sought to avoid a clash with the mass of the
peasantry. He repeated the policy of requisitions. The helpless
Bukharin saw at last – why did he not see it before? – what was
coming to him. In despair he turned even to his old party enemy
Kamenev, friend of Zinoviev and ally (in 1926–7) of Trotsky, and
spoke with horror of this 'Genghis Khan', who would destroy them
all. (Genghis Khan was a Tartar potentate who conquered China
and terrorised much of Asia. His name is a byword in Russia for
cruelty and massacre.) At last Bukharin saw that he had much
more in common with the oppositionists he had helped to destroy
than with his formidable ex-ally. It was much too late. He went under
without being able to put up any fight.

The year 1928 saw the removal of moderate economic advisers.
The able and original minds who were pioneers of economic development theory nearly all lost their jobs, and not long afterwards some
of them were arrested. Kondratiev, Vainshtein, Feldman, Bazarov . . .
the list is a long one. A few hardy individuals survived to be released
after the death of Stalin. (I met one of these few in Moscow in
1969.)

This was also the first year of 'show trials', the much-publicised
morality-story court cases in which the accused plead guilty to
unlikely but politically 'convenient' offences. Various engineers

confessed to plots and sabotage on behalf of foreign powers. But these were not yet Party men. That was to come later.

It was the last year in which open discussion of controversial issues was possible in the Party. It was in September of that year that Bukharin's 'Notes of an economist' was published, a carefully worded plea for moderation and balance in industrial planning. From then on, neither he nor any other Party leader – Stalin and his henchmen excepted – would get his thoughts into print. They could still gather and grumble, exchange letters, perhaps even conspire. But the last remaining vestige of the Party as a policy discussion forum faded away never to return, as Stalin consolidated his power and began to impose his conception of how Russia should be ruled, a conception we will be discussing and describing shortly.

In April 1929 the sixteenth Party Conference adopted the maximum version of the first five-year plan. This envisaged a huge leap forward in industrial construction. Industrial output was to rise by 180 per cent, investment by 228 per cent, consumption by almost 70 per cent, agricultural output by 55 per cent. All warnings that such figures were unrealistic were rejected as 'right-deviationist' heresy, if not treason. Stalin may or may not have believed that this plan was realisable. After all, there was no precedent in the world's economic history, and he may have genuinely thought that, by mobilising the Party and people to a supreme effort, there really were 'no fortresses the Bolsheviks cannot take', to cite a slogan of the period. Alternatively he may have believed that by these methods more could be achieved than by a balanced growth strategy, even if many of the targets were indeed unreal. Finally, he must have seen in this sort of approach great political virtues: it mobilised under his leadership a mass of Party members, to storm the heavens, to create a modern industrial society. Let us not underestimate the genuine enthusiasm which this policy generated, especially among the younger of the faithful. Whether consciously or subconsciously, Stalin must have welcomed the logic of this strategy: discipline, struggle, repression, organisation. He was at home in such a setting.

The year 1928, then, was a great turning-point. The realisation of this did not happen suddenly, it only gradually dawned even on well-informed citizens that a momentous turn was in progress. The more so as the tightly controlled press pretended that policy was unchanged, that NEP was still the basis of the Party line. Yet 'the revolution from above' was already beginning.

International affairs

The shift from moderation to an apparently left-wing policy was reflected also in the Comintern, the Communist International set up on Lenin's inspiration in 1918, to act as the general staff of world revolution, and which from the first was dominated by the Soviet Party. It may be, as Trotsky alleged, that the 'socialism-in-one-country' doctrine was the negation of world-revolutionary doctrines. It was alleged by the opposition that the Stalin faction had been prone to seek alliances with moderates, with the TUC in Britain in 1926, with Chiang Kai-shek in China in 1926–27, alliances which ended in failure. Trotsky's analysis of Stalinist policy at home and abroad was, however, gravely defective. He thought that the subsiding of the revolutionary wave, and rule by a bureaucracy, led to conservatism. He did not anticipate Stalin's left turn, domestically or internationally.

Stalin understood little of foreign countries and gave little attention to the Comintern, but the logic of his political position impelled him not only to oust the Bukharinists from their posts in the International, but also to compel the latter to adopt in all countries the extremist line which Stalin was following in the USSR. But whereas in the USSR Stalin's policy was a real (if ruthless) response to real problems and frustrations, it made no sense outside Soviet borders.

The Sixth Congress of the Comintern, in that same year 1928, obediently adopted the Stalinist theses. The international movement had followed the Soviet model, and eliminated genuine discussion in the name of Bolshevisation. Party leaders who were suspected of following a line of their own were expelled and discredited: thus the powerful German Communist Party lost its leaders Brandler and Thalheimer, and was led to its ultimate disaster by obedient (if courageous) second-raters, such as Thaelmann. The Comintern, already weak, became from then onwards a somewhat insignificant branch of the Soviet foreign office. Lenin had spoken at congresses held in his lifetime. Stalin left matters in the hands of underlings and did not bother to attend.

The left turn was made in 1928, a year of boom in the capitalist world. It is true that a year later the great crash heralded a depression, but this circumstance brought about the rise not of Communism but of Fascism. Communist Parties were forced into the narrowest sectarian moulds. Alliances with Labour or Social-Democratic parties were forbidden. Slogans such as 'For Soviet Britain' were seriously launched. The Nazi-Fascist menace was ignored. The non-

Communist left was 'the main enemy', the Social-Democrats were labelled 'social fascists'. It is hard to escape the conclusion that the sharp turn towards super-militant and sectarian policies was a mere by-product of the internal attack on Bukharin and the moderates. In this way Stalin was ensuring for his henchmen control over the Comintern, and with it also control over the world's Communist Parties, which he was cynically to use as a minor element in his political manoeuvres. It is difficult to read men's minds, especially minds as devious as Stalin's, but it may well be that he used the Comintern primarily for its effect not abroad but in the Soviet Union itself. The Party faithful took internationalism seriously. It would have been embarrassing if any Communist Party were to fall under the control of men who could not be trusted to follow the Kremlin's line.

This was of particular importance in 1928 and the immediately succeeding years because of the war scare. Official propaganda hammered away at the theme of imminent danger of invasion, intervention, counter-revolution. It is hard to say whether this was a view sincerely held. The enemy were seen as the 'Anglo-French imperialists', and also Japan. Japanese aggressive ambitions were real enough, though it was China rather than the Soviet Union which had reasons for fear. In relation to 'Chamberlain and Poincaré', cast for the role of villains (Sir Austen Chamberlain's monocle fitted the image particularly well), this was largely imaginary. True, Baldwin's government had broken off diplomatic relations with the Soviet Union in 1927, but no military action against Russia was contemplated by Britain or France. War dangers were, however, very useful for Stalin's group. They reinforced pleas for unity and discipline, it discredited any oppositionists who rocked the boat at a dangerous time, and justified ambitious industrialisation tempos, especially for heavy industry.

Propagandist links between internal repression and the international line of the party were provided by the 'Menshevik' trial. This one was a much-publicised affair, involving a number of ex-Mensheviks, ranging from Sukhanov (who had written some fascinating memoirs on the revolution) to Bazarov and other leading economic planners. They were accused, among other things, of plotting with the leaders of the Second International (i.e. of the Labour and Social-Democratic parties of the West) to intervene, wreck, invade, etc. . . . So, in line with the super-left policies adopted in 1928, prominent on the list of enemies were the non-Communist left. Leon

Blum, Ramsay MacDonald, Emile Vandervelde, leaders respectively of the French, British and Belgian Socialist (Labour) parties, were social-fascists. The real Fascists were largely ignored. Of course, the prisoners pleaded guilty, and provided evidence in the form of confessions which were false in most if not all respects. Thus one man claimed that an exiled Menshevik leader had visited Russia secretly to see him; yet at the date in question the leader was attending a conference in Amsterdam. This was an early example of a technique later to become all too common: a trial scenario written with far more regard for public relations than for facts, and the prisoners succumbing to pressure and admitting all sorts of crimes and conspiracies alleged by the prosecution. A detailed account of the preparation of this trial, written by the only survivor, is to be found in the book by Medvedev (see list of recommended reading). All an integral part of the Stalin system.

Already in 1930 the Nazis were plainly becoming a major menace in Germany. Yet until well after Hitler came to power, the official line insisted that the Social-Democrats were enemies, 'social fascists'. It is hard to judge how much help this was to the Nazis, but to say the least, it did nothing to help those who tried to resist them. Stalin had already reached a position in which no one but he could initiate or alter major policies, even in fields such as foreign relations in which his personal knowledge was small. It was becoming clear that he did not welcome advice which ran counter to his prejudices; indeed such 'advisers' could suffer punishment. No doubt this helps to explain the obstinacy with which an erroneous line was persisted in. But more of this in due course.

Stalin won both because of his skill in manipulating the party machine which he controlled, and also because he succeeded in convincing many – probably a real and large majority – of Party members that his methods and policies could cope with the many problems of the time. The foreign menace was exaggerated, and the response to it illogical and counter-productive. However, the domestic crisis was real enough: Stalin's proposed solutions seemed logical. At first the former left opposition, i.e. the exiled Trotskyists, welcomed the left turn as a recognition of the necessities of the situation. It was only later that they, and indeed many who thought they were Stalinists, paid with their lives for their misreading of Stalin's character and motives.

Chapter 2

The System Consolidated

The Revolution from Above

Stalin achieved supreme power in the process of turning the political machine towards a total transformation of post-revolutionary Soviet society. NEP was based on an independent peasantry and a tolerated private trade and petty manufacture. Stalin decided to launch the first five-year plan, to collectivise the peasantry, to eliminate private enterprise in the urban sector. Just exactly when his decisions were taken is not yet clear. They could have been taken by stages, without any initial overall conscious strategy. Thus the investment requirements of the five-year plan could have precipitated the conflict with the peasants, and experience with requisitioning led to the conclusion that coercion was both necessary and feasible. Repeated requisitioning was bound to lead to adverse peasant reaction, in the shape of reduced production, and collectivisation then became a way of ensuring that there was effective party-state control over production and sales. It is possible to imagine that Stalin drifted into his 'revolution from above' by a series of responses to emergencies. It is also possible to assert that he knew what he was doing, and that his tactics, silences and evasions were due to the need to 'sell' his policies to a party which did not yet understand them and which, until the middle of 1929, might still resist them. Official Soviet histories to this day are reticent or misleading in dealing with this sensitive subject. One day, when archives are opened, we will know more about all this (or rather we *may* know, since even archives were affected by Stalin's reluctance to speak truthfully or to allow others to do so).

Collectivisation, altering as it did the lives of well over half the people, was a fact of tremendous importance. Its consequences were many: the political system, agriculture, the terror machine, the fate of many Party members, were all greatly affected. It is not for nothing that sensitive men such as Pasternak later ascribed many evils of the system to collectivisation. It was *not* just a matter of reorganising the methods of cultivation. The essential elements which must be borne in mind are listed below.

Firstly, Stalin launched mass collectivisation suddenly and without any preparation, in his declaration of 7 November 1929. There had been no committees to inquire about how best to collectivise, or how such farms should be run. There was no Party conference, congress, meeting, at which the policy could be explained to members. Therefore no one, neither local officials nor peasantry, knew what was about to happen.

Secondly, Stalin claimed that the bulk of the 'middle peasants' were voluntarily joining the collectives. This was simply a lie, but it was a compulsory lie. It was also a necessary one. Not only Engels but also Lenin had warned against the use of force against the peasant masses. But Stalin *was* using force against the peasant masses. Therefore, since there could be no mass collectivisation without mass coercion, it was necessary to claim that it was really a voluntary process. This led to all kinds of tragi-comic contradictions: thus the Commissar for Agriculture, Yakovlev, declared that force was not to be used, but local leaders were none the less told to achieve 100 per cent collective membership in weeks or even days. How this was to be done without force was left unclear.

Thirdly, collectivisation was carried through by a predominantly urban Party machine. There were very few Party members in the villages. Ignorant zealots, or well-meaning townsmen with no knowledge of rural problems, had no common language with the peasants. Many thought that the peasants were stupid people who did not know what was good for them. Many sincerely believed that the promised tractors and modern methods, plus the abolition of the medieval strips, would lead quickly to so big an upsurge of agricultural output that everyone would be better off. Still others just did what they hoped would accord with their superiors' wishes. One Party official told them: 'Remember that if you overdo things and are arrested, you will have been arrested for your revolutionary work'. With good or bad conscience, the Party's cadres used coercion on an unprecedented scale.

Fourthly, Stalin himself intervened to make excesses inevitable. According to evidence published recently by Soviet scholars, he refused to allow any exemptions: all livestock was to be collectivised (he was later to retreat from this position, but only after extremely severe damage was done). Worse still, he decreed 'dekulakisation'. This means uprooting the so-called kulaks, the better-off peasants, breaking up families, sending millions of people to distant exile or labour camps. This was done by no sort of legal process, but on the basis of 'class analysis' (i.e. by category: you have two horses and four cows, then you are a kulak, therefore your goods are confiscated and you will be deported). It was used also as a means of enforcing collectivisation (these were the so-called 'ideological kulaks', i.e. those who opposed the official policy, whether they were 'rich' or poor). A Soviet scholar, Ivnitsky, recently wrote that instead of being a consequence of collectivisation, 'dekulakisation' became its cause; in other words, to punish and to strike fear into those who did not want to join collectives. There had been some opposition to these drastic measures, but Stalin cut it short with a vicious speech which contained the words 'when the head is off one does not mourn for the hair'. Softness was equated with disloyalty.

There developed another feature peculiar to Stalinist methods, which was to have terrible consequences. In the political as in the economic field, the party under Stalin's leadership enforced a kind of guilt by association perhaps unique in history. Men could be accused of not just being a Bukharinist or right-wing deviationist, but of 'appeasement' towards them, or of not opposing those who favoured a more tolerant attitude. Some found themselves in prison because, in not fighting this or that deviation, they 'objectively' provided 'grist to the mill' for potential enemies of the regime. Others were arrested for not having denounced some acquaintance who had been arrested for any of the above reasons. Later on the great purges were to eliminate all these categories, expanded to include relatives, colleagues, subordinates, friends, and associates of friends and so on. Analogously, there were some who were labelled 'kulak-sympathisers', or 'sub-kulak' (*podkulachnik*), which could be made to cover any person or Party member who might think that the official peasant policy was too harsh. Its harshness, of course, created enemies, and caused doubts, dismay, opposition. The so-called secret or political police (OGPU, later relabelled NKVD, or Peoples' Commissariat of Internal Affairs) came increasingly into the picture, becoming more and more indispensable as real and imaginary enemies multiplied. It was used not only against the peasants or other 'laymen' but now against Party members also.

It was in this atmosphere that the peasants were forced into collectives, amid scenes of violence and repression which have yet to be adequately documented. Eye-witnesses have spoken of threats, confiscations, cruelty, of families made destitute and then sent a thousand and more miles east in cattle trucks. There were protests too. In some areas there was particularly strong resistance. These included the relatively well-off peasants of the black-earth belt in the Ukraine and the north Caucasus, and the pastoral peoples of Kazakhstan and other backward regions in Asia. Pressure was not everywhere equal, partly because the Party was ordered to concentrate on some areas, partly because local officials reacted differently to orders. But collectivisation was bitterly resented. In the months January, February and early March 1930 Stalin's officials made rapid headway, collectivising nearly 60 per cent of all the 25 million peasant households.

The damage this might do to the spring sowing, and the danger of outright rebellion, caused Stalin to call a halt. The way in which he did it was consistent with his cynicism as a political operator, but it shocked many of his comrades. He published an article entitled 'Dizzy with success'. Local comrades were blamed for excesses. Why did they use force, when the whole process was supposed to be voluntary? Why did they collectivise all livestock? Collectivisation should be consolidated on a sound basis. Not a word to suggest that coercion was inspired, indeed ordered, by Moscow.

The peasants took advantage of this declaration by walking out of the collectives in millions. The percentage of peasant households collectivised quickly fell to 23 per cent. But Stalin ordered pressure to be resumed. By threats, more deportations, arbitrary taxes, over-assessment for compulsory deliveries, the peasants were gradually made to return to the hated collectives. As the government paid low prices for the produce which they took from the farms, their incomes were small and the peasants remained exceedingly poor. However, they were politically helpless. By 1934 the struggle was virtually over. The cost was huge. Livestock was slaughtered, or died of neglect in the collectives, with catastrophic results, as the following figures show:

	(*Million head*)	
	1928	*1933*
Cattle	70.5	38.4
Pigs	26.0	12.1
Sheep and goats	146.7	50.2

In Kazakhstan, a backward and pastoral republic, the sheep population was almost wiped out (and with it many of the Kazakhs too).

	1928	1935
Sheep and goats	19.2	2.6

Large increases in state procurements, and poor harvests, left the peasants with too little to keep body and soul together. In the terrible period 1932–3 a great many died. Local Party secretaries who warned of the danger of hunger, who tried to protect 'their' peasants from excessive requisitioning, were dismissed or arrested as right-wing deviationists. To the credit of the Party officials of those days, the number of such dismissals and arrests was large, especially in the north Caucasus and the Ukraine. Their successors were more ruthless, and millions died of hunger. By then Stalinist rules applied to the news media, and not a word about mass starvation appeared in the press at the time, even in areas where corpses were littering the streets. Indeed Soviet official histories to this day do not mention this dreadful famine at all.

It is sometimes said that Stalin deliberately starved the peasants into submission. This would not be quite fair. He faced resistance from the peasants, he thought that they were deliberately withholding supplies, the needs of the towns and of export were pressing. So he pressed. Indeed, we now know that he told the Politbureau in November 1932 that 'certain groups of collective farms and peasants' had to be dealt a 'devastating blow', to impose discipline and authority. Perhaps he thought the peasants had secret stocks and would survive. In a letter to the novelist Sholokhov, published much later, Stalin spoke of 'a war of life and death'. He told Churchill at one of their wartime meetings that the struggle with the peasantry had been a terrible one, like the battle with Nazi Germany. After 1928 Stalin never visited villages, and may not have known the horrors that were being inflicted on peasants in certain areas. Be all that as it may, those millions of deaths were the consequences of his policy, and it was on his orders that ruthlessness became standard procedure. 'Without coercion we will not get the grain and so it hardly matters if we overdo things a little'; thus spoke one of his lieutenants in the Ukraine. At least it showed to everyone that Stalin and his henchmen would recoil at nothing. Many sincere and tough Party members were horrified, but few had the courage to say so in the prevailing political atmosphere. Stalin's wife, Allilueva, is said to have committed suicide as a protest against what was going on.

While this coercion operation was in progress in the villages, the industrial five-year plan was speeded up and expanded. 'Let us fulfil the five-year plan in four years', thus went the slogan. As 1930 proceeded, more and more targets were revised upwards to ludicrous levels. Peasants fleeing collectivisation joined building brigades or staffed the new factories. They were inefficient, they smashed machines for lack of elementary training. Some were sullen and resentful, and real sabotage must have occurred, alongside innumerable reports of invented plots and treason. Others were fired with enthusiasm. Youngsters living in tents in the Siberian cold built great new factories, such as the Magnitogorsk complex, with few tools and much hard work. Productivity may have been low, waste of resources all too common, sound economic principles neglected. Yet this was a great forward leap, 'the construction of socialism', which would make Russia a great industrial power. Meanwhile what was happening in the West? Mass unemployment, financial collapse, industrial decline. Whatever was wrong with Soviet industry, it was growing, on a new basis of centralised planning. What was there that the West could teach Stalin? Could he learn from Herbert Hoover, the American President who was presiding over the greatest depression known in the history of Western industrial society? Could he learn from Western economics, which was totally uninterested, in those days, in growth or development? No wonder some Western citizens as well as Russians thought that Stalin's way was the best way. Many Western experts came to help in the process of construction.

However, the first five-year plan was overambitious even without upward amendment. Attempts to aim for impossible targets created bottlenecks, shortages, confusion. Many vast projects remained unfinished for lack of materials, skilled labour, transport. Investment grew at a tempo far exceeding anything advocated by Trotskyists in past years, and far exceeding practicable and feasible limits. Central planners imposed priorities, and the ordinary citizen's needs came lowest on the list. Tough administrators issued orders from Moscow, cajoled, threatened. Failure was all too often treated as sabotage or treason. There evolved a style of conducting affairs, which is part of the essence of Stalinism and of which much more will have to be said. There evolved also a systematic central control over production and resource use, which did not exist in the twenties and which many now regard as typical of socialist planning.

Rationing of essential foodstuffs was introduced for urban consumers by the end of 1929, life became exceedingly difficult. The great investment drive led to inflation. Goods, at fixed prices, disappeared. There developed a variety of 'closed shops', available only to employees of priority sectors, or to those with rank and influence. 'Commercial' stores were opened, to sell rationed goods at very high prices. Others sold scarce goods only for foreign currency or gold. A market for peasant surpluses was tolerated, but in near-famine conditions of 1932–33 prices were sky-high. Quality declined. Service worsened. 'Take what you're given, don't argue and don't hold up the queue'; that is how a Soviet writer described the situation of the customer. Consumer goods production suffered from shortages of materials, which were diverted to priority industries, and also from the elimination of small private businesses and most craftsmen. Food supplies were adversely affected by the consequences of collectivisation. Everything was affected by transport bottlenecks, which led to the railways being put virtually under martial law.

At the end of 1932 the five-year plan was declared fulfilled amid a flourish of trumpets. The figures were suspect. Key industrial sectors such as steel were far behind schedule. True, much had been done, and many large projects completed in the better years 1934–36 were begun during the first plan period. But the country was impoverished and exhausted. The year 1933 was hard not only in the villages. The workers too suffered, from food shortages, queues, and, finally, from rapidly rising retail prices, which outran increases in money wages. Housing became exceedingly short and overcrowded.

Typical of Stalin was a speech he made when conditions of life had reached a very low point: 'It is clear', he said, 'that the workers' living standards are rising all the time. Anyone who denies this is an enemy of Soviet power.' An excellent example of the technique of the big lie, backed by police terror. An example, too, of how to stop empirical social research: who would dare inquire into cost of living indices and real wages? No wonder it was thought politic to stop publishing such statistics. Of course it is true that statesmen do not always speak the truth, but most others, Lenin included, would have talked about the necessity of sacrifices, rather than blandly denying that any sacrifices existed.

Privilege, Inequality, Hierarchy, Discipline

Shortage, rationing, allocation, give great power to those who control. This danger was recognised by Lenin, and to guard against the corrupting effects of power he insisted on the so-called 'Party maximum'. That is to say, no Party member was to receive a salary higher than that of a skilled worker. Under the conditions of NEP, this principle meant something. But when there are 'administered' shortages, what matters is not so much the salary but the results of influence. Price-controlled and cheap goods, or rooms, or railway tickets, went to those who had the influence to get them.

At first this might seem justifiable on grounds of some sort of equity. Officials who worked hard for the common good ought not to be made to queue for necessities, just as army commanders can expect to have their food served to them or even their boots cleaned. However, what might in its origins be a necessary privilege began to be taken as a right. Such a trend is natural. What was not so natural was Stalin's reaction to it. In all sorts of ways he made it clear that dispensing privilege was an essential part of the power-mechanism, indeed of the Soviet system itself. Social historians of the future are bound to see in it a cornerstone of Stalinism.

In 1931 he made an attack on 'petty-bourgeois egalitarianism', demanding a substantial increase on wage differentials, and increases in pay of managers, engineers, officials. The 'party maximum' was abolished. All this could be justified in terms of incentives: human skills were in very short supply, and rewards were needed for those who stayed put and learned a trade. But inequalities became not only very large but were implanted in the official ideology by Stalin personally.

With the gradual abolition of rationing in 1934–35, accompanied by large price increases, income differentials became the principal indicator of real purchasing power. But privilege continued alongside, since some goods remained scarce and could be obtained only by influence. The practice also developed of issuing extra pay to officials above a given rank, this being given in a plain envelope and without any accounting. These things continued for decades, and indeed special 'closed shops' for the elite are still with us today. Trade unions, which in earlier years might have protested, were reduced to total impotence or became part of the machinery of government.

It was also under Stalin that society became increasingly organised hierarchically. Rank-consciousness is a Russian tradition, but the old ways had been apparently decisively disrupted by the revolution. The needs of government led inevitably to some restoration of civil-service ranks, just as the army needed officers and sergeants. The old names were abolished, ministers were relabelled 'peoples' commissars', officers were not called officers, uniforms were changed and simplified. Yet gradually the old ways returned. In vain Lenin in his last years fulminated against 'bureaucracy' and the resurgent habits of old officialdom. He did not foresee that the new officialdom would develop habits too.

The scope of Party and state control was not all-pervasive in the twenties because of a degree of pluralism; the Party machine did not control all organs of opinion, it was still possible for non-Bolsheviks to get a hearing and a publisher, and the Party itself still permitted some argument within its ranks. Among the leaders were brilliant intellectuals, who put their viewpoints on a high and subtle level. Even the slower-witted Stalin and his comrades had to discuss, to argue. He developed a technique of simplifying issues, of talking in the language of catechism, which was popular with the semi-educated Party secretaries. But he could not, in those days, indulge in the kinds of lies and prevarications which are only possible when no one dares to answer back.

In the twenties publications were censored, true, but there was a range of fundamental controversy. Men could and did make a name for themselves without having an official position of consequence. This was true of some philosophers, journalists, economists, historians. Academic life was still largely controlled by professors who had made their reputations in pre-revolutionary times. Literature was the scene of controversy, many schools contended. Non-Communist writers, such as Pilnyak, Zamyatin, Bulgakov, Mandelshtam, Akhmatova, were still printed. Satire flourished. In modern painting, architecture, theatre, Russia was among the world's leaders. People could still occasionally travel abroad unofficially.

There is no need to idealise the twenties, since it is not hard to show that many evils of later decades were already growing. But the contrast with the thirties is striking. Anyone who can read Russian can note it for himself, by just reading the publications of 1926, say, and comparing them with 1934 or any subsequent year. By then writers, academicians, philosophers, had been regimented. The various writers' groups were abolished and a single Union of Soviet

Writers was formed. Only one organisation was recognised in all fields, and only one 'correct' doctrine, defined by the Party. All others were illegal, incorrect, heretical.

As for the style of discussion, Stalin himself set the tone with a sharp reprimand, in 1931, to an editor of a periodical, who chose to allow some expression of a view other than that approved of by the leadership. Error must be castigated, and shown to be due to enemy machinations. Stalin's henchmen saw to it that editors and censors understood the message, and judges, lawyers and policemen too. Whichever did not follow the line was liable to be held guilty of 'objectively' aiding the enemies of the Party by not effectively opposing their treasonable plots.

The language even of academic discussion became abusive and violent. An organ of the Academy accused one unfortunate (and very abstract) economic theorist, I. Rubin, of being an agent of the bourgeoisie and the Second-International interventionists. A pair of writers who advocated a somewhat softer policy towards the peasants were accused (in the same journal) of sabotage and injecting horses with meningitis. Wreckers were to be sought everywhere. Dissent was plainly a crime.

All this had many consequences, not least for the structure and influence of rank. The state owned most of the instruments of production, so almost everyone who was not a collective farmer was employed by some state agency or other. Influence of any kind could be wielded only within officially recognised organisations and through official channels, and any published statement had to follow the line laid down. Obviously, this kind of society provided a tremendous field of power for holders of rank in Party and government. Conversely, to run such a society it was essential to organise the ruling stratum into ranks and hierarchies. Members of the ruling group developed a very strong sense of self-interest in suppressing any challenge from outside. It was not just by Stalin's orders that they eliminated all unofficial groups and ideas. The doctrine of the withering away of the state was forgotten, and Stalin was later to assert the opposite, that the state required to be strengthened.

In doing all this, Stalin and his many supporters perhaps subconsciously reflected another Russian tradition. The service gentry, the *dvoryane*, were brought into being by the Tsars, and owed their status to rank in the service of the state. The new official class, holding rank in party and state, owed it more and more to Stalin and his immediate entourage. Like their Tsarist forebears, they came to resent any pretensions to status except through rank. When Russia's greatest poet, Pushkin, was killed in 1837 and people came to pay their respects, a leading courtier of the day was said to have remarked: 'Why such a fuss about a mere junior gentleman of the bedchamber?' (that was Pushkin's court rank). In 1937 Stalin's courtiers were to pay as little attention to unofficial literary merit, with some tragic results.

Men of rank in the Soviet Union happen to be identifiable through the appointments system, which was developed by and under Stalin. Known in Russia as *nomenklatura*, it is a list of posts of political, social and economic significance, with alongside them the name of the Party committee responsible for the appointment. A man deemed worthy to hold a post on the *nomenklatura* is known by the designation *nomenklaturnyi rabotnik*, or official on the list. A British analogy would be administrative civil servant, except that the Soviet list, like the power of the Soviet party, is all-embracing. It covers officers of the Party itself, civil servants, ministers, mayors, secretaries of musicians' societies, censors, trade union officials, generals, managers, editors, collective-farm chairmen. No matter who is supposed to appoint or 'elect' them, a Party committee (in all important instances the personnel department of the *central* committee) is in fact the body which hires and fires. Or at the very least no hiring and firing can take place without its approval. The totality of all *nomenklatura* personnel covers almost every one that matters in the USSR. They are the 'Establishment' in most senses of that word. They are the elite, the ruling stratum. One can be a well-paid tenor, ballerina or nuclear physicist without being on the list, true. But these are exceptions, and even the exceptions are subject to a Party veto.

The pyramid of 'elected' Soviets which nominally ruled Russia since the revolution had lost all effective power with the coming of the one-party state, i.e. by the end of the civil war. Their role in the early thirties was so negligible that even the formalities ceased to be observed.

But what about the Party itself? With all oppositionists cowed, exiled or imprisoned, was it already an obedient instrument in Stalin's hands? Could he rely on it to glorify him, to mobilise and coerce the passive and frightened people in his name? Was it disciplined, or might it perhaps kick back at him? Members of the Party had gone through a very difficult time during the period of the 'revolution from above' (this was Stalin's own phrase, by the way).

We shall see that they were not yet totally free of the sin of independent thinking, and events showed that in taking belated action to assert themselves most of the delegates to the Party congress of 1934 were condemning themselves to death.

The Seventeenth Congress and the Great Terror

The year 1934 brought some relief to a hard-pressed population. The harvest was fair. Output of consumer goods was rising. Stalin declared that 'life was getting better, comrades, life was getting joyous'. There was in fact very little joy, but no more famine. Things were getting better. The crisis was over. The peasants were almost all collectivised. The foundations of a great modern industrial structure were laid. Great sacrifices now called for some reward. Surely, after the strains of the last few years, relaxation was called for, and also reconciliation with those ex-oppositionists who were prepared to collaborate in the building of a new and better Soviet Union.

A Party Congress, the seventeenth, met in January/February 1934, and called itself the 'congress of victors'. Stalin made the keynote speech and was duly cheered. Everyone echoed the mass media's praises of his wisdom. He was the leader, the 'architect of our victories'. Ex-oppositionists who were allowed to speak (Tomsky, Preobrazhensky) admitted errors, expressed support for Stalin. Harmony seemed to reign.

Yet an odd thing happened, noticed by few at the time. A popular and tough Party boss, Kirov, was at this time the Secretary in Leningrad. He made a speech, full of optimism. 'Our successes really are immense. The devil take it, to speak frankly, one so wants to live and live! After all, look and see what is going on! It's a fact!' He was cheered to the echo. Delegates wanted him promoted to Moscow and this was said to be connected with their desire to reduce Stalin's immense powers. There was an unreported session, and out of it came a significant relabelling: ever since 1922 Stalin held the post of General Secretary. The congress altered this to just 'secretary'. Such things are scarcely accidental. It was rumoured – one cannot document such things, but they are still talked about in the USSR – that Kirov wanted to relax the pressures, and that a majority of the Congress, and of the central committee it elected, were in favour of this. Stalin, it seems, sensed a conspiracy. Maybe we will learn one day that the majority that could have voted in secret session to clip his wings comprised those who were later to be shot on Stalin's orders.

In December 1934 Kirov was murdered in Leningrad under obscure circumstances. Stalin was one of his pall-bearers. The murder was denounced as the work of terrorists. Legal procedures were suspended. Summary executions and mass arrests and deportations followed. Zinoviev and Kamenev, helpless and out of effective political life, were forced to admit to a vague political complicity. A lull during 1935 gave grounds for some optimism. Economic conditions were improving, and Stalin himself was committed to a new constitution, 'the most democratic in the world', which was then in draft. In that year also the Seventh (and last) Congress of the Comintern switched at long last to an anti-Fascist line, as the reality of the Nazi menace was finally understood. The USSR joined the League of Nations and tried to secure alliances with the west European democracies. The former 'social fascists' were now wooed in a Popular-Front tactic. But then in 1936, the terror machine was unleashed. For the next two years, the Soviet Union was convulsed by the 'great purge', the scale of which still leaves one breathless and incredulous.

The world knew about it all through the series of show trials. Honoured leaders of the revolution, such as Bukharin, Zinoviev, Kamenev, Rykov, Pyatakov, Rakovsky, Krestinsky, were tried in public and confessed to unimaginable crimes. They, under instructions from 'Judas-Trotsky' and in association with the German and Japanese intelligence services, planned wrecking and diversionism. They caused railway and mining accidents, food shortages, industrial breakdowns; they planned the murder of Kirov, plotted against the lives of Stalin, Molotov and other leaders. They no longer had a political programme, they were – and had for many years been – mere spies and despicable traitors, who deserved to be shot without mercy.

Foreigners wondered what made these old and courageous revolutionaries confess. Was it an act of loyalty to the Party to which they had devoted their lives? Or was it torture, drugs, threats to wives and children? The charges themselves were too fantastic for any but dupes to take seriously, but some dupes were found in the West. The ordinary Russian people may have believed some of the 'evidence', and those capable of thinking for themselves were terrified by what they saw and read. In fact, as Khrushchev told us in 1956, tortures and beatings were used, and one must also allow for the demoralisation of men being destroyed by 'their' Party. That, and the fact that those unwilling to confess were anyway destroyed, explained the behaviour of these men reasonably well. Not all played their part as the script required. Bukharin tied the odious prosecutor Vyshinsky in knots on occasion, and Krestinsky did once withdraw his confession: the session was suspended, and on his return to court he had been made to change his mind. There is no doubt at all that this whole scenario was a product of Stalin's vengeful imagination.

Yet all this was but a tiny fraction of the terror. Most of it produced no public trials, confessions remained in secret files. Who was involved in this great sweep of coercion, apart from the former oppositionists?

Firstly, leading Party members, including the members of Stalin's own faction, which dominated the seventeenth Congress, who were thought 'unreliable'. By this I mean unreliable supporters of Stalin, who either voted to limit his powers in 1934, or who tried to stop the terror machine. This category includes, as we now know, the *large* majority of the central committee (at least 100 out of 130, including alternate members i.e. those who could attend without the right to vote) and of the delegates to the Congress. Here we find such men as Eikhe, Chubar, Postyshev, Kosior, Mezhlauk, and many others, including a high proportion of persons of ministerial rank, from the Commissar of Finance and the head of Gosplan downwards. The Party received a tremendous blow. Not for nothing did Leonard Schapiro call the relevant chapter of his history 'Stalin's victory over the Party'.

Secondly, the large majority of senior military officers, headed by the talented Tukhachevsky. They were supposed to have been tried by the secret court-martial, but the majority of those who were alleged to have tried them were themselves arrested shortly afterwards (Bliukher, Yegorov, etc.). All admirals commanding fleets, and all their replacements, were shot. Thousands of officers were sent to camps. The charge was treason.

Thirdly, a high proportion of managers at all levels, leading scientists, engineers; the economic damage so done is advanced as a principal explanation of the virtual cessation of Soviet economic growth in and after 1937.

Fourthly, almost every Party and state leader in every national republic within the USSR, on charges of treason, bourgeois nationalism, etc.

Fifthly, the man who headed the NKVD in 1936, Yagoda, was himself arrested the next year, and most senior police officials perished with him.

Sixthly, anyone with contacts abroad, including 'legitimate' ones: diplomats, foreign trade officials, intelligence agents, and many foreign Communist leaders resident in Russia (e.g. Bela Kun of Hungary, Remmele and Neumann of Germany, virtually *all* the Polish Communist exiles, etc.).

Finally, and numerically the largest category of all, there were those who were in some way related to any of the above: colleagues, subordinates, colleagues of colleagues and subordinates of subordinates, relatives, wives, children, friends, associates. These filled the concentration camps which were rapidly expanded.

> The stars of death shone upon us
> And innocent Russia writhed
> Beneath the blood-stained jackboots
> And the wheels of Black Marias.

So wrote the poet, Akhmatova, her husband and son being among those arrested. In fact the list is endless. It includes one of the best poets of twentieth-century Russia, Osip Mandelshtam, the finest prose writer of the Soviet period, Isaak Babel, the most distinguished stage director of his generation, Vsevolod Meyerhold, and other able men and women without number. On top of all this, the sheer scale and logic (or illogic) of the operation eventually led to a mass of denunciations, and so the terrified police, fearful of accusations of lack of vigilance, arrested persons of insignificance of all classes.

Personal tragedies could fill a library of volumes. The eminent poet Marina Tsvetayeva returned from the West to Russia with her husband and son; both were arrested and she committed suicide in despair. The former Commissar for Justice, Krylenko, was an enthusiastic alpinist. When he was arrested, so were hundreds of others who happened to be alpinists too. The wives of executed generals were arrested, separated from their children, and then were shot in their turn in distant prisons at the outbreak of war. No wonder a surviving child of a general, Peter Yakir, was later to be in the fight against the resurgence of Stalinist methods or a rehabilitation of Stalin's memory. Once arrested, the prisoner faced cruel conditions in prison and in camp, far worse than anything conceivable in the first and relatively 'liberal' decade of Soviet rule, or indeed in the reign of Nicholas II. Here Stalin himself was in part responsible: he specifically authorised torture and beatings, and many sources attribute to him the statement that prisons and camps are too soft, that they should not be a 'Kurort' (i.e. a vacation centre). This was taken by officials to be an instruction to be harsh. Prisoners in distant northern camps such as the notorious Kolyma complex in north-east Siberia suffered acutely from undernourishment, the bitter cold, scurvy. The reader may be referred to three of the best documents of the period, Solzhenitsyn's *One Day in the Life of Ivan Denisovich* and *Gulag Archipelago*, and Evgeniya Ginzberg's *Into the Whirlwind*, for vivid pictures of how things were for untold millions.

The high point of mass arrests was reached in 1937, with the coming of Yezhov to head the NKVD. The period is known to many in Russia as the *Yezhovshchina* in his name. Yet Yezhov was a creature of Stalin. When he had done his work he himself vanished, being replaced by the scarcely less odious Beria, under whom repression became systematised at a lower level of arrests. The Eighteenth Party Congress in 1939 noted that there had been some excesses, that some innocent men had been expelled from the Party. Zhdanov, a rising light in the Stalinist firmament, joked about a man who produced a medical certificate to the effect that he was mentally incapable of any deviations. A few were reinstated, but the millions in camp and prison remained where they were.

How many were shot, how many arrested, how many perished in camps and prisons? I will resist the temptation to speculate. Various computations exist, and some people, like Academician Sakharov, in his memorandum published abroad, have put total losses from Stalinist repression at between 12 and 15 million, a fantastically high figure which is yet within the bounds of credibility. No great terror in history ever went anywhere near as far. (I exclude genocide-massacres, which were different in motivation and purpose.) The 'terror' of the French revolution is as nothing in comparison. As for Tsarist repression, this too becomes negligible: a few thousand as against millions. (Sakharov's figure also includes arrests relating to periods other than 1936–8.)

Calculations are rendered difficult not only by the still-pervasive secrecy, but also because the terror hit various groups very unequally. The elite suffered most. The army is not untypical: officers above the rank of major were exceedingly likely to be arrested, junior officers less so, but only a small percentage of NCOs and men were involved: there are, of course, a great many more private soldiers than generals. Intellectuals were very hard hit: it would not be surprising to learn that as many as half of all persons with higher education were arrested, and the proportion was certainly much higher for *Party* intellectuals. Party functionaries at all levels were liquidated by the thousand. But the purge also swept up a lot of harmless members of the rank-and-file. Workers at the bench could be accused of sabotage if there was a breakdown, or of subversion for grumbling about shortages. Peasants were sometimes sentenced to eight years and more for stealing grain from 'their' farm, or for talking among themselves. A system of informers, themselves frightened by the consequences of not reporting what they heard, provided material for a police urged to vigilance against omnipresent 'enemies of the people'.

Did no one protest? Some did so. Ordzhonikidze, a close colleague of Stalin's, is said to have done so vehemently and committed suicide when he failed. Postyshev urged the end of blood-letting and was himself arrested. The machine could not be stopped, except by Stalin himself.

On top of the inhabitants of prison and camp there were yet more uncounted millions of exiles of various categories. One of these millions figures in Solzhenitsyn's *Cancer Ward*, an educated woman ordered out of her native Leningrad and earning a precarious living scrubbing floors and emptying bed-pans in a hospital ward in Central Asia. She and her like would not figure in statistics of arrests or of concentration camps, since she was not arrested or imprisoned. Yet she too suffered personal hardships and tragedies.

We must now consider two things. Firstly what was the *motive*, the purpose of the great wave of terror unleashed by Stalin. Secondly, what were its *consequences* for the Party and for society?

The Purposes of the Purge

What was Stalin's objective? He wanted supreme power for himself. Without doubt he wished to destroy all enemies, actual and potential. But other ambitious men have seldom acted with such ruthlessness, though they too aimed for supreme power. Was it just that Stalin was such a vengeful and vicious person? This is part of the answer, surely. An old Communist, who once worked in the Comintern and who thought that Stalin had been right and Bukharin wrong, said to me: 'But there was no reason why Bukharin should not have been sent to be a schoolteacher in Omsk'. In other words, political victory did not require show trials and executions. But Stalin believed otherwise.

Since he did not speak his mind, we must again reconstruct his thought processes from indirect evidence. The following might be a reasonable interpretation, but others are possible.

He and his comrades must have known or felt the intense hatreds below them. The revolution from above caused great hardship, coercion left many wounds. Many had been insulted and injured. Within and outside the Party, they might dream of revenge. Conspiracy was probable. Party leaders rendered politically impotent by Stalin might seek to exploit the situation. The danger of war with Nazi Germany, growing every year, might give them their opportunity. *Ergo*, cut the danger off at the roots. Trotsky, it is true, spoke always of defending the Soviet Union. But he also once advanced the 'Clémenceau thesis'. Clémenceau had urged vigorous action to overthrow the French government during the First World War for failing in its duty to the nation (and, of course, he ultimately led France to victory in 1918). Oppositionists, then, might wish to overthrow Stalin after some military failures. So: liquidate them all in good time, destroy them and their reputations.

To achieve all this Stalin had to have control over the terror machine. The OGPU had been renamed 'People's Commissariat of Internal Affairs' (NKVD, from its Russian initial letters) in 1934. But from Stalin's point of view the NKVD itself was of uncertain loyalty. Its traditions were those of the founder of the secret police, Dzherzhinsky, a dedicated fanatic of unimpeachable integrity. True, his successors were of a much lower species, but Stalin did not feel safe until the NKVD had become his own personal security organ. The old OGPU-men were in the main replaced by new recruits, loyal rather than intelligent. He knew that the NKVD was staffed by men of limited brain-power. How could they identify an enemy? The purge had to be adapted to imperfect executors. So Stalin's unique concept of security evolved: deal with categories rather than people. Was there any past associations with any opposition? Was there a record of any statement which was off the Party line? Was he reported on unfavourably by a neighbour? Did he receive a visitor from abroad? Did he, by serving abroad, have the opportunity of meeting some foreign agent or Trotskyist? Was he a colleague of, or appointed by, any of the above? When the great blood-letting was in progress, did he express doubts as to its wisdom? Was he by any chance a son or wife or father of someone caught in the net? Then play safe: detain, deport, isolate. To provide a sort of reason, compel him to confess. All these people *could* have a reason to hate the regime. Once arrested, they could not be released, as they had a grievance. Guilt or innocence is irrelevant. Better a hundred innocent men in jail than let one guilty man escape.

This is no fantasy. Look at two characters in Solzhenitsyn's great story. Ivan Denisovich himself was arrested – why? Because he had escaped from a German prisoner-of-war camp. If the Germans *had* recruited him as a spy, he would have claimed to have escaped. So: to a camp with him in distant Siberia. His fellow-prisoner the naval officer had received a parcel from a British admiral with whom he was a liaison officer in the Arctic. Who knows, he *might* have been recruited by British intelligence? To a Siberian camp with him! In these years Greeks were deported from the Black Sea area, Chinese and Koreans were sent to prison camps from East Siberia, just in case. I heard of a man in Karaganda who received a letter from abroad in a language no one at the local NKVD could read: so they arrested him, 'just to be sure'. A Russian told me that, travelling in a train, he heard two fellow-passengers speaking French. He understood French. So he hastily bribed the conductor to move him to another compartment, in case he was arrested for not reporting what they might say!

Stalin feared war. Yet he liquidated most of his best military officers. Contradiction? Not entirely. Tukhachevsky, Uborevich, Yakir and others of the best generals had established military reputations, knew and trusted each other, had the loyalty and respect of their subordinates. These were indeed useful qualities in war, but made them potentially effective conspirators. They *could* challenge Stalin if they wished. In modern strategic jargon, they had that capability. Therefore, though there was in fact no conspiracy, they had to be destroyed. Every one was deemed to have appointed 'his' men to work with him, so thousands of staff officers met the same fate as their commanders.

Stalin believed in obedience. He believed also in their being one answer, the correct answer, to any question. To be wrong, or indeed to disagree with the official view, was another indicator of potential treason; 'he thinks too much, such men are dangerous'. Technical conflicts of view about cruisers versus submarines, or on fuel policy or economic planning, would and did lead to accusations that one side to the argument was in the pay of the enemy. He systematically eliminated the very notion of non-subversive disagreement.

Stalin believed in Stalin. He was sure that only he could rule, and steer Russia through the dangerous shoals and rocks that lay in her path. He was doubtless jealous of the intellectuals he destroyed, but he could have only contempt for their political sense and realism. How could they run the USSR? He pursued with single-minded vigour his own glorification. Poems, cantatas, pictures, novels, presented him as the embodiment of wisdom. History was rewritten to make of him the co-leader, with Lenin, of the revolution in which he played a worthy but second-rank part. Was this only to please his vanity? Not only, surely. Russian tradition was autocratic. A great charismatic leader was needed to keep everyone in line, whom the ignorant common people and the scarcely less ignorant local officials could worship. His authority and glory could not be questioned, for that would be a danger to the state in dangerous times.

Issues had to be made simple. Then the Party secretaries could impose the proper policies. It would never do to start allowing a statement of two sides to a question. Intellectuals had to be kept in a straitjacket.

Society as a whole required to be mobilised, individual convenience was unimportant. By all his actions Stalin showed that he believed in Hierarchy and Discipline as essential virtues. Privilege too, but privilege was dispensed to those who served well, and was not, under Stalin, a secure right. Stalin was many things, but surely not the expression of the narrow self-interest of the bureaucratic elite. He feared their consolidation, and punished them without mercy. They were proportionately the principal victims of the great terror. Their lives, property and privilege depended on Stalin's whim and everyone knew it.

The state was said to embody the proletarian dictatorship, but the ordinary worker in town and village was suppressed as never before. Western commentators used to say that Russia of the thirties was not a political democracy but was an economic democracy. This was a total error. It is not just that trade unions were emasculated and free speech vanished. Workers were treated with arbitrariness and brutality. Living conditions, works canteens, sanitary arrangements, were often appalling. Foul language, threats, abuses, were the rule.

Why? Did Stalin wish it so? This leads me to another question. Can one really blame all these things on Stalin personally? Surely one man could not do it alone? Indeed not. Few could deny Stalin's major responsibility before history, least of all Stalin himself. But

there were many other factors which combined to bring about the
phenomenon which we are discussing here.

There was the logic of a revolution from above, of all-out mobilisation for economic growth, based on mass coercion. This is a police-
state logic. There was the low cultural level of the whole country,
and also of the Party membership. In the twenties many tough and
uneducated members of the civil-war period were promoted to
Party and state jobs. Khrushchev was one such man among many.
Stalin was for them a suitable master. They followed his lead blindly.
With him they knew where they were. They could rule in their sphere
as mini-Stalins, eliminating or silencing anyone who dreamt of
questioning their authority.

Russia at the revolution had a relatively thin stratum of educated
people. Many died or emigrated. Some who remained were of
doubtful loyalty. Party intellectuals questioned and argued. The
great purge was, among other things, the revenge of the semi-
educated petty bosses on these damned argumentative literati, with
their superior airs. How well this suited Stalin! How well Stalin
fitted in with the needs and aspirations of the new men! True, their
careers were at risk. If they offended the big boss they would vanish.
But on the one hand there were excellent opportunities for promotion (so many of their superiors dismissed, arrested, shot), and, on
the other, Russian and other history knows of many absolute monarchs who mercilessly punished their servants, but whose servants
none the less revered them and the absolutist principle. The great
purge brought such men to the top by eliminating the more independent minds from the ruling elite.

The rise to power of a stratum of self-made and poorly educated
men gave its imprint to the whole style of Soviet politics and society
of the thirties. The crudities, the swearing, the disregard for the
rights and conveniences of subordinates, were the consequences of
the promotion to authority of what could be called the sergeant type.
It should be recalled that sergeants are men of the people, and that
they usually bully and bawl at the men under them. They also value
and cling to their hard-won privileges. In one Soviet novel, a minor
official was promoted to a job which gave him access to the managerial dining-room; 'from that time on he regarded every proposal to
improve the feeding of ordinary workers as a personal insult'.

This argument should not be misunderstood. It is not being
asserted that the old Russian ruling classes were kind to soldiers,
serfs and workers, for there are many examples to the contrary. Some

of the most humane of the Bolsheviks were those of working-class origin. But the civil war and then the horrors of the revolution from above ensured, as by a survival of the fittest, the emergence of the tough and brutal species. The men with moral standards and scruples went into the wilderness or to the wall. So did the old intelligentsia, few of whom survived the thirties. Furthermore, the brutalities of Peter and of Nicholas I were in due course softened by the influence of 'Europe' and of liberalism. In 1849 Dostoevsky was taken out for execution and pardoned at the last second. Many soldiers were flogged to death. Thirty years later such acts were no longer conceivable. The prison regime of Alexander II or Nicholas II, especially for 'politicals', was relatively civilised. But the liberal elements were wiped out by the revolution, and in Stalin and his henchmen we saw a sort of revival of what might be called the Asian-despotic element of an earlier Russian tradition. Hence the unspeakable conditions in prisons or camps. Hence also the refusal to provide any privileges for the 'politicals'. Under the Tsars these were likely to be gentry, or educated people, and therefore better than the criminals. But for a Stalin or Beria their social origin and education compounded the offence, while criminals were men of their own kind. So what matters it if criminals in camps robbed the helpless 'politicals' of warm clothes and food? Indeed, the criminals were deliberately given the softer jobs and positions of authority in camps.

The social origins of the new rulers, and the folk traditions which they brought with them, help to explain important elements of Stalinism, and also the crude ways in which power and privilege were used. But this was not without certain dangers for the regime.

Stalin may also have been conscious of the need to prevent the ossification of a privileged caste. In this respect he resembled Mao, who launched his 'cultural revolution' largely to bring about the downfall of the Party-machine men. Mao called in the mob and the army to help him. Stalin operated through his control over the police, and by playing individuals and groups off against each other.

Stalin produced a theoretical justification for his repressive measures. The state cannot wither away in a hostile capitalist environment. On the contrary, as socialism becomes victorious the intensity of the class struggle grows, as the desperate enemies seek to destroy the Soviet system. Therefore what was needed was more vigilance, more severity. In other words, for the state to wither away its power must first be maximised.

He found enough people willing to do his bidding, some for

careerist motives, some because they sincerely believed that despotic demagogic government under Stalin was the best way to rule the Soviet Union.

His immediate circle were a mixed bunch. Molotov, who was Prime Minister, was a man of education and some culture. Voroshilov was a hard-riding, hard-drinking military crony of civil-war days. Kaganovich, the only Jew in the leadership after the defeat of various oppositions, had the reputation of a trouble-shooter, but was ignorant and crude. Mikoyan, an old Armenian revolutionary, concentrated on questions of trade rather than high politics. Zhdanov, son of a schoolteacher and literate, was a hard organiser who after the war acquired the reputation of being censor of the arts. There was also Shcherbakov, a rude individual of limited intelligence whom Stalin used to impose the party line on literature in the thirties. Khrushchev, who was sent to the Ukraine when the purge swept away the republican leaders, became a Politbureau member in 1939. Beria, a man of vicious habits and low cunning, became chief of the NKVD (police) in the same year. Younger stars included Malenkov, who rose through Stalin's personal secretariat and was at least educated, and Voznesensky, able and vigorous successor of executed chief planners. Perhaps a sentence should also be devoted to Kalinin, nominal president, a pathetic old man without power who was once trusted by the peasants.

Of these, only Molotov had played some significant political role in the first ten years of the revolution, and he was totally devoted to and dominated by Stalin. All the rest of Lenin's comrades-in-arms were dead by the end of the decade. Stalin's henchmen were intellectual pygmies compared with the great minds who argued over major issues during the revolution and in the twenties. Perhaps this is one reason why they participated joyfully in the destruction of the great minds. How could crude and uneducated practical men like Kaganovich or Voroshilov stand up and argue with Bukharin and Preobrazhensky? Their political future depended on gagging and destroying men far superior to themselves. Stalin made sure that no one in his entourage had or could acquire any stature. He was to be the supreme arbiter in all matters.

The Cultural Counter-Revolution and Neo-Nationalism

I have already referred to the degeneration of public debate to the level of simplified dogmatic statements of an infallible and undiscussable Party line, a process in which Stalin himself took a leading part. At first no very clear pattern could be discerned, other than the glorification of Stalin, the suppression of dissent and praise for the stupendous victories of socialist construction. Organisationally everything was put under tight control.

The twenties had been a period in which many cultural ideas competed with one another. Modern art, theatre, experimental 'Dalton-plan' schooling, advanced forms of musical composition, flourished. Historians such as Pokrovsky rewrote Russian history in terms of class war. Intellectuals like Alexandra Kollontai advocated free love. Divorce was easy.

These tendencies were disapproved of by some influential party members, and ran counter to puritan and national traditions among the people. But at first it seemed natural that various schools should contend. Thus Lenin once wrote that he was no admirer of Mayakovsky's poems, but 'of course' he was quite incompetent as a literary critic.

In the thirties, however, Stalin's Party began to claim omniscience in all matters. The destruction of the Party's own intellectuals meant that control was to be exercised by the boorish tough-guys, who saw no value in culture as such – though they did invest large sums in education, especially technical education. They would set no value on the life and work of some poet who seemed of doubtful loyalty.

In 1934 the first Congress of the newly formed Union of Soviet Writers adopted the principle of 'socialist realism'. Stripped of verbiage this amounted to an instruction to writers to serve the Party's interests, to be 'engineers of the human soul', to mobilise and inspire, and to write in a manner which the newly literate masses could understand. 'Realism' did not mean a frank statement of the real situation. One should see the future in the present, i.e. discern what ought to be rather than what is. The key principle was *partiinost*', which is inaccurately translated as 'partisanship', since it means expressing the essence of the Party's line and world-view, and also obedience to the Party's dictates on the cultural front.

In 1934 the satirists Ilf and Petrov imagined a writer who sent to the publishers a story called 'A Soviet Robinson'. Shipwrecked on a desert island, he surmounted difficulties, grew crops, raised rabbits and was in due course rescued by a Soviet ship. The publisher liked the story, especially the bit about the rabbits, since the party was running a campaign to increase the rabbit population. But Robinson had no social content. A girl? No, no, that would be cheap romanticism. There must be a trade union chairman, secretary and treasurer and also a fireproof safe. 'What,' cried the author, 'this spoils the whole story. Why the safe, anyway?' The publisher replied: 'To keep the trade union dues'. 'Who would steal them?' 'Well, the chairman, or the secretary, or Robinson.' The author then said: 'If a safe is to be washed up from the wreck, you might as well have a table, a green cloth and a little bell for the chairman to ring at the trade union meeting.' The publisher replied: 'No, no, I never said the cloth should be green. We do not limit literary freedom!' Such a satire could not have been published after 1934.

The effect on the censorship of the new line was not merely to tighten up political vigilance – this was inevitable as the terror grew in intensity – but also to drive publishers and censors into refusing to allow the appearance of harmless works which were not 'positive'. Thus a poem about love or the beauty of nature, by Akhmatova for instance, could be suppressed because it did nothing to help socialist construction. Sadness was 'out', because it did not 'mobilise'. The job of authors was seen as participating in the great effort to mobilise the people to fulfil the tasks set by the Party. Of course this was not always applied in its full rigour, but the damage done to literature was certainly severe. It is unfortunately the case that the present generation of Soviet officials are still inclined to look at literature in this way: 'Is it, or is it not, useful for us?'

Music suffered too. Stalin himself attended a performance, in 1935, of Shostakovich's opera *Lady Macbeth of Mtsensk* (*Katerina Ismailova*). He did not like it. There is no reason why he should: modern music upsets many people, even with a much more developed cultural sense than Stalin had. But, unlike Lenin, he erected his taste into compulsory principles. The opera was suppressed. Other officials, whose musical ideas were doubtless as primitive as Stalin's, joined in the hunt. Music, too, was to be joyous and positive. Symphonies should be in a major key. Poor Shostakovich wrote songs in praise of the happy life of onward-marching Soviet Man. Had not Stalin said that life had become joyous? Shostakovich continued to write serious music, of course, and high-quality propaganda-music was written by Prokofiev (his score for the film 'Alexander Nevsky' is justly famous). The world renown of these composers protected them, though they were attacked for 'formalism' by Zhdanov after the war. Later on, the 'positive' pseudo-folk-song became the political fashion, and mediocre composers of ditties on happy collective farmers became rich and famous. (I am not suggesting that

Western pop and country-and-western songs are on a higher level than this, but their authors do not become secretaries of the Union of Composers and do not exercise a veto on the publication of serious music.)

The theatre suffered exceedingly from the arrest of eminent directors, and also from the espousal by the Party of one style, that of the Moscow Arts Theatre. Experiment, modernism, symbolism, were wiped off the stage. Talented playwrights, even if not arrested, had plays banned. Stalin is on record as having gone to see one play, Mikhail Bulgakov's *Dni Turbinykh* (produced in England as *The White Guards*) no less than fourteen times. Yet the author's other plays were suppressed, and even this one was confined by the censorship to one theatre in Moscow.

Bulgakov himself told a story about how he dreamt that he was called by Stalin into the Kremlin. Seeing that he was destitute, Stalin (in the dream) ordered that he be given clothes, and decided to telephone the director of a theatre to instruct him to put on a play by him. In Bulgakov's imagination, Stalin said the following: 'Hello, is this the director? Stalin speaking . . . Well? Is no one there? Have I been cut off? Fetch the Commissar for Posts and Telegraphs immediately! Hello? Who is on the line? Who? The *deputy* director? Where is the director? Dropped dead? Just now? Well, well. Why are people so nervous in our country?' (This tale was published long after the death of both Stalin and Bulgakov, but gives us a taste of the atmosphere of the time.)

The drive against modernism in all branches of the arts was due not only to the old-fashioned tastes of officialdom but also to the help given them by second-rate jealous men in the ranks of the intellectuals, who persecuted their colleagues with a zeal which makes extremely painful reading. There were far too many such cases.

This was also the case in painting. It is not just Stalin but ordinary second-rate painters who ensured that the works of Chagall, Malevich and other distinguished 'moderns' were relegated to cellars, where most of them still are (though some were shown when old Chagall himself re-visited Russia in 1973). Artistic conservatism comes naturally in an alliance between uneducated politicians and routine hacks of the art world. For them even French impressionists were too advanced. Everything should be clear, straightforward, optimistic, on the Party line. Peasants and workers should march onwards and upwards. Stalin had to be painted in oils in appropriate poses. Revolutionary scenes showed Stalin standing behind or beside Lenin, with all 'enemies of the people' omitted. If history could be rewritten, as we shall see, why should art not follow suit? The hack painters also produced a mass of copies of approved Russian masters of earlier years, which hung in many a hall and corridor through the Union. It was Prince Mirsky, one-time lecturer in Russian literature in London, who explained the dominant taste in architecture and decoration as derived from what a peasant once saw as he looked from outside into the houses of the gentry. (Mirsky returned to Russia in the thirties and vanished in the purge.) This is a conservative outlook. In architecture it favoured a kind of monumental and grandiose neo-classicism, a Russian translation of municipal Gothic.

But to turn to other subjects. The author of the history of the Party vanished. The leading Marxist historian Pokrovsky, after his death from natural causes, was reviled, his theories cast aside. So were the legal theories of such famous Marxists as Pashukanis. Many lawyers, historians, philosophers, vanished into camps. Sociology became a dirty word, partly because it had been used several times by Bukharin. The chief legal luminary became the unspeakable Vyshinsky, prosecutor at the show trials, who hurled abuse at and mocked his helpless victims, and who must have been well aware that the scenario he was enacting was a pack of lies.

Of course there were many honest men who did their best to keep their heads high and who never said or did anything dishonourable, during a period when it required courage to avoid joining in the hunt for 'enemies'. Some paid a high price for their integrity. The great geneticist Vavilov was in the end hounded out by the charlatan 'biologist' Lysenko and died in prison.

Education was re-modelled on traditional lines, with the old marking system, formal teaching, uniforms. The virtues of family life were again stressed. Abortion was made illegal. Divorce was made more difficult. Patriotism was declared a key virtue. It was almost like adopting Pétain's slogan of '*Travail, Famille, Patrie*'.

This leads us to the new line on history and nationalism. There was a total rewriting of the history of the revolution, the civil war and of all that had happened since. Not only was Stalin glorified, but his victims either disappeared from the record or were presented as criminals and plotters. Since they included the large majority of Lenin's closest collaborators, this compelled Stalin's historians to write travesties of well-known facts. Trotsky ceased to play any role in 1917–20, except as a disorganiser of the Red Army. Lenin's own works were edited and expurgated. 'Histories' of the Civil War had to omit the names of almost all the Soviet Commanders, since most of them had been shot in the purges of 1936–38. Documentary evidence which would show the falsity of the newly imposed legends, such as the record of the Party Congresses of Lenin's time, were removed from library shelves, along with the writings of any and all victims of the Stalin terror.

Stalin's imposed orthodoxy extended also to the pre-Soviet period. The attack on Pokrovsky's work was followed by a new history text-book, which, as far as Tsarism was concerned, followed lines which could have been accepted by a nationalist liberal historian. Stress was laid on the continuity, greatness and even goodness of the Russian state. Peter the Great, Ivan the Terrible and other successful Tsars ceased to grind the faces of the poor and became positive figures. The war against Napoleon was a great patriotic war once again. The emphasis on Russia and things Russian could be seen as part of psychological preparation for a threatening war. It certainly accorded with a widespread feeling among cadres and people. It did, however, create a problem. Many inhabitants of the USSR were not Russian. Stalin himself was not Russian. Of course, there was much talk of the *Soviet* people, of Soviet patriotism, but the various other nations' histories had to be rewritten, so that Russia appeared as their protector. Thus she saved Georgia from the Turks, the Ukrainians from the Poles, and this was good. True, Tsarist Russia was 'a prison of the peoples' (Lenin's words), but this was taken to mean that the Tsars oppressed everybody. It was still good and 'progressive' that Russia had annexed various territories, if only because otherwise they would not be part of the great progressive Soviet Union.

There was careful watch on real or alleged 'bourgeois national-ism', and national parties and governments were purged again and again. Georgia had been a victim of Stalin's Muscovite centralism when Lenin was still there to protest about it, in 1923. Despite his own origins, Stalin launched or authorised a particularly severe repression in Georgia in 1937–38. I was told years afterwards that the Georgian intelligentsia suffered terrible losses, and that Beria was the man who did the job. The same happened in other republics too. This was not, or not yet, Russification. All were encouraged to shout 'Long live the great Stalin' in their own languages.

Stalin sought to restore Russian traditions in matters great and small. Thus in 1936 he restored military rank designations, more or less on the old pattern (Lieutenant-general instead of *Komkor*, Corps-commander, and so on). The exceptions were in most cases a move away from German, e.g. 'Sergeant' instead of the pre-1917 *Feldwebel*.

He spoke, too, of ranks in the Party itself, analogous to miltary ranks, though only as a (none the less significant) figure of speech.

So the period of the great terror smashed the old Party, largely replacing it by a disciplined and obedient body which would serve the autocrat without question. Stalin institutionalised a police-and-informer state. He eliminated or isolated even potential critics, thereby depriving the country of the services of a large proportion of its more intelligent inhabitants. There were important achievements also, and we will be speaking of them. However, the terror was not only a fact, which had a profound effect on its victims and the survivors alike, but is an integral part of the impact and final triumph of Stalinism in the Soviet Union. Is this an exaggeration? Not at all. Of course, terror is not all that happened, and many worthy people built, taught, worked, because they felt they were doing a good job for the community, or maybe just because they hoped to earn more or be promoted. Yet never in peacetime history were a people subjected to such convulsions and so much suffering as the Soviet people in the thirties. At the beginning of the decade repression was accompanied by acute material privation. By 1937 material conditions had improved markedly, but the terror raged across the land. And there were still greater tragedies to come in the forties.

As the French saying goes, '*un peuple heureux n'a pas d'histoire*'.

Foreign Policy Turnabouts

'Social-fascism' survived the coming to power of Hitler. Perhaps Stalin thought that Hitler would not last, alternatively that he could do a deal with him. Unofficial military links, which existed with the Weimar Republic since the early twenties, were not cut off instantly. He was oddly slow in realising just how dangerous Hitler was going to be for him. Anti-Fascist Popular-Front tactics seem to have begun more or less spontaneously, in France in February 1934. Only later did the Moscow line swing in that direction, and some Party members were being expelled for premature anti-Fascism even at the beginning of 1935 (for instance in Czechoslovakia).

Then the line changed decisively. The Seventh Congress of the Comintern was held in Moscow in July 1935. No one dared suggest that the ultra-left line of earlier years was wrong: the Party line changes with the changing situation. It was admitted that some comrades were somewhat too sectarian. Almost overnight the 'social-fascist' Léon Blum and other Social-Democrats became potential allies. Never content with half-measures, the Party line stretched rightwards to embrace alliances with liberals, and even with the moderate right, provided they opposed Nazi-Fascism. This Comintern policy was an accurate reflection of the logic of Soviet foreign policy at the time. For Stalin hoped that the Nazi menace could be contained by an alliance with the West. The new tactic began in 1935 with a pact negotiated with the then French premier, Laval. This blossomed into a 'collective security' policy, with Litvinov, the Foreign Affairs commissar, making able speeches in Geneva on the theme: 'peace is indivisible'.

The Communist parties of the West were caught by surprise when the foreign-policy line changed. Thus in France they had opposed Laval and arms expenditures. Shortly before he was killed in 1940 I met the French novelist, Paul Nizan, when we were both in our respective armies near Lille. He had by then broken with the Communists, but in 1935 he was close to the leaders. He told me that the French party had sent a deputation to Moscow to ask timidly to be told in advance in future when such changes were to occur. Nizan said that they got a contemptuous reply! 'We taught you Marxism, work it out for yourselves.' The parties adjusted obediently to the change. Stalin was surely right not to take their leaders seriously. Those who were in Russia as emigrants were in many cases shot during the purges. The Western Communist leaders were tied to Moscow above all by the knowledge that their followers identified Communism with Russia, basked in the reflected glory of the revolution and of the much-publicised achievements of the five-year plans. Splinter groups set up by dissidents, or by Trotsky's followers, were small and impotent.

The adoption of the 'Stalin' constitution in 1936 was perhaps partly motivated by the need to present the USSR as a fit partner for the democracies. Certainly its terms – full of fine phrases about freedom of speech, of assembly, from arbitrary arrest – contrasted very strangely with the facts of terror.

The Popular-Front tactic struck a responsive chord in the West. The Nazi menace was deeply felt, and the weak response of Western conservatism inclined the left towards an alliance with the Communists. The fear of Hitler caused many in the West to close their eyes to the despotic or oppressive features of Stalin's Russia. Some were genuinely naïve, were victims of propaganda. Some believed what they wished to believe. Some even thought that Stalin had killed the really dangerous 'international' Communists and was now just a national Russian dictator, with whom a deal was possible. There were plenty of delusions and illusions. It is easy, by hindsight, to condemn those who hoped that the Soviet Union was basically or potentially on 'our side' against the rising tide of brownshirt barbarism. Faced with the feeble appeasement policies of Neville Chamberlain, good and honest men in despair turned hopefully east, and thought they saw progress.

Stalin was careful to suppress independent sources of information and to cut off his people from any contacts with the West. Soviet scientists stopped attending conferences, personal unofficial contacts became a punishable offence, an exit visa almost impossible to obtain. Who would dare to tell the truth to a foreign delegate or tourist?

Western sympathies with the USSR increased when she alone went to the aid of the Spanish republicans when the civil war broke out. Popular enthusiasm for the Spanish cause was real enough among the left, and in Russia itself. The miserable tale of 'non-intervention', and the appearance of German and Italian forces, strengthened the popularity of the Soviet Union among the Western 'left', and also strengthened Soviet and Communist influence in Spain itself, although the Communists had been weak – far weaker than the Anarchists, for instance – when the civil war began.

Stalin's policies in Spain provide invaluable evidence about his tactics and aim at this period. He used Soviet arms to establish political influence, through a Communist Party totally subservient to him and willing to do the NKVD's bidding in suppressing Spanish left-wing dissidents. Thus, the semi-Trotskyist POUM, led by Andrés Nin, was liquidated and Nin himself killed in an unofficial Communist prison. A son of the old Menshevik Abramovich went to Spain as a volunteer and was kidnapped and never heard of again. This attack on innocent children of political enemies was a feature of Stalin's way; two sons of Trotsky, one totally non-political, were murdered. The International Brigade was very tightly controlled. The whole political balance in Republican Spain was shifted towards the Communists. But they occupied no key positions; even in 1938 the President was a liberal, the Premier a (compliant) socialist, the Army Commander non-political. Furthermore, the Communists insisted upon a very moderate line in internal affairs: expropriations, requisitions, nationalisation were opposed. What mattered, it seems, was political control, not social revolution, perhaps because the latter would scare the potential allies of the Soviet Union out of participating in an anti-Nazi coalition.

In its volume Soviet aid was insufficient to turn the balance of the war, and, unlike the Italians, the Russians sent no actual formations of 'volunteers'. Advisers, technicians, pilots, were there. They suffered severe repression when they returned, probably because anyone who had been abroad was suspect in 1937–38. It is odd that Antonov-Ovseenko, the Soviet consul-general in Barcelona and the probable organiser of the killing of Nin the 'Trotskyist', should have been recalled to Moscow and shot, as an alleged Trotskyist!

There is a certain parallel between the Party line on Spain and that followed by Communists in other Western countries. Under 'Popular-Front' cover they busily penetrated other organisations of leftish complexion or of no political colour: they were even in control of parts of the Student Christian Movement! But their influence was not used in any specifically Communist direction, except – big exception! – to express Soviet policy on collective security and anti-Fascism, and to wage implacable war upon anything smelling of Trotskyism. I recall an argument (in a Paris métro train, of all places) with an earnest Party organiser, who said – 'for me, Trotskyism *is* fascism!' But he was perfectly willing to sit alongside a Tory duchess who was supporting a foreign policy which suited Moscow.

It seems reasonable to conclude that Stalin was exceedingly concerned with the military danger to the USSR, and that he subordinated his tactics abroad to the task of finding support for an alliance which would save the USSR from facing Germany, or Germany and Japan, unaided. This time no one can doubt or deny that the danger was real. No one can blame Stalin for trying to avert it, whatever one's views as to his methods.

Economic Policies in the Mid-Thirties

In a speech made as early as 1931, Stalin said:

'We are fifty or a hundred years behind the advanced countries. We must make good this distance in ten years or we shall go under.' It so happened that there was just ten years. It is true that he mistook

who the enemy was to be. It is also true that the excesses and im-
balances of the first plan are not to be excused by a sense of urgency:
if the runner in a 5,000 metres race covers the first 200 metres in 23
seconds, he cannot justify such excessive speeds merely because he
had to win the race. Such behaviour is counter-productive, and so was
much that was done in the first years of the decade on the economic
front.

We saw that 1933 was a terrible year. Things then began to go
better. The second five-year plan was more realistic and paid greater
attention to consumer goods. By 1937 material conditions had greatly
improved, the more so because this was a good harvest year. Planning methods and farm organisation settled down. There was much
inefficiency and waste, but all critics agree that there was a vast rise
in productivity from the abysmal levels of 1933.

Planning was centralised, resources were allocated by state and
Party organs, the market played no part in deciding the direction of
investment. Prices, except in the (legal) peasant market, were fixed
by the state. In its essentials the Soviet economy was already
functioning on the same principles on which it functions today,
though there have been many changes in detail since then. The
Party exercised its control partly by its grip on all appointments in
the economic sphere, partly by direct intervention via the central
committee's officials, with Stalin himself the supreme arbiter in
matters great and small.

The results of the sacrifices of the early thirties bore fruit. Huge
new industrial complexes came into operation, including the Ural-
Kuznets metallurgical combine, the Stalingrad and Kharkov tractor
works, and most important, a powerful engineering ('machine-
building') industry. In the first plan period much of the capital
equipment had to be imported, and the export of foodstuffs to pay
for that equipment was among the causes of the hunger of those
years. The aim was to achieve much greater self-sufficiency. In terms
of economic orthodoxy this may have been unsound, but it accorded
with the harsh realities of the Soviet Union's strategic situation. In
the First War the Tsarist armies suffered terribly through shortage
of weapons, and it was very difficult to expand or even maintain
production because the machinery and equipment was so largely
imported. Even if Britain and France were allies – as they were in
the First War – the fact of geography would impede the flow of
supplies. And no one could be sure what allies, if any, the USSR
might have in the event of war.

Centralised planning of the 'Stalinist' type has many inherent weaknesses: bureaucratic deformation, arbitrary interference with insufficient knowledge, disregard for economic cost, a tendency to use 'campaigning' methods to achieve results by a given date (with resultant neglect of other and perhaps equally important activities), and a lurching from bottleneck to bottleneck. Managerial ingenuity had to be diverted to getting supplies to fulfil plans, by fair means or foul. One of Stalin's sayings was: 'The victors are not judged'. In other words, get away with it if you can, provided you fulfil your plan. Plans were in aggregate units, such as tons, roubles, etc., and quality and the needs of customers tended to be neglected, unless the very top of the political machine was sufficiently concerned to exercise direct supervision, which could not be done systematically.

Yet with all its defects, the system had an overwhelming advantage: that of enabling the leadership to concentrate resources on its priorities, without being deflected by considerations of profitability, private-enterprise interests or the pressure of public opinion. The terror ensured the acceptance of the priorities of the regime, since any questioning was evidence of subversion and could result in a long involuntary journey to Siberia. In peacetime this concentration on priorities is difficult to achieve under a democracy. In wartime we have centralised planning in the West also, with many of the bureaucratic distortions which inevitably accompany it, but we put up with these distortions because they are a necessary price to pay for mobilising everything for war. Stalin was engaged in the thirties in organising a war economy in peacetime.

The Soviet financial and price system facilitated his task. Investment was nearly all financed out of the state budget. The state revenue came very largely through prices, especially via turnover tax, a purchase tax levied on consumer goods. By increasing prices at which it sold its goods the state could obtain the necessary resources with which to finance the expansion of industry. Voluntary savings and managerial choice played an insignificant part in investments. It was a most effective way to ensure a high rate of (forced) savings in a relatively poor country.

Terror and despotism had also some severe economic costs. Thus experts failed to give proper advice for fear of being dubbed traitor or deviationist, which is why impossible plans were sometimes adopted. There was fear of responsibility, which paralysed initiative. Finally a very large number of skilled managers and engineers were arrested;

Stalin said that 'Cadres decide everything', yet he had thousands of the best and scarcest cadres sent to remote concentration camps.

But, whatever its faults, Stalin's overall strategy and the means available to impose this strategy had a certain rationality, given the objectives pursued. Surely Stalin's ghost would argue this, and probably add that the destruction of possible oppositions, the mobilisation of the arts and sciences and his own supremacy were part of the same package.

The recovery in agriculture had been due to a species of compromise with the peasants. Collectivisation was maintained, and so was compulsory delivery of produce at exceedingly low prices. (The state resold them to the consumer at very much higher prices.) The new tractors, owned and operated by the state, replaced the horses killed during collectivisation. But apart from grain and some industrial crops, the farms and the peasants were left largely to their own devices. Each peasant household was allowed a small plot of land and a limited number of animals (a cow, a sow, several sheep and goats, etc.), and in 1937 the bulk of livestock was in fact in private hands. The peasants were free to sell their own produce in the market. They derived from their collectives a very small cash income and bread-grain, in payment for collective work. Their little 'private enterprise' supplied the rest of their money and produce. It cannot be said that this arrangement was popular. Collective work reminded them of the old *barshchina*, work for the lord under serfdom, which entitled them to cultivate their allotments. None the less life was becoming more tolerable.

Unfortunately, as from 1938 there was a turn towards greater pressure on the village. This may have been due to the exigencies of rising army expenditures, or because Stalin now felt that agricultural production had recovered sufficiently to resume the offensive; his policies suggest a definite tendency to disregard peasant welfare even more than that of other citizens. Be this as it may, 1938 began a process of imposing large delivery quotas of more and more types of products (even including sheep's-milk cheese) at low prices, and requiring the farms to build up their livestock herds. With fodder short, this led to a reduction in privately owned animals. On top of this, taxes on the farms and on the peasant allotments were increased, and a compulsory minimum of collective work imposed. The intense unpopularity of these measures, taken on the eve of war, might help to explain why many peasants met the German invaders of 1941 with the traditional bread-and-salt of welcome.

The working class of the thirties was greatly 'diluted' by recent arrivals from the countryside. Their numbers very greatly exceeded original expectations, partly because the labour productivity plans had been over-optimistic and partly due to the flight of peasants from collectivisation. Housing plans were underfulfilled. Consequently overcrowding was appalling. The ex-peasants, rootless and unskilled, needed to be turned into an industrial labour force. We have already noted one method used to achieve this: larger inequalities of income, to provide a reward for acquiring skills. We must now mention two others, both typical of the attitudes of High Stalinism.

The first of these was 'Stakhanovism'. Called after Alexei Stakhanov, a miner who overfulfilled his work norm fourteen-fold, the original purpose of the campaign was to encourage and glorify high productivity. There was indeed plenty of scope for the tightening up of work norms and increasing effort. However, this campaign rapidly degenerated into publicity-seeking and artificial record-breaking. Managers would arrange things to enable one of their men to become a Stakhanovite, depriving other workers of materials and opportunities for extra earnings. This is only one example of the distortions engendered by party campaigns in any field – it became more important to report the success of this particular campaign than to achieve sound results overall. In agriculture this could take the form of: 'never mind the potatoes, the campaign right now is for milk', or vice versa. The chase after record-breaking caused much annoyance, and there were cases of Stakhanovites beaten up by fellow-workers.

Needless to say, the distortions were not willed by Stalin, not as such. But a man must be deemed to will the probable consequences of his own acts. If one exerts pressure on Party secretaries to run campaigns then their behaviour, in endeavouring to obey, is reasonably predictable. Similarly Stalin's drastic statements on the need for vigilance against Trotsky-Bukharin traitors within the Party was bound to lead to the arrests of thousands of individuals whom Stalin himself had no sort of reason to arrest. But he programmed the machine, and its acts are still attributable to him.

The second method was the imposition of sterner discipline. This initially took the form of denying factory housing and social insurance benefits to 'flitters' and absentees. An internal passport system, residence permits and 'work books' were introduced, as control measures. Then, amid much propaganda about duty to the socialist state and the disorganisers of production, sterner measures were taken, culminating in the decrees of October 1940, which forbade changing one's job without permission, made the holders of many jobs subject to direction, and punished 'flitting', absenteeism and arriving late to work as crimes. Being late three times equalled absenteeism, which meant prison in some cases, 'compulsory labour at place of employment' in others.

The imposition of this law, passed 'at the request of the trade unions', ran into difficulties, because managers tried not to report the 'criminals', and prosecutors and judges did not apply a law which contradicted the habitual sense of right and wrong. Whereupon a campaign was mounted, and managers and judges who failed in their duty were themselves punished. This led to wild excesses, since the terror was still fresh in everyone's minds. Extenuating circumstances no longer counted. Cases were in due course reported of women arrested for absenteeism in the ninth month of pregnancy, of prison sentences passed on people who were in hospital, or looking after a sick child at home. A long list of unbelievable 'judicial' acts can readily be compiled from the columns of the legal periodical *Sotsialisticheskaya Zakonnost'* for 1940. Of course, a halt was soon called to such absurdities as these. But one learns something of the atmosphere of Stalinism from the fact that they could occur at all. How scared must managers be to report as an absentee someone who is so sick as to be in hospital, or having a baby! Doctors were frightened of signing medical certificates of unfitness. Judges, with plain evidence before them, were terrified of being regarded as soft on absentees and flitters. These were instances of the cost of a campaign method allied with terror.

The whole idea of tying a man to his job and imprisoning him for leaving it or for being absent could perhaps be regarded as due to the imminence of war, and sure enough some reference to an emergency was sometimes made. But the arguments of official propagandists did not stress this, but rather the duty of citizens of a socialist state to be disciplined, in effect to do what they were told. It is arguable that a labour force of this kind was part of Stalin's model of a properly organised hierarchical society. (If soldiers are not to be free to choose where to go, why should workers or peasants be? This was what Trotsky had argued way back in 1920, when he favoured militarisation of labour. Not, of course, that Stalin was influenced by his arch-enemy.) In any case, the decrees were not finally repealed until after Stalin's death. He also introduced fees for higher and secondary education, contrary to the constitution, which guaranteed free

education at all levels and cut down on social benefits, such as
maternity leave. These things too remained uncorrected until after
his death. Of course there could be no word of protest.

It has already been pointed out that growth tempos declined
greatly in and after 1937, and one cause was mentioned: the disruptive effects of mass arrests. There was another: the effect of a
sharp upswing of arms expenditures. In the early thirties the investments in heavy industry were intended to create the means of
making arms, but actual direct spending on arms was modest.
Naturally it speeded up as Hitler's Germany armed. The effect on
the highly strained industrial structure was to create bottlenecks and
to diminish the civilian production of capital goods. To take one
example among many, tractor output in 1937 was less than half of
that in 1936, because tractor factories made tanks. Shortages of
consumer goods also became severe in 1940. These consequences of
necessary war preparations cannot, of course, be blamed on Stalin.

Unfortunately, he was responsible for disrupting arms production
too, by shooting and imprisoning military leaders and some leading
planners and engineers. Thus Tupolev, the famous aircraft designer
('TU 104' was to be his) was for a time in prison, though he was
released. Worse still, he replaced talented generals with loud-
mouthed nonentities. Voroshilov was commissar for war, and his
three deputies, key men in organisation, armaments and supplies,
were Kulik, Mekhlis and Shchadenko, all of whom later showed
themselves totally incapable. Stalin himself took an active part in
choosing weapons, and a leading manager (Emelyanov) has told us
in his memoirs about how he personally supervised the testing of
various kinds of armour-plating for tanks. New and modern types of
weapons were chosen in due course, but both in tanks and in planes
the equipment of the Red Army in 1941 proved far inferior to the
German.

Chapter 3

War

Munich and the Nazi-Soviet Pact

Stalin has been blamed for cynically trying to embroil the West with Germany and for signing a pact with Hitler. Here, oddly enough, he has a fairly good defence for his actions in terms of Soviet security. Let us now put the case for him.

Whatever propagandists may say, it was becoming exceedingly doubtful, even before Munich, whether Britain and France would in fact join in an anti-Nazi coalition. France seemed paralysed, and Britain under Chamberlain's leadership was pursuing the policy of appeasement. It was unlikely that Laval, or Daladier, or Chamberlain would lift a finger if Germany and the USSR came to blows. They might well say: 'may they exhaust each other'. Therefore it was by no means unreasonable for Stalin to contemplate a deal with Hitler, though it did contradict the official anti-Fascist line of Soviet and Communist propaganda media. It was said in 1937 by a senior Soviet intelligence officer who defected to the West, Krivitsky, that Stalin was already then thinking along these lines.

Whether or not this was so, the fact remains that the Soviet government did try to link up with the Western powers during the Czech crisis of 1938, and that in the Munich agreement the Soviet Union was deliberately snubbed and ignored.

After this, two things happened. Stalin took over the Premiership from Molotov, and Litvinov was dismissed, with Molotov replacing him. A clear signal of a change of line.

When, after the German occupation of Prague, the British guaranteed Poland, negotiations for an Anglo-French-Soviet military pact began. But Stalin had justified suspicions about them, supported by all that we now know from archives about Chamberlain's intentions. Justified too by what in fact happened in 1939 when Germany attacked Poland; the Western allies did nothing, even though they did declare war. There is absolutely no reason to believe that they would have done more if Hitler had invaded the Soviet Union in 1939.

Hence in the harsh terms of great-power politics the Nazi-Soviet pact made sense. By twentieth-century international standards of behaviour it was not worse than many other things that were done in and by the West.

This said, there were, however, some highly questionable consequences of the new policy.

The first was the unfolding of a programme of Soviet expansionism. Not just into eastern Poland, where at least it could be claimed that the inhabitants were Ukrainian and Belorussian, but into the then independent Baltic states, into Romanian Bessarabia and also parts of Finland. Wider horizons were discussed with the Germans by Molotov. This might be justified as strengthening Russia at a dangerous time, by adding territories into which Germany might well herself expand. There was also the strong, if ideologically impure, motive of recovering territories lost during the revolution, and conscience was saved by the organisation of 'votes' in Latvia, Lithuania, Estonia, in which the inhabitants were prevailed upon (polite words) to join the Soviet Union voluntarily. Finland was another story. The motive here was originally the moving of the frontier further from Leningrad and the setting up of a Soviet base at the entrance to the Gulf of Finland at Hanko. When the Finns refused, Stalin ordered his troops forward and set up a so-called Finnish people's government in the first village which they occupied, Terioki, under a Finnish Comintern official, Kuusinen. This seemed like a bid for a takeover of the whole country. However, the campaign went badly for the Russians at first, the Finns resisted skilfully, and the Terioki 'people's government' was quietly forgotten; it is not to be found in any Soviet histories of the period. In the spring of 1940 a major offensive in Karelia finally broke Finnish resistance, and Stalin opted for a moderate peace, which left Finland an independent country. It is significant that the Anglo-French forces which were so inactive in helping the Poles made plans for an expeditionary force to help Finland against the USSR, with whom they were not at war; this on the eve of a German attack upon them. Western leadership at this time was neither realistic nor intelligent. Stalin made mistakes as we shall see, but he was not alone in so doing (but these particular

Soviet mistakes would ensure that Finland as well as Romania would join the German invasion in 1941).

A second consequence was the abandonment of anti-Fascism. This greatly confused the Western Communist parties and caused many members to leave. It was bad enough to be told that the USSR had signed a pact with Hitler. Maybe this was a response to harsh necessity. But this did not make the Nazi system any less detestable, or any less a menace. Yet when the war began the Communists were instructed to oppose an imperialist war, and the official line suggested that Britain and France were somehow more blameworthy than Germany. Communist front organisations demanded a 'people's peace', whatever that was. The ban on the French Communist Party saved it from making a public fool of itself. There is evidence that when the French armies collapsed in 1940 the illegal Communists hoped to have their activities legalised by the occupying power! The Germans (naturally) would not play.

This whole policy seems to have been an almost classical example of the inflexibility of despotism. For it was certainly in the Soviet interests to have the West resist Germany effectively. In so far as Communist opposition weakened the French war effort and contributed to the ease of the Nazi victory, it brought nearer the day of reckoning for Stalin's Russia. But no doubt Stalin shared the illusion of many, including Churchill, about the strength of the French army, and the events of May–June 1940 were a shock to him (as they certainly were for the writer of these lines, who was nearly captured). None the less, Molotov did not fail to send Germany his congratulations, and the Party line did not change until 22 June 1941.

In Russia itself it was the same thing. Anti-Fascist news disappeared from the press. When Ehrenburg returned from France after the fall of Paris, he was appalled to discover that any critical references to the Nazis were censored, and he was expected to lecture in the presence of representatives of the German embassy. Nothing could be said about Nazi atrocities. Trade with Germany boomed. Everyone was given to understand that relations were good and friendly. Incredibly, the Soviet authorities handed over to the Germans some of the German Communists who were in Soviet jails! One such, Margarete Buber-Neumann, widow of purge victim Heinz Neumann, has written about this disgraceful episode; her book includes a valuable comparative study of Soviet and Nazi concentration camps. All this was no sort of preparation for the conflict to come! Behind the scenes, it is true, defence preparations went ahead, but without the urgency which the situation demanded.

Security measures were taken in newly occupied Western territories. Polish officer prisoners were massacred. There was a mass round-up of 'suspect' categories, hundreds of thousands were sent by trains to exile, thousands went to labour camps from Riga, Tallin, Vilna, Lvov. Was this a military precaution, or was this simply the 'normal' Soviet police technique at work in an incorporated area? Probably the latter. Anyway, the remaining inhabitants of these areas welcomed the Germans in 1941.

We now know that Hitler began to plan the invasion of Russia soon after the fall of France. However, plans are but plans. The decision to prepare must be dated from Molotov's visit to Berlin in November 1940. Beneath the formal courtesies the atmosphere was cool. Molotov had large ambitions for Soviet expansion and was concerned about German activities in the Balkans. Hitler's reaction could be summarised by the phrase: this means war! 'Operation Barbarossa' was mounted.

German troops appeared in Romania, occupied Yugoslavia (to the Soviet government's visible chagrin), edged into Finland, concentrated quietly in occupied Poland. German ships were ordered out of Russian ports. Soviet intelligence agents reported all this, as did their embassy in Berlin, frontier-crossers in Poland, troops near the border. German planes flew over west Russia taking photographs. By late May 1941 the signs were unmistakable and were all pointing one way.

Stalin's Biggest Mistake

He would not believe it! On June 14 he ordered a statement to be issued that rumours of impending conflict with Germany were unfounded and provocative in intent, and that relations remained normal. Indeed, Soviet deliveries of materials to Germany continued right up to the fateful night of 21/22 June. We know from the memoirs of Russian generals that no secret warnings were sent out, to counteract the effect of such a statement. In fact there were repeated warnings in a contrary direction: beware of provocations, do not deploy troops, do not fire, do not send alarmist reports. True, there was much German disinformation. True also that Stalin did move some troops towards the threatened regions. But there was no general mobilisation, and no state of emergency. It was not until literally a few hours before the attack was launched that a warning of imminent trouble was sent out to the various headquarters. But before it reached most of the actual formations and airfields the bombs had begun to fall. Soviet divisions, in any case far weaker in equipment, training and experience than the Germans, had to meet the attack with soldiers asleep in barracks and many officers on leave.

Of course we know that another country, America at Pearl Harbour, was caught off guard by Japan later in that very year. Yet Stalin had more and better information than Roosevelt, and at the least Roosevelt did not ban anti-Japanese propaganda and lull people into a sense of false security.

How could Stalin not see? He would understandably discount British warnings, as his reading of the situation was that the British wished to embroil him in war with Germany. Other warnings seem to have reached him in diluted form. He appears to have been confused partly by deliberate German disinformation, but most of all by being surrounded by his own cronies, who would not tell him what he did not wish to hear. Beria's intelligence, as reported to his master, did not sound too alarming. It may be deduced from Zhukov's memoirs that the chief of military intelligence, General Golikov, was not passing on all the evidence either. He cannot be entirely blamed for this. He knew that 'the boss' thought that the Germans would not attack, or anyway not that year. He knew that thousands of officers had been shot on the boss's orders only a few short years ago. It was very risky to tell the truth.

Stalin's terror, his choice of second-rate and timid men as colleagues, therefore contributed to his inability to see.

A great drama can be written about June 1941. The German blow was being aimed. Soviet officers could discern the danger, intelligence men in the field could see it coming and reported even the day of the assault. Yet there was lack of reaction. Some army commanders deployed their men on their own responsibility, the fleets were put on to alert in time, but over most of the front the Germans achieved total tactical surprise, thanks largely to Stalin's obstinacy or lack of information.

How much of the resultant catastrophe can be laid at Stalin's door? What, in fact, were the decisive factors in the initial defeat, indeed virtual destruction, of the bulk of the Soviet forces in the West?

They were caught literally asleep, and no doubt this made a

difference. Some units which would have put up a respectable resistance were overwhelmed as they struggled to get to their positions, or even into their clothes. The air force suffered a shattering blow, with hundreds of planes destroyed on the ground in dawn raids. A Soviet Air-Marshal put losses on the first day as one thousand aircraft. On all this there is no dispute. What follows is in part more controversial, and my interpretation could be challenged, though it can be backed with a good deal of evidence.

Firstly, there was a very large qualitative discrepancy in armaments. The total number of Soviet planes and tanks matched the Germans; but those Soviet planes that flew (for instance the I-16 fighters, or the heavy and slow TB-3 bomber) were hopelessly outclassed by the Messerschmitts, which could shoot them down at will without damage to themselves. Very much better planes were coming off the production line but few were operational and hardly any pilots yet knew how to fly them. Most Soviet planes were not then equipped with radios. In all these circumstances numbers meant nothing. It was like bows and arrows facing machine-guns. The purges could have been the decisive factor in delaying the introduction of new planes (the I-16 had done well in Spain). The same picture is broadly true of tanks. When the new Soviet tank, the T-34, became available it did very well, but the standard Soviet army tank of June 1941 was notably less well armed and armoured than the German.

Secondly, the Soviet commanders were strikingly inferior in the means of mobility. Lorries were far too few. Fuel dumps were grievously inadequate, means of moving fuel were primitive, and preparations had not been made for a retreat. This last point was a by-product of the hurrah-atmosphere of the previous years. 'If any pig dares put its snout into our Soviet garden, we will show him!' that was the burden of much official propaganda. Commanders who talked of fuel dumps deep in the rear were liable to be accused of defeatism and panic-mongering. For this Stalin had indirect responsibility. The result was the abandonment of almost all the vehicles and tanks of outflanked armies in retreat. Lack of mobility ensured that Soviet responses to breakthroughs were too late to save the situation. In any case they had great difficulty in conveying orders, owing to shortage of radios, when the German advance cut telephone lines. Staffs lost touch with their formations.

Thirdly, Zhukov and others stoutly maintain that the Germans **also** had substantial *numerical* superiority. The Soviet government had not ordered general mobilisation until after the war had begun. Soviet divisions in the west were below strength, many others were too far from the threatened area to affect the outcome. So it was not possible to make up for qualitative deficiencies by using masses of men, since there was an inferiority even in numbers of infantrymen. The latter were armed mostly with ordinary rifles, against German automatic weapons. Numerical superiority in the sectors chosen by the Germans for their advance was crushing (on this at least there is no dispute).

Then, and here Stalin's responsibility is obvious, many Soviet commanders were of poor quality, hastily promoted to replace those shot in the purges. By common consent, the three principal front commanders on 22 June, F. Kuznetsov, D. Pavlov and Kirponos, were at best competent second-raters. Lower formations were led by men with minimum staff training, or none. Facing a situation which would have taxed the ingenuity of a Napoleon to the utmost, it can hardly be surprising that many of them failed. Of course, there were some able men in command positions, and gradually, learning from experience, there was a very marked improvement in the quality of leadership, but only after catastrophic losses.

Finally, morale. More than one Soviet general refers to lack of confidence between soldiers and officers because so many officers had been recently arrested. (One writer of memoirs, Gorbatov, had himself been sent from a concentration camp in Siberia to command an infantry corps in 1941.) Also there had been no propaganda build-up to prepare the troops for an attack by the Germans. There were illusions about proletarian solidarity, too: German workers would not shoot, they hoped. There was widespread discontent with the Soviet regime, though in fact the collapse of resistance was not attributable to the refusal of men to fight. Mass surrenders, when they occurred, were generally explicable by an already hopeless local situation. But they may have fought harder if they had known what sort of treatment awaited them. They had to learn this the hard way. Many civilians, including even Jews, stayed behind hoping that life under the Germans would be tolerable, unaware until too late of how Germans treated 'undermen'; Soviet propaganda had been silent on this point since 1939.

It may well have been that any well-organised German attack was bound to score initial victories whatever the Soviet leaders did. Military experience, a higher level of training and education, the traditional qualities of the German soldier, a higher level of technology and a much larger industrial base (including that of occupied Europe), were great advantages. The initiative lay with the attacker. The achievements of Soviet industrial growth, while impressive, still and inevitably left gaps which were militarily damaging. They could no doubt have done more to produce lorries and radios, for instance, but only at the cost of cutting back the development of something else of military importance.

Disasters multiplied. While the southern front did hold for a short while, the northern and western defences were broken on the very first day, and German mobile columns penetrated very deep. By 28 June, a mere six days after the advance began, the Germans were far into the Baltic states, had captured Minsk, and quite obviously would advance hundreds of miles further before effective resistance could be organised. Yet Stalin remained silent. It has been alleged that he fell into black despair, that he felt that all was lost. It was indeed a remarkable silence. It had been left to Molotov to broadcast that war had begun. The people seem to have been left leaderless as the armies were shattered. Then at last Stalin spoke. On 3 July 1941 he went to the radio, and said: 'Brothers and sisters . . .' He spoke of deadly dangers, declared a scorched earth policy and urged all-out resistance. In a subsequent speech, on 7 November, he further invoked 'our great ancestors': Alexander Nevsky, Dimitry Donskoy, Suvorov and Kutuzov, among others. This was indeed a patriotic appeal to Russian tradition.

Alexander Nevsky, who defeated the Teutonic knights in the thirteenth century, was a prince and a saint of the Orthodox church. Dimitry Donskoy defeated the Tartars in the fourteenth century. The other two were distinguished generals in the Turkish and Napoleonic wars. This appeal could be seen as the culminating point of the 'patriotic' turn of history and propaganda, which had begun well before the war. The danger *was* deadly, and German atrocities were showing all too clearly what would have been in store for the people had Hitler won. It was logical and necessary to mobilise everyone and everything in the name of Holy Russia. The people responded.

Stalin the War Leader

Stalin recovered his nerve, sacked some incompetent generals, had some officers shot, including the unfortunate staff of the west (i.e. central) front, appointed better men to take charge. He became

Commander-in-Chief, and his own staff (*stavka*) functioned along-side and above the general staff. The large number of military memoirs published in recent years give a picture of Stalin's role as Commander. All agree that he was genuinely in command, that he took advice but imposed his own decisions, that he was not a fool who directed operations on a globe, as Khrushchev claimed in an excess of anti-Stalinist zeal. Mistakes were made, certainly, but it is wrong to ascribe these only to Stalin and the successes only to his staff officers. It is, of course, always easy to prove that any plan for victory did not originate with the Commander-in-Chief but had been pro-posed initially by someone else: one of his own staff, or by some subordinate commander. But it is the job of the c-in-c to decide what to do on the basis of proposals put before him.

In early July Stalin faced the necessity of further large retreats. So many troops and weapons had been lost already. Evacuation of plant from threatened areas was undertaken on a vast scale, but many factories could not be moved, and those that were could not resume production for some months. Meanwhile the loss of produc-tion and the disruption of communications reduced the productive capacity of Soviet industry, and for a time made it impossible to make up the losses and create a tolerable balance in hardware. Though the Russians succeeded in halting the Germans in the centre, in battles in the Smolensk area, the northern front was rolled back all the way to Leningrad, which was surrounded within six weeks of the outbreak of war. In the south, Soviet troops fell back to the Dnieper, holding on to Kiev. The armies in the southern Ukraine were defeated and surrounded near Uman, while the armoured columns of the central front turned south and threatened the rear of Kiev from the north (map 1). The Soviet commander saw the coming disaster and tried to get permission to retreat in time. Stalin committed the grave error of refusing, apparently in the hope that a counter-attack would succeed. German armies duly closed the trap, and an entire Russian army group was to all intents and purposes annihilated. The commander, Kirponos, nearly all his staff and the party leaders of Kiev were killed in trying to break through eastwards. The Germans claimed 600,000 prisoners. This disaster made effective defence of the industrial areas of Kharkov and the Donets basin impossible.

The Germans then struck at Moscow. Here the Russians had managed to assemble a fairly formidable defence, with two army groups (or 'fronts') astride the main highway covering the capital.

BARENTS
SEA

BALTIC
SEA

Murmansk

WHITE
SEA

FINLAND

Leningrad
Tallin
Tikhvin
Pskov
R. Volga
Riga
Kalinin
Kaunas
Vilnius
Vitebsk
Moscow
Vyazma
Ryazan
Smolensk
Tula
Minsk
Bryansk
Warsaw
Pinsk
Orel
Gomel
Voronezh
R. Dnieper
Lvov
Kursk
Kiev
Kharkov
D O N B A S
Stalingrad
Kremenchug
R. Volga
Dnepropetrovsk
Astrakhan
Kishinev
Zaporozhye
Nikolaev
Rostov
Odessa
Kerch
Grozny
Krasnodar
Sevastopol
Simferopol
Ordzhonikidze
Novorossiisk
Tbilisi

Petrozavodsk
Saratov

BLACK   SEA

■■■■■ Soviet line
         22nd June 1941

▲▲▲▲ Front line end
         November 1941

●●●●● March 1942
         (After Soviet counter
         offensive near Moscow)

xxxxxxx Line reached by
         German advance
         in South (Oct. 1942)

⬤ Surrounded
    Soviet troops

⟫ German
    attacks

➤ Soviet
    attacks

Scale 100 0 100 200 300 km

Map 1

But these troops lacked mobility and air-power, and, despite all the bitter experience of German enveloping movements, were too far forward. The bulk of both these army groups were surrounded near Vyazma in yet another disaster, in the first days of October 1941. The encircled troops were able to distract the attention of the Germans for a week or two by their attempts to break out, but most of the men and all their equipment were lost. At this time there was literally no effective formation between the Germans and Moscow. Stalin ordered Zhukov, who was then in Leningrad, to take charge of the defences. Matters were not improved when the Bryansk army group south-west of Moscow, was unable to hold Guderian's tanks, which advanced rapidly towards Kaluga and Tula, south of the capital.

On 16 October, government offices and foreign embassies were ordered out of Moscow to Kuibyshev, and panic broke out among the civilian population. The Germans took Kalinin and advanced on Moscow, the drive from the north-west reaching a point which travellers today can see marked by a memorial barrier. It stands *between* Moscow's international airport and the city. It was touch and go.

At this moment Stalin was seen at his best. He did not leave the Kremlin. His nerve did not break. A meeting of the Party was held in an underground station. On 7 November, with the enemy just outside the city, he took the salute at the march-past of troops on the anniversary of the revolution. Despite appeals from hard-pressed generals, he held back enough of the reserves, which had been ordered to Moscow, to mount a counter-attack. Winter had come. The Germans, overconfident, did not have adequate clothing, and had been exhausted by the stout defence which Zhukov had been able to improvise in the nick of time. Morale had been greatly strengthened by patriotic appeals, and by German atrocities. Like their ancestors of 1812, men stood fast and died: 'Russia is vast, but there is no room for retreat. Behind us is Moscow.' German losses mounted, and they were ill-prepared for a serious counter-attack from an army which Hitler had declared destroyed. The Soviet offensive of December drove the Germans back 100 miles in places. An invaluable breathing space had been won. Tragically, Leningrad could not be relieved, and its defenders suffered horribly. With hardly any food or fuel, nearly a million civilians died in the siege. But the city held out.

Stalin prepared for the 1942 campaign in the hope of being able to drive the Germans further back. But the balance of forces was not in his favour. Industry was still disrupted by the consequences of losses of territory. Allied aid began to arrive but made little difference at this point of time. New formations were still not trained, and the huge losses of regular troops and almost the whole of their supplies and armaments could not yet be replaced. Attempts to take the offensive failed with heavy losses. One such attempt, in the Kharkov direction in May 1942, led to the destruction of the attackers and dangerously weakened the southern front, where the Germans had concentrated a powerful attacking force. Stalin has been blamed for insisting, against advice and appeals from the local commanders, that the Kharkov attack be made. This, and the Kiev disaster, could have been his responsibility, especially as his staff officers at head-quarters found it difficult to change his mind when he made it up. The German attack disrupted the southern front completely. Men simply fled. Khrushchev later recounted that some soldiers could only be assembled if they were hungry and there was a soup-kitchen. Again there was a large haul of prisoners and equipment. The Germans drove through to Rostov, across the Don, into the fertile Kuban and to the foothills of the Caucasus. Stalin felt, with reason, that here was another major crisis. He issued stern orders, the death penalty was carried out for unauthorised retreat, every effort made to restore discipline. The German drive reached the outskirts of Stalingrad in mid-August 1942.

Gradually, the Soviet production effort began to redress the balance of forces. This was a fantastic achievement. The arrival of goods on lend-lease helped overcome certain vital production bottle-necks, and was valuable in providing lorries and radio equipment, to mention two items of importance. But the fact that, by the end of 1942 the Russians were actually producing more planes and tanks than the Germans, and often they were better planes and tanks, was due primarily to the self-sacrifice and hard work of the people. Just how great the sacrifices were is simply not realised in the West. Food was short, since the best agricultural areas were occupied and transport facilities greatly strained. In rear areas many people were hungry. They lived in overcrowded hostels and several families to a room. Overtime was long, and military discipline was imposed on the civilian population. Production of consumer goods stopped, and clothes and other necessities were almost unobtainable. In no other country was such total priority given to the waging of war. For this purpose, Stalin's political system and economic planning mechanisms were invaluable. But they would never have succeeded had the people not responded. It was tragically unnecessary to continue the methods of terror and police rule, yet continued they were. The novelist Simonov described an episode in which a unit fought its way out of encirclement, made its way east in good order, despite tremendous difficulties, yet when they reached the Soviet positions they were not thanked but disarmed by the NKVD and sent to the rear for interrogation. On the way the Germans attacked the column, and these unarmed men suffered severe losses. One would have thought they deserved better.

It does not matter too much who originally conceived the idea of attacking the German flanks around Stalingrad. A glance at map 2 will show that the position suggested this possibility to anyone on the staff. Hitler was mesmerised by the name 'Stalingrad', and sent large forces to attack it. They were resisted heroically in the streets by men of the 62nd Soviet army. On either side of the German advance were weaker forces, including allied Romanians, Italians, Croats. The Soviet problem was how, while holding on at Stalingrad, to assemble in an open plain in winter, with no hard-surface roads and one railway, a sufficient force to attack the flanks of the Germans, and to conceal this from the enemy. Stalin showed iron nerve in withholding more than minimal reinforcements for Stalingrad itself, despite the fact that the defenders had nearly been driven into the river.

On 19 November 1942 the blow was struck and the tide of war turned once and for all. Paulus's 6th Army was surrounded, the Italians and Romanians were destroyed, a huge gap opened on the German southern front. The skilful von Manstein extricated his troops hastily from the north Caucasus and fell back in fair order westwards. Hitler forbade Paulus to retreat, relief attempts failed, and on 2 February 1943 the 6th Army surrendered. This was an immense triumph for the Red Army, and for Stalin the Generalissimus.

On the eve of the victory he took a step which again symbolised the stress he put on national tradition: the army's uniform was made to conform closely with Tsarist pattern, including the stiff 'shoulder-boards' (epaulets, in Russian *pogony*) for officers. In the civil war the *pogony* had been objects of hatred and derision. Now they were Soviet, and senior officers were henceforth far smarter than they had been, and infinitely better dressed than the men. Indeed there were few armies where rank distinctions and privileges were so pronounced.

Legend:
xxxxxxx German positions 18th November
Soviet concentrations
● German and allied units surrounded
Soviet advance by 31st December
The first Soviet attack
Soviet attacks
German counter attacks

R. Volga

STALINGRAD

ROMANIAN 4th ARMY

GERMAN 6th ARMY AND 4th TANK ARMY

R. Don

ROMANIAN 3rd ARMY

Kotelnikovskii

R. Don

Millerovo

ITALIAN 8th ARMY

Voroshilovgrad

Scale

0   100   200km

Map 2

Stalin himself never went to the front. But he exercised control through appointing and shifting generals, and he supervised all major operations. Often supervision over carrying out his orders was entrusted to a 'representative of the *stavka*', who kept in touch with Stalin by telephone. Vasilevsky and Zhukov often acted as such representatives.

Political control was concentrated in a small defence council, which virtually replaced governmental and Party organs. Since most of its members were later politically disgraced, the post-Stalin histories published in Russia do not mention its composition. It is therefore worth noting who they were: Stalin, Molotov, Beria, Malenkov and Voroshilov.

They were each given important sectors to supervise. Beria naturally had security, Malenkov was entrusted with armaments, especially aircraft production, and so on. Some members of the Politbureau were in effect chief political officers ('members of the military council') of fronts and army groups. Thus Zhdanov was in Leningrad, Khrushchev at Stalingrad and later in the Ukraine. (Brezhnev was with the 18th Army in the Caucasus.)

The rest of the war was an almost uninterrupted series of Russian victories. Only once, in May 1943, a German counter-attack scored a significant success, recapturing Kharkov. But they soon lost it again. In August 1943 the Germans made their last great effort; in 'operation Citadel' they tried to break through in the Kursk-Belgorod area. Forewarned, the Soviet high command took the necessary precautions, and after the failure of this attack the initiative remained firmly in Soviet hands. Stalin signed triumphant communiqués announcing the capture of important towns, which were read over on the radio and were accompanied by artillery salutes: Kiev, Sevastopol, Odessa, Minsk, the list grew. The Leningrad siege was finally raised, and Soviet troops during 1944 penetrated into Poland and the Balkans. Victory was coming. Since the Germans were in full retreat long before the Western allies landed in France in June 1944, it is not surprising that Stalin and Russians generally claim with pride that they bore the brunt of battle. The cost was enormous. More died in Leningrad alone than the total of British and Americans killed from all causes throughout the war. Soviet military casualties must have been of the order of 10 million, and of these perhaps 3 million died of hardship in German prisoner-of-war camps. To these must be added roughly 10 million civilians, some killed by the Germans (this applies particularly to the Jewish population of western areas), others by starvation and sickness.

Stalin's name became associated with taking Russia out of the jaws of disaster into victory. At home he became accepted even by many of those who suffered at his hands in the purges. Abroad his stock also rose. In 1943 he met Churchill and Roosevelt at Teheran. In February 1945 he was host to the same allied leaders in Yalta, in the reconquered Crimea. Stalin recognised at Yalta the primacy of Western interests in a number of areas, including Greece. He obtained from the Western leaders agreement on a predominant Soviet interest in eastern Europe, including Poland, whose borders were to be moved far westwards. He agreed in words about democracy and elections. The strains which were to become the cold war were still beneath the surface.

The war had complex effects on internal policies and human attitudes within the Soviet Union. It gave, as was inevitable, a very strong impetus to Russian nationalism, and the victories were a source of national pride. It also strengthened the conservative or even reactionary aspects of Stalinism. To cite two examples, a decree sought to end co-education, to provide separate curricula for boys and girls, using justificatory arguments which would have pleased Lord Palmerston and Mrs Beeton. Then in 1944, there was a new decree on family life, which freed men from any responsibility for children fathered outside marriage. While giving state allowances for 'single mothers' and introducing honorific titles (e.g. 'Mother Heroine') for mothers of many children, no doubt due to the very heavy war losses, the decree reintroduced the stigma of illegitimacy for children born out of wedlock. These were further steps on a road which began several years earlier. An example of another kind of severity was mass deportations of peoples accused of disloyalty: Chechen-Ingushes, Kalmyks, Crimean Tartars and some others were transported wholesale, under very hard conditions, and their autonomous republics liquidated, with the war still in progress. On a more positive note, the war in alliance with Western democracies gave ground for hope that the regime would relax its severities after victory. Many peasants believed that collective farming would be liberalised or even ended. Intellectuals hoped for a less rigorous censorship. A new unity between rulers and ruled could perhaps have emerged from the terrible trials of war, in which the people showed by their sacrifices their loyalty to the state.

In April/May 1945 the Soviet armies entered Berlin, met the

Americans on the Elbe, and victory was celebrated in Moscow with a great parade at which captured German standards were thrown at the feet of Stalin, who took the salute on Lenin's mausoleum.

What, then can we finally say of Stalin as a war leader? After his initial loss of nerve, he did hold firmly the reins of military leadership. Despite some tragic blunders, his basic ideas were in the end vindicated. The great awe and fear that he inspired, and the fact that all men who might have challenged him had been executed, helped to keep the Soviet Union fighting and united in the face of the catastrophies of 1941 and the summer of 1942. Let us not forget that both the scale of the defeats and the degree of civilian hardship exceeded by far those that brought about the fall of Tsarism in 1917. This is not a justification of the great terror. It is nonsense to say that 'Stalin destroyed the fifth column' in 1936–38; millions of his victims were totally innocent, and the scale of repression created discontent which was of use to the invading Germans, in the Ukraine and elsewhere. The fact that the Germans misused their opportunity, imposing their own brand of racialist terror, was Stalin's good fortune. Stalin also had the wit and sense of self-preservation to appeal to patriotism and tradition. But it can be argued that only a discipline both harsh and credible (i.e. based on past experience of ruthlessness), plus faith in a leader built up for years as a demi-god, saved the Soviet Union from collapse.

There are those who say that the victory proves the basic correctness of the whole Stalinist line: collectivisation, industrial growth, the destruction of the opposition. I heard one such argue that the results of the battle of Stalingrad proves that Stalin's policies were right. A critic retorted: 'For all we know, but for Stalin's policies the Germans would not have got as far as Stalingrad'.

Chapter 4

The Last Years of Stalin

The Brief False Spring

Joy was unbounded when peace came. There was hope of change. True, the regime and its police was basically unaltered, most of the prisoners remained in camps, soon to be joined by perhaps millions of repatriated prisoners of war and labourers deported by the Germans. But for a short time hope persisted. Stalin made a major speech at a victory banquet. In it he thanked the people, and singled out the Russian people. He drank to them, speaking, as always, with a strong Georgian accent:

> 'Let me propose one more toast to you. I would like to drink a toast to the health of our Soviet people, and principally to the Russian people. I drink to the health of the Russian people because it is the outstanding nation amongst all nations of the Soviet Union. I drink the toast because not only is the Russian nation the leading nation but its people show a sharp intellect, character and perseverance.'

Yet the Russians constitute only about half of the population of the USSR. There are over a hundred other nationalities, some Slavs (Ukrainians, Belorussians), others of quite different and ancient cultures (Lithuanians, Georgians, Armenians), still others of Turkic or Tartar origin (Uzbeks, Kirghiz, Bashkirs, Azerbaijans, etc.). Stalin was here asserting and emphasising the primacy and dominant role of the Russians in the multinational Soviet state.

Life was inevitably exceedingly hard. People returned to ruined towns and villages, reconstruction began amid universal shortages. On top of everything, 1946 was a year of drought. Many still went hungry. But this was not seen as a repetition of the grim year 1933, since current sufferings were plainly due to the aftermath of war. Great efforts were made to restore tolerable conditions of living.

But early in 1946 the reimposition of stern Stalinist controls began. Some would link this with the beginning of the cold war. Indeed, as we shall see, it was already then becoming clear that relations with the erstwhile allies were going to be difficult. However, while not wishing to deny a connection with external strains and internal repression, it seems to me that Stalin's whole conception of government required him to stamp on 'liberal' illusions and restore total discipline, whatever line was being adopted at the time by Truman or Attlee. It is perhaps easier to discern the influence of foreign policy on economic plans at this period: a great stress was laid on the reconstruction and development of heavy industry. Stalin, more than ever isolated in the Kremlin, showed little awareness of the appalling conditions in which people were living.

Two blows were struck in 1946, signalling the end of any 'liberal' nonsense, one against the writers and the other against the peasants. Zhdanov, who was to become a species of cultural commissar, launched a violent attack on two literary journals in Leningrad, and also on two distinguished Leningrad writers, the poetess Akhmatova and the humorist Zoshchenko. He showed particular concern for the elimination of actual or imagined reflections of 'bourgeois' ideas, of alleged admiration of anything Western. He demanded the elimination of the unpolitical, the strictest subordination of the arts to the dictates and needs of the Party. Zoshchenko had written a harmless funny story about a monkey who found everyday life in a Soviet city so difficult that it decided to return to the jungle or the zoo. Zhdanov denounced this as a slander on noble Soviet men and institutions. The stage was thus set for the narrowness and extreme national-conservatism of the late-Stalin period, which extended to all branches of the arts and sciences, and which will require further examination in a moment.

The attack on intellectuals was closely followed by the decree of 19 September 1946, on 'breaches of the collective-farm statute'. It was there noted that on many farms the private plots of peasants had been increased in size, contrary to the rules, and the lands in question were to be returned to the farms. Various unofficial ways of making life easier were stamped on. It is true that the decree also reaffirmed the 'democratic' basis of collective-farm management and denounced officials for illegally taking away collective property. However, the main purposes of the decree was to tighten discipline, and *personal prejudice*

a council for collective-farm affairs was set up to ensure that regulations were strictly observed. Needless to say, it did not bother with collective 'democracy', save perhaps to ensure that the party's nominee for chairman was voted in unanimously by a peasant meeting (in some cases even this formality was not observed).

This was only one indication of Stalin's strong bias against peasants as a social group. Two more examples: in wartime some peasants had opportunities to sell the produce of their allotments to hungry townsmen at very high prices, and so it was entirely proper to levy a high tax on the allotments and on privately owned livestock. However, the tax rates remained at high levels also after the war, and were in fact increased in the last years of Stalin's life. The resultant burden was the greater if one recalls that compulsory deliveries at very low prices were levied on the peasant household as well as on farms, that (for instance) milk had to be delivered whether or not the peasant family possessed a cow. According to Khrushchev, when he tried to reason with Stalin, the latter accused him of a pro-peasant *narodnik* (populist) deviation.

Another example relates to the currency reform. No doubt it was true that large sums had accumulated in certain civilian pockets during the war, and action was needed to 'devalue' these savings in preparation for the abolition of rationing. But what was in fact done was to wipe out nine-tenths of the value of savings held in cash (savings banks and bonds were treated more favourably). Most cash savings were in peasant hands.

Stalin imposed harsh policies on low-paid townspeople also. The bad harvest of 1946 delayed the abolition of rationing for a year, but when it came the new prices reflected to the full the shortages of 1947. Ordinary bread cost $3\frac{1}{2}$ times the prewar price. He did authorise an increase in wages for the lower-paid, thereby diminishing the excessive differentials in pay. None the less, average wages were still only 65 per cent above the 1940 level, and so living standards were exceedingly low. Of course, Stalin could say in his defence that life was hard because of appalling shortages occasioned by the war, and that his price policy strictly reflected reality. Furthermore, as goods became more abundant, retail prices were reduced year after year. This is a good defence, though in most countries it was considered politically necessary to mitigate such severities by rationing or subsidies. Stalin had no reason to fear public opinion, however.

There is, of course, some connection between the economic situation and political repression. However, the relationship is anything but simple. Terror enables a leader to impose unpopular policies. It may have been the precondition of a very high rate of 'primitive socialist accumulation'. But such a relationship holds only on the general level, not for particular dates or events. Thus there is no correlation between a bad economic situation and terror. The wild excesses of 1936–38 took place when living standards and productivity had reached the highest point of the decade, far above the 1931–34 level. Similarly, the high-point of postwar repression was being reached when postwar economic recovery was far advanced.

Stalin and the Cold War

It can be plausibly argued that Stalin's economic and cultural policies after 1945 were intimately connected with the developing cold war. True, there is much evidence that Stalin's whole conception of government, including his own aim to achieve personal despotic power, was in a very real sense independent of a hostile environment. None the less, the Stalin regime justified itself and its own severities by reference to this environment, and many Party officials certainly thought that both dictatorship and Stalin were an unavoidable consequence of danger from without. How far Stalin's own policies increased this danger is another question.

As for the origin of the cold war, many volumes have been and will be written on this theme. Perhaps it is enough to say that deep suspicion of the 'imperialist' West was always present in the mind of Stalin and the bulk of the party, and the wartime alliance seemed likely to be temporary. Despite a certain euphoria plus some illusions about the wartime ally 'Uncle Joe', many highly placed Westerners considered that the USSR was likely to be a postwar menace. Certainly this was true of Churchill well before the war ended, as his memoirs bear witness. Therefore, once the common enemy was destroyed, strains and stresses were bound to arise. Stalin's actions in Eastern Europe exacerbated the situation. In Poland and Romania especially Soviet policy very quickly showed an insistence on the total domination of Soviet nominees and the negation of normal democratic procedures, which Western leaders thought had been agreed at Yalta. In East Germany the Social-Democrats were destroyed and a Communist regime installed under the aegis of the Soviet occupation authorities. These actions prompted Churchill's famous Fulton speech in March 1946, on the Soviet menace. A freer atmosphere at first prevailed in Hungary and Czechoslovakia, and its extinction may well be best seen as coming at a somewhat later stage of the cold war, intensifying it further. Soviet policymakers also exerted pressure on Turkey and Iran, which alarmed President Truman in particular.

By hindsight it would seem that Stalin was engaged in consolidating the Soviet sphere of influence, while gaining ground where he could. He did not interfere in Greece when British troops crushed the Communists in 1944–45, because Greece was assigned to the Western sphere by the Yalta agreement. He could not see that he was in breach of his obligations by imposing his nominees upon countries which Yalta had placed in *his* sphere. Suspicious by nature, he was ideologically predisposed to expect imperialist plots. American lend-lease ended abruptly in 1945, with the defeat in Japan, and the offer of Marshall Aid seemed to Stalin to be a bid to extend American influence, especially into the vulnerable area of the recently-occupied or liberated East European states. The fact that some of their governments wished to accept Marshall Aid was, for Stalin, further proof of the urgent need to establish firm and obedient Communist governments there. This in turn led to, or accelerated the process of, the establishment of party dictatorships in Czechoslovakia and Hungary, a process completed in the first half of 1948. This in turn brought a strong hostile reaction in the West.

A very important aspect of Stalin's policy was his estimate of the American nuclear threat. In the first postwar years only America had the bomb, and for long after they were greatly superior in means of delivery, with bases all round the USSR. Might they not use it to prevent the USSR from ever challenging America in the future? It is instructive to recall that at this period even Bertrand Russell advocated some such policy (in order to avoid the danger of a future war between nuclear powers). Stalin's fears were not absurd. In 1973 there was published in America a report from the then US ambassador in London, to the effect that Churchill had been advocating the use of nuclear-bomb threats to force a Soviet withdrawal from Central Europe. Soviet losses had been huge, the country was exhausted. It was said that the USSR 'did not disarm' after the war. This was not so. The army was greatly reduced in size. But Stalin's consciousness of weakness caused him to adopt a tough posture, and also to reinforce secrecy, to conceal weakness.

He succeeded all too well. The Western countries felt themselves to be weak, in disarray, menaced by the Soviet giant. A system of alliances designed to deter the Communists was brought into being.

Action and reaction now followed thick and fast. American bases were established, and the western zones of Germany were organised gradually into what ultimately became the federal republic. An early stage in this process gave rise to a conflict over Berlin, which was isolated inside Soviet-occupied East Germany, apparently as the jointly occupied capital of a future German state. This marked perhaps the high-point of Stalin's tough policy, and it strengthened Western alarm and military preparations. By now both sides were fully engaged on propaganda war and believed the worst of each other. Relations deteriorated. In retrospect, Western weakness and Soviet strength were alike overstated, and the belief that the USSR was planning to overrun Europe was unfounded, in the sense that Stalin had no such intentions and made no preparations designed to secure such an objective. But the more the West prepared to meet a largely imaginary threat, the more Stalin believed that the West must be preparing to roll back the Soviet forces from Central Europe, or go even further.

Relations were made worse still by the Communist triumph in China in 1948–49. It is by now accepted that Stalin did very little to help his Chinese comrades, perhaps foreseeing that a huge country like China was bound eventually to challenge Soviet hegemony among Communists. But at the time it appeared that the 'world Communist conspiracy' was scoring large gains and threatening the whole world. The very next year, 1950, saw the outbreak of the Korean war. Once again, most experts today will accept that Stalin allowed the North Koreans to attack in the expectation of an easy victory and American inaction. He seems to have misread a speech by Acheson, the then Secretary of state, which omitted Korea in a list of countries which America would protect. It is now also clear that Mao Tse-tung had nothing to do with the decision, that he was not consulted and perhaps not even informed. However, the North Korean attack set in motion a major American response, which ultimately brought China in and still further worsened the already grim international atmosphere. In Washington a major war with the Soviet Union appeared quite likely in 1950–51. Hence the policy of economic embargo, and intense military preparations.

While relations with the West were deteriorating, Stalin launched his campaign to tie the 'satellites' firmly to the Soviet Union. The first stage was to put Communists in power, but Stalin did not trust Communists; did he not have hundreds of thousands of Soviet Party members shot? And these were foreigners, in contact with God knows whom? So soon followed a second stage, that of purging the parties and establishing leaders whose obedience to Moscow was certain, and reinforced by control of Beria's secret police over the repressive apparatus of each country.

This caused a clash with Yugoslavia. Though Belgrade had been liberated largely by the Red Army, the Yugoslav partisans led by Tito had an outstanding and heroic military record, and had not returned to their country in the baggage train of the Russians. Their pride, morale, national appeal, stood high. So when Stalin's henchmen demanded Soviet control over police and other state organs, Tito decided to say 'no'. Overconfident in his power over the minds of Communists abroad, Stalin thought he could destroy Tito by declaring his hostility. Tito responded by imprisoning the few who were prepared to take Stalin's side. A furious Stalin broke relations, and Tito became a 'fascist monster' in Soviet propaganda declarations.

Among his sins was carrying on discussions with Bulgaria about a Balkan federation. To Stalin this seemed treasonable, a possible ganging up to weaken Moscow control. A great purge was launched to destroy real or imagined Tito-ites, or National Communists, or potentially disobedient persons, from the parties of the satellite states (at this period very clearly satellites). In Bulgaria, Hungary, Czechoslovakia, Romania, heads rolled. Stalinist terror methods were imposed, with public trials and abject confessions. Many were arrested, some executed, and Communists suffered most of all. The extent of repression varied. In Poland some (including Gomulka) were arrested but the local leadership prevented a bloodbath. In East Germany the ultra-loyal Ulbricht avoided any major purge. In China, Mao Tse-tung could not be treated as a mere satellite, both because of the sheer size of China and because he and his comrades had won through with hardly any Soviet help (and indeed against Stalin's advice). However, during Stalin's life the Chinese deferred to Moscow and to Stalin, in public at least.

All the ruling Communist parties in Europe were, by the end of 1949, wholly ruled by and from Moscow, and Stalin-worship and endlessly repeated protestations of total loyalty to the Soviet Union became universal. So was a total copying of Soviet institutions and methods, even in absurd detail. It is hard to say whether Stalin exactly willed this, or whether, like the purges themselves, there were excesses due to over-zealous and frightened comrades. In such an atmosphere, people denounced each other, tried to prove loyalty, some to save themselves and some to secure promotion. There was competition in imitating every Muscovite method, speech and policy. Western opinion was outraged.

There is evidence to show that Stalin became alarmed by the scale of Western response to his policies, and that he tried, from 1950, to negotiate a reduction in tension. Even the 'peace campaign' he launched was, in all probability, not only a political manoeuvre but a rather clumsy effort to appeal for a less bellicose atmosphere. But by then nothing could stop the momentum of the cold war.

Political and Cultural Repression at Home

Stalin's character in the last seven years of his life underwent a deterioration. Already in the thirties his thirst for despotic power may have had paranoiac features. After the war, his intense suspiciousness verged increasingly on clinical abnormality. Perhaps worship as a demi-god not only goes to but affects the head, after a time. Stalin hardly ever met people outside the narrow circle of his drinking-companions who were the Politbureau, and everyone was required to tremble and obey. Party organs such as the central committee hardly ever met. Party Congresses were no longer called – none met between 1939 and 1952. In this hothouse atmosphere there was plenty of petty intrigue, with some comrades ready to whisper to Stalin and to Beria about the real or alleged intrigues or plots of other comrades, to get nearer to the despot's favour and to edge others out of it.

Zhdanov had been put in charge of the cultural sector, and we have seen how he began the clean-up of alleged liberal elements in Leningrad in 1946. The purge extended to the musicians. Respected and world-famous composers, Shostakovich, Prokofiev and others, were accused of 'formalism' and lack of party spirit. Hack writers of optimistic pseudo-folk songs and party-line oratorios, were extolled. It all made most painful reading, and can be read in its devastating detail in Werth's *Musical uproar in Moscow*. As always, the despicable careerist hacks rushed to denounce their superiors. Someone even accused a composer of writing a 'formalist fugue'. Luckily none was arrested, but life became difficult for musicians.

Zhdanov was a possible successor to Stalin. In this capacity he inevitably competed with Beria and the rising Malenkov. In August 1948 he suddenly died, almost certainly a natural death. As we shall see, the cultural 'line' was in no way changed, and this suports the view that he was carrying out general Party (Stalin) policy, rather than initiating his own.

His death was followed by the mysterious 'Leningrad affair'. For reasons not yet clear, the Party leaders in Leningrad, who had led the organisation during the terrible siege, were all shot. So were many others in Leningrad. The purge also reached out to eliminate the chief planner, Voznesensky, on charges still unknown. The only common denominator in these executions was that they all had at some point some association with Zhdanov and with Leningrad.

The terror wave rose again, not to the hysterical and public levels of 1937, but silently arrests mounted. The Jewish anti-Fascist committee, set up during the war, was liquidated, apparently because they had suggested the Crimea (whence the Tartars had been deported) as an area of Jewish settlement, and some diseased mind thought of treason. The foundation in the same year of the state of Israel (originally with Soviet support), and the welcome given to Golda Meir, the first Israeli ambassador, re-inforced suspicions. This led, in 1948, to the arrest of the most eminent Yiddish writers, and for good measure the old commissar Lozovsky, whom the Party had put in to control them. Most of them were shot, after three or more years in prison, in 1952, Lozovsky among them. In 1948 the surviving Yiddish institutions (theatre, press) were closed. A campaign against 'rootless cosmopolitans' acquired increasingly anti-semitic overtones.

This was part of the ever-tightening and narrow cultural controls. Theatre critics were warned off by an article about 'anti-patriotic' criticism in *Pravda*. Writers, economists, painters, historians, were attacked and corrected. Hurrah-nationalism became *de rigueur*. 'Kow-towing before the West' was a crime. All good things came from Russia, now and in days of old. It was discovered that Russians had invented almost everything, from the steam engine to radio, not excluding the aeroplane. Scientific contacts with the West, tenuous for years, became impossible. Cultural contacts were minimal. After the Moscow Dynamo tour of 1945, even football matches with the West ended.

In science there was the destruction of genetics, in that disgraceful meeting at which the pseudo-scientist Lysenko claimed that, in denying the very existence of genes and chromosomes, he had the authority of the Central Committee and of Stalin behind him. Some Western Communist scientists, like J. B. S. Haldane, found this too much to bear. A bold Soviet geneticist, told to recant on the authority of Molotov, dared to reply: 'But does Comrade Molotov know more about genetics than I do?' He was dismissed, as were many eminent scientists. Luckily very few of them were arrested, despite much abuse. Now the situation is improving: for example Dubinin, whom Haldane knew, is now director of a revived institute of genetics.

Ignorant commissar-types invaded other sciences. Various modern ideas, from resonance-theory to cybernetics, were branded as bourgeois reactionary nonsense. In each branch of knowledge some dead Russian was extolled as a great originator, and some living Russian was put in charge to watch for heresy. In economics the original mind of Varga put forward ideas about possible changes in Western capitalism. In 1948 he was dismissed and his Institute of World Economics abolished. One hack-economist attacked the very notion of using compound interest as anti-Marxist. A budding mathematical-economics school was silenced.

Einstein was attacked too, but, with scientists hard at work to devise the Russian nuclear bomb, sheer necessity protected the physicists, while pure mathematics avoided trouble because so few commissars could understand it.

It is hard to compute the damage done by this deliberate Stalinist campaign to secure total obedience of intellectuals to the Party line, and to cut Russia off from all Western influence – and so also from Western science and technology.

After 1946 there was ever more stress on *Russian* nationalism, pressure to Russianise increased. Stalin seemed to forget all he might have learned from his own Georgian nationality, and from his own old theories on the national question. He aimed at centralised sub-ordination to himself as the leader of a new *Russian* 'socialist' empire, which was still internationalist in theory. But how could it be so in practice when Stalin had a law passed making all marriages between Soviet citizens and foreigners (*any* foreigners) illegal! Yet such a law *was* adopted, in 1947.

Old titles restored included, in 1946, the formerly hated title of *minister*. Uniforms for diplomats, uniforms for miners, for railway-men, emphasised rank by braid and epaulet. Stiffness and formality grew stiffer and more formal.

Over all this Stalin presided, working largely at night, with officials throughout the USSR sitting in their offices until dawn in case the boss telephoned with orders or questions. Much was decided at all-night dinners, amid crude jokes and guffaws of drunken cronies.

He hardly ever appeared in public, hardly ever spoke or wrote. A major exception was his essay in 1950, on linguistics, written perhaps because the pretensions of a philosopher-king require an occasional exercise of the philosopher's art. Stalin insisted, not unreasonably, that language did not significantly depend on class, and denounced crude oversimplifications, as well as intolerance in matters scientific. The 'linguistic' content in Stalin's intervention was hardly earth-shattering, but the sycophants rushed in to praise him to the skies as a genius of unique proportions.

Stalin's remarks on the need to tolerate differences of opinion in scientific questions is one of many instances of what looks like lying hypocrisy of gigantic dimensions. Who else but he had insisted on the enforcement of Party-line orthodoxy, who else had backed Lysenko? One supposes that lies of this kind came naturally to a man who, long ago in the twenties, invoked 'Party democracy' whenever it suited him in the battle against Trotsky and other oppositionists. In the same spirit he coerced the peasants while drawing attention to abuses in the democratic provisions of the collective-farm charter. Similarly, at a time of the most acute overcrowding (1948), he announced that in Moscow they had 'abolished slums', a lie so bare-faced as to take one's breath away. No wonder no statistics on housing could be published until well after his death.

The cultural and political scene of the late-Stalin period was grim, and it is hard to find any extenuating circumstances. Super-patriotism, drum-beating and semi-scientific nonsense became compulsory, and so was endlessly repeated adulation of Stalin in matters great and small, relevant and irrelevant. The author of a doctoral thesis on mathematical statistics (if he wished to pass) would have to include quotations from the 'leader and teacher of the peoples', such as a remark that 'statistics is very important'. He would have to expunge every reference to Western statistical works and theories, to avoid 'kow-towing'.

In his last years, Stalin's isolation and paranoia grew worse. He allowed or ordered Molotov's wife to be arrested, and Molotov himself, with Mikoyan, may have fallen out of favour. Even Beria was quite possibly threatened. (No reliable evidence for this period is yet available.) Certainly a new purge of some kind was in the wind. Judging from the trial of Slansky and his associates in Czechoslovakia, it was to have an anti-Zionist and anti-Semitic 'angle', but would involve many others too. The discovery in January 1953 of a largely Jewish 'doctors' plot' showed the way things were going. By then

Stalin's mind must have been so abnormal that any defenders of his record would have to plead insanity.

Economic Progress and the Nineteenth Party Congress

By contrast, economic progress was rapid, at least in the urban sector. Growth rate statistics always look impressive in a period of postwar reconstruction, but Stalin must have been gratified at the speed of recovery and the achievements of industry. In his speech in 1946 he envisaged realising by 1960 the following targets:

	(*million tons*)	
	1945	*1960*
Steel	12.25	60
Oil	19.4	60
Coal	149.3	500

In actual fact these targets were exceeded:

	(*million tons*)
	1960
Steel	65
Oil	148
Coal	513

Nor was progress confined to heavy industry. The industrial consumer goods sectors were quickly restored to their (admittedly inadequate) prewar levels, and a start was made in creating the capacity to produce consumer durables, hitherto virtually unavailable to the population. Retail prices were reduced in every year from 1948 to 1953. Life, while still hard, began to get better, though housing was still appallingly crowded.

Two reasons can be given for the good economic performance. One is the inflow of reparations from defeated countries. These included much dismantled equipment, rails, materials, and also (temporarily) technicians to train Russians in new skills. For example most of the Zeiss works in Jena were moved east and eventually Russians were able to make good cameras, for home consumption and export. But the most important reason, surely, was the hard work of the people, and the devotion to duty of a great many middle-grade managers, and officials. There were petty bureaucrats and careerists in plenty, but there were others too. I recall once meeting the chief architect of the city of Kiev, who was plainly an enthusiast for the task of rebuilding it and he and his colleagues doubtless made wholehearted efforts to do the job well. The war strengthened the feeling of patriotic pride. It caused heavy loss in manpower, but many acquired new skills in the increasingly mechanised school of war.

The economy had to rely heavily on women. A source of great unhappiness was the disproportionate numbers: almost twice as many women as men in the 20–40 age-groups at the end of the war. Women made great progress educationally and many became engineers and technologists, whilst dominating numerically the professions of teaching and medicine. However, they also had to do the hardest and most disagreeable work, which perhaps was natural in a country of peasant tradition, for field work was always a feminine occupation.

Agriculture did not do well. There were several reasons. One was the wartime destruction of villages, equipment, livestock. Another was that shortage of men was particularly acute in rural areas. But the trouble in large part was due to the neglect of agriculture by the planning organs, and the persistence of paying very low prices for farm produce. Delivery obligations and taxes rose, incomes remained exceedingly low. A so-called 'Stalin plan for the transformation of nature' was introduced with a flourish of trumpets in 1949. It was supposed to cause a change of climate of the arid south-east by huge plantations of forest shelter-belts. Orders were given, peasants were compelled to plant seedlings, but almost all the effort was wasted, due partly to the technical unsoundness of the scheme (Lysenko had a theory that trees of the same species do not compete for light and food!), partly because no material incentives were provided. In due course the 'plan' was quietly forgotten.

In 1949–52 pressure on the peasants increased, with heavier taxes on their own animals and produce. Recovery was halted. Poverty-stricken villages and miserably low productivity were the legacy of Stalin's successors. Stalin in his last years was still continuing his policy of neglecting the interests of the peasants and of agriculture.

Perhaps he would claim that the cold war left him with little room for manoeuvre. From 1949 Soviet military spending rose. The numbers in the armed forces went up, and great efforts on the part of scarce scientific manpower were being devoted to ending the American nuclear-arms monopoly at the earliest date. As tank output rose again, that of tractors declined, in 1951–2. Indeed, the performance of the whole economy (except agriculture) was the more creditable, if one bears in mind the growing strain of the arms race in the last years of Stalin's life.

Stalin's last work proved to be his contribution to, or outline for the preparation of a textbook on economics, published under the title of *Economic Problems of Socialism in the USSR*. Amid theoretical formulations concerning the law of value, two points stood out. One was his emphatic warning to the economics profession to keep clear of practical matters of management and of resource allocation, for this was the province of the political authorities. The other was his belief that the area of 'commodity-money relations' (or spontaneous economic forces) should be gradually reduced. These ideas were anachronistic and did not long survive his death. At the time, however, they were hailed as the finest flowering of human wisdom.

In October 1952 there assembled in Moscow the nineteenth Party Congress, the first to be held for thirteen years. Stalin was there, greyer and older, but he spoke only very briefly. The main report was presented by the man who was presumably intended to be his successor, Malenkov. The five-year plan for the period 1951–5 was submitted and approved, over a year late. The delegates acclaimed Stalin and passed all resolutions with customary unanimity. All seemed as before. Some must have forgotten that even great despots are mortal.

The End of an Era

Death came on 5 March. It may have saved Russia from another purge, it probably saved some threatened individuals, and so inevitably a rumour arose that death was not natural, though there are no grounds for doubting that the tough old dictator was struck down by disease in a medically normal way. There were widespread expressions of genuine sorrow at the passing of a man who dominated the history of his country for thirty drama-packed years, who had led it to victory and in whose name many had worked and died. Huge crowds gathered for the lying-in-state and the funeral. Speeches were made by Malenkov, Beria and Molotov, the three most likely to succeed. Stalin's body was laid to rest beside that of Lenin in the mausoleum in Red Square. What was the measure of his achievement?

measure of his achievements?

Stalin rose to power in the aftermath of a great revolution, in a country bled white by war and just beginning to recover from almost total economic ruin. He died at the head of one of the world's two super-powers, with a Soviet hydrogen bomb in the making, with an industry second only to that of the United States in its total output. The borders of the Russian Empire were almost everywhere restored, Soviet troops and Communist governments were established in the heart of Europe. The most populous country in the world, China, was ruled by Communists, even though their long-term loyalty to the Moscow leadership could not be guaranteed. All this was achieved under Stalin's guidance. So was almost universal literacy, a great expansion of education, a social security system.

His economic strategy made possible the survival of the Soviet Union in a desperate military struggle with Nazi Germany (Stalin's ghost would argue). This meant sacrifice, discipline, coercion, particularly against peasants. But did not peasants elsewhere have to bear the burden of industrialisation? Where was industrialisation carried out with 'consensus'? Did anyone ask British farm labourers or hand-loom weavers for their opinions during our industrial revolution? Did *they* have the vote in 1800? The whole process in the USSR could have been less arduous and more easily accepted if it were not for the need to hurry, a need due to the hostile environment, the overwhelming urgency of military security.

Stalin (his ghost would continue) organised a potentially anarchic land. He harnessed the people to the huge task which faced Russia, and gentler methods would not have succeeded. His opponents were very clever, but they could not rule. They were good at arguing and agitating, and criticising, but could they build? Imagine Bukharin organising something! Why, he was a professor by nature, or perhaps an inspired journalist. Rykov? A drunkard with no real backbone. Trotsky was a non-starter, an outsider who could not command the loyalty of the Party cadres, and he pursued unsound policies. No doubt (Stalin's ghost would perhaps admit) he and his supporters were not in the pay of foreign intelligence services; this was crude morality-play stuff for the ignorant masses. But Trotsky had been wrong at a time when it was very dangerous to be wrong.

Who else could have saved the country in 1941? Potential opposition was wiped out and it would have been perilous to allow it. True, the terror paralysed the initiative of many, but where would Russia have been without iron discipline, firm leadership, indeed semi-religious faith in the leader?

Mistakes? Unnecessary cruelties? Innocent victims? Certainly. Would Russia have been happier if the character of Stalin had been different? Possibly, but people cannot be divided into parts. His qualities and his defects were indissolubly bound together. *On balance* (his supporters could claim) he must be seen as a positive figure in twentieth-century Russian history. And not only Russian history, in view of his part in freeing Europe of Nazi Germany.

This sort of line could be taken by apologists for Stalin. For Brezhnev and his colleagues it is hard to avoid falling for this argument, as they had all been Party or state officials under Stalin, and too much stress on the negative features of his rule might undermine the legitimacy of the entire Soviet state, which he did so much to create.

Another line of defence is traditional-nationalist in character. Stalin, like Ivan and Peter before him, was a ruthless moderniser, who made his country great. Indeed there have been a number of old-style Russian nationalists who found it possible to accept Stalinism. A variant of the above is frequently encountered among German scholars: Russia can be ruled only with the whip; Stalin is the kind of ruler these people need, and deserve. Did not the Tsars rule as absolute monarchs, with the help of a service gentry who owed everything to them? Stalin's 'service (and servile) comrades' were part of the warp and weft of Russian history.

But there is a formidable 'case against'. There was, first, his ruthless disregard for human life. His victims number many, many millions. It is absurd to argue that they *had* to die to ensure the success of Soviet policies. It is arguable that these very policies would have been pursued more effectively if they had not been massacred.

A Communist or Socialist should see Stalin as one who perverted the original ideology of the revolution and destroyed the Communist Party that Lenin knew. Hierarchy, rank, privilege, the deliberate creation of vested interest as a political ploy, these are part of an *anti*-socialist way of life. Concealment of facts, censorship, a pretence of democracy and of continuity of revolutionary ideology, were part of the essential lying and dishonesty of Stalinism. The destruction of most of the intelligentsia did inestimable harm to society, to the economy, to culture. Not the least harm was done to Marxism itself. It is due to the Stalin terror that original Marxist thought atrophied in Russia, and so the recent interest in Marxist ideas in the West and in developing countries has kindled no Soviet contribution or response worthy of the name.

Furthermore, Stalinism *destroyed the Party* as an organism capable of thought and discussion. It is clear that any body of thought, or of men, are kept sharp by competition with persons who argue against them. The *advocatus diaboli* of Catholic theologians is a recognition of this need. Stalin's reign lowered the general level of argument and understanding in the Party at all levels. Party secretaries who did not obey and who argued did not remain Party secretaries for long. Yet the passage of time and the rule of seniority has brought the former middle-grade secretaries to positions of supreme power. Khrushchev, as we shall see, was an 'original', a character, but he was unique, and his undistinguished bureaucrat-colleagues got rid of him. What we have now, as an illegal Russian ballad has it, is rule by men who 'became bosses through learning that silence is golden', but who now have nothing to say. How Stalin towers in retrospect over the pygmies who have succeeded to his empire! It is the fault of his system that they virtually *had* to be second-raters. This is in sharp contrast with the scientists, men of world class, products of the best of Soviet and Russian education. The gap between the politician-type and the true intellectuals, which exists in all countries, might well be dangerously large in Russia now.

It is also attributable to Stalin's system that Party-state officialdom represents a powerful vested interest in the maintenance of 'administered privilege'. They control what is produced and to whom it is distributed. They have become conservatives, waving a red flag on high days and holidays. Stalin used their self-seeking for his own purposes, while punishing and purging them without mercy. They held office at his whim. After his death they demolished the terror machine in the interests (*inter alia*) of personal and job security, and now they do not fear. But the net effect is that power is in the hands of a new class which has lost revolutionary dynamism and which is no longer impelled by an autocrat. It is not clear where they go from here. Hardly towards 'world revolution', whatever that might be.

Critics can also seize upon the *economic* weaknesses of Stalinism: over-centralisation, a clumsy supply-and-production bureaucracy, lack of rational criteria for choice, the enthronement of arbitrariness. Above all his agricultural policies were cruel and counter-productive, and collectivisation is something for any country to avoid. If the pace and strategy of economic development by his methods required the horrors of terror and purge, then the pace and strategy were wrong.

Stalin's foreign policy too could be attacked, on grounds not of morals but of effectiveness. His refusal to see the menace of fascism, his attacks on Social-Democrats, helped Hitler to power. His policy towards Finland and Romania in 1939–41 may have impelled both into an alliance with Hitler, to the military detriment of the USSR. Enough has been said of his disastrous error in failing to see the imminence of the Nazi assault in 1941. The origin of the cold war is a complex subject, but at the least Stalin's policies certainly contributed to mobilising American opinion for the waging of it. His obstinate misinterpretation of 'decolonisation' caused Soviet policy to miss opportunities: for too long people like Nehru were seen as imperialist agents, a mistake quickly corrected by his successors.

So there were great errors as well as crimes, to set against the successful consolidation and enlargement of the Soviet state.

So where does all this leave us? Stalin achieved much. His rise, his methods, his successes and his brutalities all need to be understood in the context of Russian history, of Russian 'political culture', of the fate of the Bolshevik revolution in a backward and peasant country under conditions of international isolation. Having achieved power, he imprinted his personality on many events. His style of work was widely copied, his vengeful cruelty brought much avoidable sufferings to millions of people. Yet for all that, if the cruel and vengeful Tsar Peter can be called the Great, so will not future generations give to Joseph Vissarionvich Djugashvili, called Stalin, this same title, and with as much or as little reason as to that ruthless modernising despot of bygone days? It may be objected: we live in a more civilised century. But do we?

A Digression: What Explanation for Stalinism?

How did it come about that a libertarian revolution, made in the name of Marxian socialism, brought forth Stalinism? Some reasons have been advanced already, but it seems worth while to recapitulate and to try to generalise.

One category of explanations lays stress on the specific features of the *Russian political tradition*, of which Stalin showed himself well aware. Like Peter the Great, Stalin sought to mobilise the human and material resources of a backward country to catch up with the West, by barbarous means. This was linked with the logic of the Leninist concept of *seizing power in a backward country*, and then creating the pre-conditions for socialism from above. While a one-party state was not part of the original ideology, it became an objective necessity if one were to retain power and to transform the social structure, in a country with a large majority of peasants, uninterested in or hostile to such a transformation. For this purpose the *Leninist concept of the party*, as a tightly organised, centralised and disciplined organisation, was particularly well suited, and of course Stalin as General Secretary was at the strategic centre of the party's organisational role of ruling, coercing, transforming. It will be endlessly argued whether Stalinism was the natural and logical outcome of Leninism, or whether on the contrary Stalin destroyed Lenin's party, as he certainly destroyed physically most of Lenin's comrades. Perhaps the most reasonable judgement is that Lenin's strategy and methods created the opportunity for a Stalin, provided him with organisational and ideological weapons, but that Stalin then used them in ways which surely would have horrified the founder of Bolshevism. ('If Lenin were alive today he would be in prison', to quote words attributed to his widow.)

Also relevant was the *low educational level* of the citizenry in general, of the bulk of party members in particular. The Europeanised intellectuals were few, and it was surely no coincidence that Stalin's rise to power was followed by the violent deaths of most of the party intelligentsia. Men promoted from the ranks brought with them the conventional views so typical of high Stalinism, on topics as different as art, history, women, punishment, Jews, education and what I have called the sergeant-major-type attitude to subordinates. It may also be proper to add the unfortunate effect of the militant denial – by the left-wing intellectuals themselves – of the principles of traditional morality. Truth, justice, conscience, were for years mocked, presented as bourgeois prejudices. *Salus revolutionis, suprema lex.* This cleared the way for the extremes of ruthlessness and injustice to which they themselves were soon to fall victim.

We must now take on board the explanations which relate to *socialism in one country*, and the linked questions of *forced accumulation and industrialisation* under conditions of perceived military danger. Stalinism is then seen as a system of highly disciplined mobilisation, which can be linked with the already mentioned historical tradition relating to catching up ('Peter the Great was the first Bolshevik'), or to the specific contradictions and problems faced by Soviet Russia in the twenties and thirties (or, of course, both).

Then what of *Marx and Marxism*? Space does not permit a full discussion, but the reader is referred to the valuable symposium edited by Robert Tucker, which contains a discussion of this question by L. Kolakowski and M. Marković. One now condemns Marxism, the other still basically supports it. But they have some points in common. Neither considers Stalin's (or Brezhnev's) Russia to be consistent with Marx's ideas on socialism, but these ideas contain much that can be regarded as utopian, or internally inconsistent. It was not explained how the 'proletariat', the real working class, is supposed to liberate mankind. It was not the case that political disagreements arise only out of class struggle or conflict over private property, and the unanimity which, according to Marx, would be typical of a classless society could only be an imposed unanimity. The elimination of 'commodity relations', that is, of a market economy, involved the setting-up of a system of *centralised planning*, which, contrary to Marx's expectations, had to be both *hierarchical and bureaucratic*. This is because, if a market does not co-ordinate the millions of decisions taken by thousands of managers, an elaborate and complex command structure is the only alternative. Its very existence, its all-inclusiveness, greatly strengthened the power of the party and state organs which managed the economy and allocated human and material resources. Stalin's officials dominated the lives of the rank-and-file citizens (and of the more junior officials too), because the state-and-party were the supreme managers as well as the political bosses: anyone who falls foul of Authority falls foul of the only employer. The poet Mandelshtam, penniless in his exile, dreamt of owning a cow, for then he could survive even though the state refused to publish his works. At the same time the very need to co-ordinate economic activity consciously provides powerful functional reasons for the concentration of decisive power at the top. Where but at the top can one see the interconnections and complementarities of the various industries, or even just guarantee that orders are given to ensure the supply of a dozen different materials to, say, the chemical industry or the Urals machine-building plant?

Finally, what of the role of *Stalin's own character*? Medvedev wrote: 'though there were objective reasons for the cult of personality, much depends on the personality'. That is to say, the rise of a Stalin is largely explicable by impersonal circumstances, but once he achieved the status and power of a supreme despot there was much that he could arbitrarily decide to do. He surely did so decide. The scale and nature of the terror of the thirties has no precedent even in Russia's rather bloody history. Never before had returning Russian prisoners-of-war been treated as criminals and sent to concentration camps. These extremes of ruthlessness can be contrasted with what followed: after Stalin's death and the execution of Beria and a few other senior police officials, political executions virtually ceased. On a different plane, Stalin's death was immediately followed by a change in his anti-peasant policy. These facts suggest that Stalin's personal role was in certain respects decisive. And if, as some analysts do (for instance, Stephen Cohen in his very interesting contribution to Tucker's *Stalinism*), one regards the terror as *the* essential feature of Stalin's system, then naturally this helps one to draw a clear distinction between Stalinism and the methods of rule which preceded and followed Stalin's.

Chapter 5

Stalin's Heirs and Stalin's Legacy

A difficulty inevitably faces the successors of a mighty tyrant, and furthermore one who cut down any potential rivals. The men who follow were brought up in the shadow of the despot, and reached their high positions by subservience. They were known to the public for many years in their capacity as servants who extolled the virtues of their great master and denounced his enemies. The public had been told *ad nauseam* that every achievement was due mainly or wholly to the unique wisdom of Stalin. No wonder there was fear of 'panic and disarray' when the news had to be broken that the great dictator was no more. No wonder the security forces were mobilised to ensure order, though in fact the only disorder was accidental: the vast crush of people during the funeral ceremonies were hard to control and many were trampled on. But this was not a political demonstration, except perhaps of a pro-Stalin sort. For, as a bitter Soviet critic of Stalinism had ruefully to admit, the despot was widely popular. Many a sincere tear was shed.

Who could succeed? Let us look at the line-up as if we had not benefit of hindsight. Who were the front runners?

Lenin had been followed by a brief triumvirate of Zinoviev, Kamenev and Stalin. Three men made the speeches at Stalin's funeral ceremony, and seemed likely to become the new triumvirate: Malenkov, Molotov and Beria.

Georgi Maximilianovich Malenkov was just over 50 in March 1953. He it was who was thought to be Stalin's successor-designate, since he presented the main report to the Party Congress in October 1952 in Stalin's presence. This was the first Party Congress to have been held since 1939. He seemed to speak with the voice of authority. Yet he was an unimpressive-looking man with two if not three chins. Of intellectual origin, with a degree in electrical engineering, he had served in Stalin's Secretariat, and was thought to have played a sinister if minor part in the purges of 1936–38, and a rather larger part in the mysterious purges which eliminated Voznesensky and the 'Leningraders' after Zhdanov's death in 1948.

Except when he was a member of the key State Defence Committee during the war, and as such had been directly concerned with armament production, he at no time held a post of direct responsibility for anything, working all the time in the Secretariat of the Party. (I met Malenkov later on, in 1956, and he struck me as an intelligent man who had no great presence; he certainly seemed to lack positive qualities of leadership.) Perhaps Stalin preferred him to the others precisely because he had no independent standing whatsoever.

Vyacheslav Mikhailovich Molotov (63 years old in 1953) was another matter. One of the few surviving old Bolsheviks, his real name was Scriabin; he was related to the composer. He had been a leader of the Bolsheviks in Petrograd in 1917 when the Tsar fell, but this was less because of the strength of his personality than because older and bigger men had all been arrested. When Lenin came back in April 1917 he criticised the cautious line which had been pursued by Molotov and his colleagues. Stalin came to dominate Molotov after his (Stalin's) return from Siberian exile, and thereafter he was Stalin's indefatigable supporter. He had the reputation of being a colourless but efficient organiser, a reliable bureaucrat. In the thirties he was Prime Minister, until Stalin took this office on the eve of the war. He was at times Foreign Minister, and in this capacity he became well known in the West for unyielding and humourless obstinacy. In Stalin's last years Molotov was said to have fallen out of favour, and his wife was arrested. By seniority he was, nonetheless, a weighty candidate for the succession.

Lavrenti Pavlovich Beria (54), Georgian, had a career in the secret police, rising in 1938 to succeed the ruthless Yezhov as head of the NKVD. Though under him the purges were less drastic, he nonetheless presided over the great prison-camp empire and over the country's vast and oppressive security network, first as minister and then as 'overlord' of the Ministries of Interior and of State Security. He was said to have many unlovely personal characteristics, and fed Stalin's paranoiacal suspiciousness. While some of the stories told against him may have been concocted by his enemies after his fall, he seems to have been cruel, boorish, ignorant – but also ruthlessly efficient. In a struggle for the succession, the combination of being a Georgian and a policeman was a serious handicap. Many did not want another Georgian succeeding Stalin and feared and disliked his police associations. His command over the security troops, and the secret files he had on his rivals, were advantages which must have caused these rivals deep concern.

So much for the triumvirate. Who else was there? Kaganovich had been a vigorous and ruthless Stalinist in the thirties, but had faded somewhat since. Mikoyan, an Armenian, was an able and astute operator, who did much for Soviet trade, but was never a real challenger for the leadership. One of the elder statesmen was Andrei Andreyev, but he was colourless and not a contender. Less senior than most of the above, but in a strong position behind the front runners, was Khrushchev, of whom much more will have to be said. Let us look at how he appeared in 1953.

Nikita Sergeyevich Khrushchev was already 59. An almost un-lettered youth at the time of the Revolution, he received his schooling and Party training as a promoted worker. His first steps up the Party ladder were under the patronage of Kaganovich, in a district of Moscow. His upward moves coincided with the Purges. He admitted subsequently that he was then a wholehearted Stalin-supporter. He was not important enough to be held responsible for the massacre of the party cadres, but he stepped into dead men's shoes. In 1938 he succeeded the disgraced Postyshev as Secretary of the Ukrainian party (he had been born in Russia proper, but near the Ukrainian border and he liked to wear Ukrainian embroidered shirts). In 1939, he became a member of the Politbureau. Two years later the Germans invaded and occupied the Ukraine. Khrushchev spent the war as a political officer with various army groups in the South, and he was at Stalingrad and with the army that recaptured Kiev. After the war he resumed the Secretaryship in the Ukraine, save for a brief and painful moment in 1948 when he seemed to have lost Stalin's favour and was replaced by Kaganovich. Then in December 1949 he was called to Moscow as one of the Secretaries of the Central Committee and also as First Secretary of the Moscow Party Provincial Committee. Both in the Ukraine and in the Secretariat he took a particular interest in agriculture. Indeed in 1950 he proposed the creation of 'agro-towns', urban settlements for peasants, an idea which was disavowed by *Pravda*, a distinct blow for its author. He did not seem a dangerous contender, and it is quite probable that the triumvirate allowed him to advance after Stalin's death because they feared the capture of the Party machine by one of their own number. They either did not consider him to be a menace, or preferred to risk him than to endure one of themselves. His bluff and hearty manner suggested the ex-peasant rather than an intriguing statesman.

No one else seemed even remotely likely to challenge for the top places. Kosygin, it is true, had been a member of Stalin's Polit-bureau, but in 1952 he was demoted. Brezhnev had been serving his time in the provinces (Party Secretary in Dnepropetrovsk, then Moldavia). He had become one of the Secretaries of the Central Committee in Moscow in October 1952. He was still quite junior, 46 years old, and at Stalin's death was appointed deputy head of the political department of the Soviet armed forces. Voroshilov, old crony of Stalin's, was a political nonentity. Suslov aspired only to the status of senior ideologist, a role he still fulfils today (1975). Bulganin, the future Prime Minister, was a lightweight.

How far did it matter who succeeded? It is hard to deny Stalin some influence on the course of Russian history, however much one notes – as we have been noting – the importance of tradition and the logic of circumstances. But these lesser men would surely be swept along by the currents of prevailing opinion and the needs of the moment? What difference would it make if the policies dictated by the situation were carried out by Malenkov, Molotov or Khrushchev?

The question is at least worth asking. We shall shortly be discussing the legacy of Stalin, the problems and challenges which were faced by his successors. In seeing how they tackled their task, we should always bear in mind the extent to which there were choices, and the influence of the individual in command upon the choices that were in fact made. Again, as in identifying Stalin's special contribution, we should not forget that certain species of leaders are apt to make certain kinds of choices, and that the emergence of this species is usually no accident. That is to say, in explaining why something is done or not done, it is often the case that alternatives *did* exist, but the individuals in command did not see them as alternatives, or were extremely likely to reject them. Thus though President Ford has the physical possibility of nationalising some major American industry, it is evident that no Republican would have been adopted as presidential candidate if he was suspected of harbouring such a thought. So a Soviet leader in the fifties was unlikely to try to solve the agricultural problem by de-collectivisation or to declare a new NEP for small-scale industry, or allow a second political party, though a case could have been made for such actions and they were not 'impossible' (in the sense in which, for instance the restoration of the British Empire is impossible).

What were the problems facing Stalin's heirs? In no order of importance, they were the following.

1 *Foreign policy and the cold war*

Though the USSR was developing nuclear weapons, it was far behind America both in number of warheads and in means of delivery. American bases ringed the Soviet Union. Many countries in Europe, the Middle East, and Asia, were in American-led military alliances. Latin America was wholly in America's sphere. The Korean war was still dragging on, with China heavily engaged, but Soviet arms and prestige also involved. Soviet-backed or imposed regimes ruled in Eastern Europe by Stalin-type terror, but a bitter and counter-productive quarrel raged with Yugoslavia. Soviet influence in non-Communist countries, including the ex-colonial countries, was minimal. Stalin's successors needed to find some accommodation with the West, since a confrontation in the nuclear age was far too dangerous. The Korean war had to be brought to an end, if only to take some steam out of Western military effort, which was now including German rearmament. The new leaders needed to re-think their relationship with their satellites. They had to give thought to the evolution of relations with China, a country far too large and proud to be treated as a satellite. An effort to win friends and influence people in the developing countries was clearly overdue, if only to challenge pro-American governments in those countries and thereby reduce the threat from American bases.

2 *The terror*

At home it was at a pathological and intolerable level. The general sense of insecurity extended also to the leadership. Only a few years previously Voznesensky and the Leningrad Party leadership had been summarily executed. No one felt secure. This affected the conduct of government business, but also other aspects of life. New ideas in any sphere were inhibited by fear. The wall separating the Soviet citizens from Western contagion kept out also the flow of desirable technical information, and contributed to technological backwardness. Vast numbers of people, many of them above average in education, were held in labour camps, where they produced little and required a large number of guards. It was very likely that Stalin's heirs would consider the creation of a greater sense of security, amnesties, some effort to gain the confidence of the intellectual community. This applied not only to the scientists and technologists, whose services were obviously essential, but to the writers too. Insistence upon Party-line literature had become quite evidently counterproductive. Plays or books showing happy peasants eating goose contrasted so blatantly with the real situation in the villages that they had no effect. Some sort of relaxation had to come.

3 *The 'Stalin' political system and the Stalin image*

How far could any relaxation go without endangering the Soviet state, the monopoly of power of the Party, the many vested interests associated in that monopoly? By 'vested interests' I mean not only the fact that senior officials of Party and state benefited from material privileges, but also their security from criticism from below. Thus a provincial Party Secretary was monarch of all he surveyed, controlling the local press, judiciary, local government, and subject only to removal from above. A convenient state of affairs for the beneficiaries. The one-party state had existed since Lenin's time, and for most people it seemed normal, even natural. ('What', said a Muscovite when a foreigner suggested a multi-party system, '*several* parties? Isn't *one* bad enough?'.) This linked up with the older Russian tradition of firm rule as the one alternative to anarchy and confusion. This tradition was greatly strengthened by the Stalin despotism, not least because it had eliminated those elements of free discussion that survived into the twenties. People were accustomed more than ever to tremble and obey. How much relaxation, then, would be safe? And what of Stalin himself? He embodied the repressive system, and at first he remained infallible: his embalmed body was laid to rest in the mausoleum beside that of Lenin. To criticise him was dangerous. Dangerous to those of his successors particularly closely identified with his policies and his crimes. Dangerous also because it was bound to lead to embarrassing questions: if he committed errors and crimes, how is it that his colleagues tolerated him for so long? How, too, could they admit that the Soviet Union was led through a critical period of its history by a despot whose ruthless suspicions bordered on the pathological? On the other hand, to dismantle some parts of the Stalinist structure without publicly criticising Stalin was likely to be neither convincing nor effective. Not surprisingly, the leaders oscillated rather nervously between criticism of and silence about Stalin's crimes, before finally settling (under Brezhnev) for silence. Another important political issue faced them: how to organise the selection of the leadership itself. Lenin and Stalin had died. Hardly anyone had been able to resign or to retire into private life: the way out from the top was to prison or before a firing-squad. The Party Congresses had virtually ceased to meet, and these unwieldy assemblies were no more than mass meetings anyway. The Central Committee under Stalin's rule seldom met either, though much was declared and decided ostensibly in its name. An orderly procedure for succession had to be devised.

4 *The economy*

i *Living standards.* Stalin's system paid little attention to the needs of ordinary citizens. They came last in the scheme of priorities. While of course the output of consumer goods was rising, and Stalin may have sincerely desired that people should live better, in fact the quality of the goods available was often deplorable, shops were few and shortages many, housing conditions were abominable (not only in the space available per family, but also because repairs and maintenance were shamefully neglected), consumer services primitive. Rural standards were particularly low. All this contrasted with the undoubted achievements of Soviet heavy industry. It was both feasible and politically necessary to improve the consumer's lot, and Stalin's successors were bound to seek the credit for doing this.

ii *Industrial planning.* Stalinist over-centralisation had a number of negative features, already remarked upon. Increasingly it seemed impossible to run a complex modern industry by orders issued from ministries in Moscow. The achievement of quantitative plan targets was too often at the expense of quality, and inefficient solutions were frequently adopted for want of being able to identify better ways of achieving given objectives. Stalin's doctrine that the 'law of value' does not apply to transactions within the state sector seemed to justify arbitrary pricing of means of production: for if value categories did not affect the production and allocation of materials and machines, it did not seem to matter what their prices were. Yet planners in fact chose between alternatives by comparing costs. In choosing what appeared to them the cheapest variant they could be misled by irrationally fixed prices. The planning system was also 'conservative'. This statement may seem strange if one considers that industrialisation was a primary objective of the Stalin regime, yet it was so because planners planned by using 'material balances', i.e. they based themselves on past experience in determining material and fuel requirements. This led to neglect of new and progressive materials and fuels: oil and natural gas were backward, while emphasis continued to be given to solid fuels. Chemicals were backward too, with little attention to synthetics and plastics. In transport, the steam locomotive predominated until after Stalin's death. Consumer demand failed to find due reflection in production programmes. The latest and most modern machines were few, it being simpler to fulfil plans by making obsolete models. There were serious problems of co-ordination between plans made by different ministries. The wage system was in chaos, there being no one at the centre responsible for wages policy. Yet Stalin's 1940 decrees tying workers to their jobs were falling into disuse even before his death. So there were plenty of perplexities facing his successors, even while they could continue to boast of high growth rates.

iii *Agriculture.*   The weaknesses here were very noticeable, despite strict censorship and statistical silence (or misleading and exaggerated claims based on a mythical 'biological yield' of grain). Poor and lopsided mechanisation, very low harvests, gross misuse of labour, appallingly low incomes for collective work, farms very short of money because of low prices paid for produce, very inadequate supplies of fertiliser, and finally heavy tax and delivery burdens on the private allotments and animals which formed the basis of the collectivised peasants' livelihood, all these cried out for remedy. Food supplies to cities and raw material supplies to industry were adversely affected. It is not surprising that the first major measures decreed by Stalin's successors were concerned with agriculture.

Thus there was plenty on the agenda for Stalin's successors, whoever they might be.

Malenkov Outmanoeuvred: Khrushchev Wins Power

Malenkov spoke first at Stalin's funeral. He appeared to be taking over the direction of the Party and the state. Yet in a few days he ceased to be Party Secretary, retaining the Premiership. How he was compelled or persuaded to give up a key post – *the* key post – remains obscure. Leadership was to be collective, we were told. It was reasonable, in this context, for his colleagues to require that no man could hold the two top positions, that he had to choose one or the other. Did he in fact choose the Premiership, because he thought that it would be the decisive position to hold? If so, he was mistaken. It was an odd mistake to have made, for one who spent most of his political life in the Party Secretariat. More likely he was denied the Secretaryship by his comrades, as part of a deal.

This is suggested by the fact that no First Secretary was appointed at this time. What happened was that, of the Secretaries that remained, Khrushchev was senior. Other leading Party figures took key *ministerial* posts: Molotov (Foreign Affairs), Beria (Interior and Security), Bulganin (Defence) and Kaganovich all became Deputy-Premiers. Mikoyan and Kosygin were among the other Ministers. The Politbureau (Presidium)[1] of the party at this date consisted of Malenkov, Beria, Molotov, Voroshilov, Khrushchev, Bulganin, Kaganovich, Mikoyan, Pervukhin and Saburov, in the order in which they were then printed. Perhaps it was this massing of top leaders in the government as distinct from the Secretariat of the Party that helped to convince Malenkov that, as head of the government, he was in a strong position.

He began to evolve a policy of concessions to the citizen. Lower retail prices in the spring of 1953 and 1954 seemed to follow Stalinist precedent, since Stalin had lowered prices several times from the high levels of 1947. However, Malenkov's cuts were excessive, in that they made shortages of some foodstuffs worse. He launched a campaign to increase output of consumer goods, revising the five-year plan target figure upwards. The relative rate of growth of producer goods and consumer goods were altered, giving more emphasis to the latter. He announced a new deal for agriculture and the peasants, though it was his rival Khrushchev who was to carry through the detailed measures and to take the credit for their success. He made pacific overtures to the West.

Beria, it appears, was willing to go further yet. It is odd to imagine a man with such a police record opting for an ultra-soft policy, and of course he was never able to explain his policies or defend himself once he was attacked. But his enemies accused him of aiming dangerously to weaken collectivised agriculture and of urging too drastic concessions to the West, particularly over Germany. The riots in East Berlin (June 1953) may indeed have been a consequence of the appearance of a loosening of the Soviet grip on East Germany, a state whose unpopular regime particularly required Soviet troops

---

[1] The Politbureau was renamed 'Presidium' in 1952, and became known as the Politbureau again under Brezhnev. To avoid confusion, we will call it the Politbureau throughout.

to maintain itself in power. Anyhow, Beria fell. On 28 June 1953 his name was omitted from the list of top men attending a performance at the Bolshoi theatre. Innocent observers might have surmised that he did not like the programme, or that he had a cold. But at this period lists of top men on such formal occasions served to inform officials throughout the land about ranking (in those days Malenkov still came first), and absence from such a list without explanation was rightly interpreted by Kremlin-watchers as a sign of demotion, if not worse.

The circumstances of Beria's arrest is a subject of contradictory off-the-record statements. He may well have been detained at a meeting of the Politbureau with the commander of the Moscow garrison participating, to ensure that security troops could not help their fallen chief. He was certainly suspected of using his position as security chief to seize power. The others must have feared him and his security empire. Under Stalin it was subordinated only to Stalin himself, not to the Party or government. They feared that, with Stalin gone, Beria would try to rise to supreme control, so he and his empire would have to be cut down to size. The formal accusations against him were traditional-Stalinist: he had been a foreign spy, and so on. He was allegedly tried and certainly shot, the shooting quite possibly preceding his 'trial'. With him went his senior deputies (such as Abakumov, who featured in Solzhenitsyn's *First Circle*) and some republican and provincial security chiefs. The executions of these executioners proved to be the last *political* executions to date. (I except the shooting of a spy, Penkovsky, and a series of executions for criminal offences such as stealing government property.) Few could feel much sorrow at the elimination of the administrators of terror, and many must have rejoiced. Beria was succeeded as security chief by a professional policeman without political ambitions, Ivan Serov. Serov's record, however, included supervising deportations from territories annexed in 1939–41, reminding one that few could achieve high office in the Stalin era and keep their hands clean.

In August 1953 the Supreme Soviet met and was addressed by Malenkov. It was then that he announced new agricultural policies.

But it was at the plenary session of the Central Committee of the *Party* in September that Khrushchev showed that *he* was in command of agriculture, and in an increasingly strong position generally. He vigorously criticised the existing state of affairs. There was a shortage of grain (the audience might have remembered Malenkov saying, to the Nineteenth Party Congress in October 1952, that 'the grain problem is finally solved'). Livestock numbers were below the levels of 1928 and even 1916, and the number of cows was falling. Taxes on the peasants were too high. Prices and incomes were too low. He announced measures to relieve the situation. Procurement prices were raised. Taxes were cut. Investment in the needs of agriculture, and peasant incomes too, would go up. The Party's role was vigorously stressed, the inadequacies of the Ministry of Agriculture were stressed too.

Early in 1954 Khrushchev launched the first of his many agricultural campaigns: to increase grain supplies quickly by ploughing up vast tracts of virgin and long-fallow land in an area stretching from the Lower Volga to the Altai, but mainly in Kazakhstan and southern Siberia. The drought risk was high, but it seemed a quick way of remedying the grain shortage, while the task of providing more fertiliser to raise yields in existing areas was bound to take many years. This campaign was launched on Khrushchev's authority as Party Secretary. Malenkov remained silent.

Khrushchev's authority was being gradually enhanced. From just being 'secretary' (though the chief one by virtue of seniority) he became known as 'first secretary' in September 1953, and later as 'First secretary', the capital letter being a signal to all who could read and understand. He steadily established his supporters in key positions in the party. For example, he weakened Malenkov by shifting Andrianov, Malenkov's protégé, from the Leningrad Party Secretaryship into obscurity. Malenkov remained Premier, and judging by Khrushchev's later actions most ministerial positions were not held by men who followed Khrushchev. But by stressing the role of the Party and exercising increasing control over its organisations, Khrushchev was becoming a formidable force in Soviet politics.

A sign of Malenkov's weakness was the appearance of an odd pseudo-fairy-story in a literary monthly: 'A sparrow was appointed Eagle. Then the other birds wondered: "Is he really right for the job?" (Even I noticed the significance of this in distant Glasgow. The point will not have been lost on Russian readers.)

However, industrial policy remained under Malenkov, who continued to stress the need to produce more consumer goods ('on the basis of the successes of our heavy industry'). Foreign policy, too, was at this time in the Malenkov-Molotov bailiwick. Some successes were achieved in the direction of détente: the Korean war finally ended (July 1953), and the Austrian peace treaty signed (but only in February 1955). Further progress, especially on the complex German question, was blocked as much by Western intransigence as by Molotov's unyielding obstinacy. This was the John Foster Dulles period of American policy, when the very idea of an agreement with the Soviet Union was considered immoral, and no proposal the USSR would possibly accept was made from the Western side. Whatever Stalin's responsibility for starting the cold war, the West was now firmly committed to waging it, and Malenkov's rather tentative gestures were not heeded. He was able to announce, soon after becoming premier, that the USSR had the H-bomb. While he must have thought that this was an essential deterrent, it hardly added to the Western sense of security, especially as exaggerated accounts of Soviet strength and intentions were current.

Other unsettled problems seemed to be left in abeyance. First steps were taken to woo the Third World, but it was not until after Malenkov's fall that decisive steps began to be taken. Similarly, while mass arrests were no longer made, and the 'doctors' plot' story abandoned and discredited, there was no amnesty, and those in camps and in 'eternal exile' stayed where they were. Nor was anything done to alter the industrial planning system.

Malenkov, then, seemed to be suffering not only from the power-manoeuvres of the energetic and much more colourful Khrushchev, but also from lack of decisiveness, standing and influence. His consumer goods policy could easily be presented as unsound. How could the standard of living grow rapidly without massive *investments* – in agriculture, in the consumer goods industries themselves, in housing, in trade facilities? At the same time, Party conservatives were upset by the apparent downgrading of heavy industry, 'the foundation of our military and economic might'. It was in fact over this issue that Malenkov was attacked, and over this issue Khrushchev could count on the support even of men like Molotov and Kaganovich, old Stalinist hard-liners, as well as the industrial planners-in-chief Saburov and Pervukhin. The decision to remove Malenkov from the Premiership was presented to the public at a meeting of the Supreme Soviet (February 1955), in which a statement was read to the effect that Malenkov resigned, giving as a reason his administrative inexperience. In this statement he took responsibility for past agricultural failings, but was made to deny responsibility for the 1953 reforms which he had himself announced in August of this year. It is interesting that, though present, Malenkov himself said not a word. He was appointed Minister of Electric

Power Stations, and retained his seat on the Politbureau. The new Premier was to be Nikolai Bulganin, an amiable man with a little beard, carrying little authority and evidently expected to do Khrushchev's bidding.

So the events in February 1955 established an important precedent: they were non-sanguinary. Malenkov was not executed or imprisoned, merely removed, nominally by the Supreme Soviet, actually by the Party (Central Committee). It was a peaceful outcome. A year later, Malenkov came to Britain as head of an electricity delegation, and this astonished old Kremlin-watchers: 'What? Allow the fallen Premier out of Russia? Stalin would not have done it!' Others may have recalled that there had been a time when Stalin *did* allow his future victims to become ambassadors abroad, and Bukharin had visited Paris two years before his execution. However, times really had altered. The leaders must have agreed to avoid blood-baths. They had all been under heavy strain in the reign of the late dictator, and wanted no such things to happen again.

The supremacy of the Party, and of the Party's First Secretary, was strongly reasserted. Khrushchev had come to power. But it was still power with strings attached, since the Politbureau was virtually unchanged: it still included Molotov, Malenkov, Kaganovich, Mikoyan, Voroshilov, Saburov, Pervukhin, all of them men who did not owe their positions to Khrushchev and who could be a majority against him when and if they chose. Indeed, throughout Khrushchev's period of rule moments occur at which it is unclear whether a given decision was Khrushchev's own, or whether it was forced on him (or watered down) by his comrades. This was so at times even after the events of 1957 enabled him to dispose of his more obstreperous colleagues in the leadership.

But Malenkov's removal had other aspects. It was carried out by methods which were secretive; no word of any disagreement appeared in the press until after the *fait* was *accompli*, there was no debate, Malenkov made no public defence, and everything was said to be unanimous. This reasserted the principle that the Party was always to appear to the people as monolithic. There was to be no return to the Party debates of the twenties – and indeed this has not happened yet and shows no sign of happening in the near future.

In retrospect, Malenkov was surely an unsuitable choice of successor; he really was a sparrow failing to hold the job of an eagle. Yet he did manage to project to the people the idea that he stood for higher living standards, and this may be illustrated by a kind of folk-tale heard in Moscow in 1956. According to this tale Malenkov was visited, shortly after Stalin's death, by his mother, who was an old intellectual, a doctor. She said: 'Georgi, you have done much harm to the Russian people, but now you are in power, you can do good.' 'Very well, mother, I will try,' replied Malenkov. And he tried. So 'they' got rid of him.

Apocryphal? Imaginary? Certainly. The significance does not depend on the truth of the story, merely in the fact that such stories circulate about 'them'.

Khrushchev's Policies and 'Destalinisation'

Khrushchev's personality was unique. Under Stalin a whole breed of functionaries arose who gradually lost such individuality as they may have possessed, at any rate in their reported utterances. Whatever its content, a speech by Molotov, Kosygin, Malenkov, Saburov and most of the others was depersonalised, standardised, full of predictable, prefabricated phrases. Mikoyan was to some extent an exception; perhaps an Armenian was allowed to express humour (there have been many 'Armenian jokes' in Russia for a hundred years or so). But here was Khrushchev, informal, bullying, cheerful, folksy, shrewd. In a world which, under Stalin, was protocol-minded to the *n*th degree, Nikita Sergeyevich's bluff chatter was a very radical departure from precedent. It shocked many, both colleagues and ordinary people, who expected dignity and remoteness.

Here are some typical extracts from a Khrushchev speech, as it was reported at the time (it was said afterwards that his colleagues frequently had to insist that his words be edited and toned down before publication).

'We all know the huge role of women in all sectors of communist construction. But in this hall there are very few women. Can't even see them without binoculars. How can we explain it? People say: those present here are mainly the directing cadres. So – men direct and women work? Clearly not an adequate explanation.'

'Some might say: "what's this, has Khrushchev come to criticise us and tell us off?" What did you think, that I'd come to read you Pushkin's poems? You can read poetry without me. I have come to show up defects, to urge you to freshen up some organisations, to blow some wind of change at some of the directing cadres.'

'Suppose someone like a skilled mechaniser receives a tractor. In his hands, a tractor is like a violin in Oistrakh's. But I know some tractor-drivers who treat their machines differently. If such a one starts up the tractor, I want to shout to him: "Switch off, the nerves can't stand it!"'

Not the style or words of address usual in Party circles, at least in public! He spoke often, at great length, toured the country, harangued, stirred up local officials, criticised subordinates in front of their subordinates.

What is it that Khrushchev tried to do? Wherein did he differ from the other leaders? Did his personality affect policy? Again we return to the role of personality in history. Writing about Lenin a Soviet author (writing for *samizdat*, i.e. illegally circulating literature) remarked that his personal qualities, such as a liking for Beethoven and modest kindliness, were of as little importance in themselves as an ex-peasant general's liking for cabbage soup and dirty jokes. What matters is what people do, and how it fits into the historical circumstances. Can the same be said of Khrushchev? What does it matter if he introduces an agricultural policy with a cheerful speech about his grandmother's views on cooking, if the policy he actually introduces would also have been adopted had he been replaced by any of five or six comrades in the leadership? Was there a Khrushchevian policy? If so, what was it, and how could it be distinguished from that of Malenkov, Molotov, and later from that of Brezhnev?

One clue is provided by the changes which occurred after Malenkov's fall. The priority of heavy industry was reasserted. But Khrushchev gave increasing priority to agriculture, greatly extending the virgin lands campaign and also investment in farm machinery, and later also in fertiliser. Prices were increased again, causing a further rise in incomes of collective farms and peasants, though the levels were still modest by later standards. In July 1955 Bulganin raised major questions concerning industrial efficiency and managers' authority, though without finding a solution. In the same year a state committee on labour and wages was set up, to bring order into the confusion of wages rates. (Kaganovich was made its first head, his last post before his political demise.) There followed a whole string of social legislation of a progressive kind. A housing drive was launched, which at last gradually began to add to the pitifully low area of housing space per head in cities. A minimum wages law benefited the lower-paid. Revised regulations greatly increased the pensions and disability benefits of the ordinary worker and employee. The law forbidding workers to change their jobs without permission was repealed. Maternity leave, which had been cut to 70 days by Stalin in 1940, was restored to the original 112 days. Tuition fees in secondary schools and in higher education, also introduced by Stalin in 1940, were abolished. One must assume that Khrushchev urged or supported these measures.

Agriculture is primarily a supplier of consumer goods – foodstuffs. Housing and social services benefit the citizen. It is therefore futile and misleading to contrast Malenkov's concern for the consumer with Khrushchev's emphasis on heavy industry. He may have somewhat downgraded manufactured consumer goods as against agriculture, and he had to emphasise heavy industry if he was to secure the 'conservative' support he needed to throw out Malenkov. But his emphasis was unmistakably towards doing something visible for the citizen.

The 'conservatives' were likely to have been less pleased by another measure which followed Malenkov's fall: releases of political prisoners and exiles. In 1955 and 1956 most prison camps were closed and their inmates returned home, many after seventeen or more years of suffering. Few families indeed existed in which no one had been arrested in the Stalin period. Many perished, of course, but a great many survivors came back, especially among those who had been arrested or re-arrested in 1949–52. These were all sorts and conditions of people; two whom I met included an economist who had a total of fifteen years of prison camps, and also a peasant who told me he had been sentenced to fifteen years for stealing grain on 'his' collective farm. As they came back and spoke to their families and friends it became difficult to avoid some official statement about the repressions and terror of the Stalin era. Khrushchev found it both necessary and convenient to act accordingly, as we shall see.

Khrushchev continued the policy, very cautiously begun soon after Stalin's death, of encouraging the intelligentsia to think for themselves. Censorship remained, of course, but was somewhat relaxed. Criticism was now tolerated, not of the regime as such or of its top leaders, but of many abuses, shortages, inefficiencies. Critical works on agriculture flowed from the pens of literary men like Ovechkin, Dorosh, Yashin. Ilya Ehrenburg caught the atmosphere of the time with his novel *The Thaw*. Needless to say, Khrushchev himself was an ignoramus as far as the arts were concerned. (In 1956 I saw how he talked his way through a 'command-performance' solo by David Oistrakh at a Kremlin reception, while paying undivided attention to army folk-dancers.) But he sensed the need to win the trust of the artistic as well as the scientific intelligentsia, and up to a point he allowed them some scope, and is known to have caused concern not only to his more cautious colleagues but also to the literary bureaucrats. For, as experience shows, few are more conservative and negative than officials of the writers' and painters' unions.

In foreign relations, Khrushchev took pride in a very liberal visa policy for foreign visitors, who were no longer to be shunned like the plague by ordinary Russians. (But exit visas for Soviet citizens remained very hard to come by.) Scientific and cultural delegations were exchanged with many countries. Already in November 1955, he and Bulganin visited India and Burma, and began a policy of economic aid for developing countries, which at first yielded political dividends, because of novelty and the USSR's anti-imperialist reputation, and also because American aid was at this time heavy-handedly linked with anti-Communist military alliances. Khrushchev was also able to utilise a clash between the Western powers and Egypt to establish an important political and military bridgehead in the Middle East. This led to some rather naïve attacks on 'Soviet economic penetration' from the West, with indignation about Soviet arms sales, as if it is a law of nature that only Western arms should be supplied to the Middle East.

While these moves were undertaken in the Third World, Khrushchev also attempted accommodation with the West. Adenauer was invited to Moscow in 1955 and diplomatic relations were established with the German Federal Republic, though real agreement over Germany was still very far away. In 1956 he visited Britain with Bulganin.

Continuing to develop nuclear weapons, Khrushchev ordered a substantial cut in conventional forces, and the number of Soviet troops diminished, from well over 5 million to 3,600,000 between 1955 and the end of the decade. (I heard much talk of this among Russians in 1956. Some expressed the view that the compulsorily demobilised officers 'would have to do some real work for a change'.)

Meanwhile, back to internal affairs. Khrushchev promised to observe Party rules, to follow the procedures so neglected by Stalin of calling regular Central Committee meetings and regular Congresses. A Congress was held in February 1956, the Twentieth Congress. It was this gathering that Khrushchev chose as the occasion for a secret speech attacking Stalin. Years afterwards, a Soviet academic told me that, in his view, Khrushchev's 'debunking' of the Stalin legend was his great service to his country. Let us see how he came to make his attack and the form which it took.

The successors of Stalin, as already indicated, faced a problem, and vacillated in their treatment of the dead dictator. A long article could be written tracing the zigzags of policy from 1953 to the Twentieth Congress. Cautious criticism of some of his ideas alternated with a reassertion of his services, but more common was silence: thus neither the anniversary of his birth nor of his death was celebrated, while Lenin was built up steadily into the unique father of the Soviet state. Gradually the phrase 'cult of personality' was born, as a way of referring to excesses by Stalin and fulsome praise of Stalin. The country was therefore not wholly unprepared for a steady downgrading of his semi-divine attributes. Nonetheless Khrushchev administered shock treatment.

The 'secret' speech was read to Party meetings and to selected groups of non-party people in the months that followed the Twentieth Congress. It had a most profound effect. Some rejoiced. Some wept, for they had sincerely worshipped Stalin. Some, relieved at the end of despotic terror, were alarmed: could the resultant shock-waves be controlled? It was made known also through Party channels in Eastern Europe, China and to other Communists in the world. It leaked to the West and was published in full in several Western newspapers.

Khrushchev roundly accused Stalin of despotic rule, of morbid suspiciousness, of crimes against innocent Party and military leaders. Many loyal comrades had been shot or imprisoned, on false evidence or on no evidence. He told harrowing stories about individual cases. He said that beatings and torture were widely applied after 1936, and that the murder of Kirov, which gave the signal for the purges, was a mysterious and suspicious affair. He accused Stalin of blindness in the face of the Nazi German attack in 1941, of self-glorification, of historical falsification.

Some extracts from the speech can give some idea of its effect on men and women brought up for a generation on the Superman Stalin myth:

> It was determined that of the 139 members and candidates of the Party Central Committee who were elected at the 17th Congress, 98 persons, i.e., 70 per cent, were arrested and shot (mostly in 1937–8). (*Indignation in the hall.*)

What was the composition of the delegates to the 17th Congress? It is known that 80 per cent of the voting participants in the 17th Congress joined the Party during the years of the [Bolshevik] underground before the revolution or during the Civil War; this means before 1921. By social origin the basic mass of the delegates to the Congress were workers (60 per cent of the voting members).

For this reason it was inconceivable that a Congress so composed would have elected a Central Committee, a majority of which would prove to be enemies of the Party. The only reason why 70 per cent of the Central Committee members and candidates elected at the 17th Congress were branded enemies of the Party and of the people was that honest Communists were slandered, accusations against them were fabricated, and revolutionary legality was gravely undermined.

The same fate befell not only the Central Committee members but also the majority of the delegates to the 17th Party Congress. Of 1,966 delegates with either voting or advisory powers, 1,108 persons were arrested on charges of counter-revolutionary crimes, i.e. decidedly more than a majority. This very fact shows how absurd, wild and contrary to common sense were the charges of counter-revolutionary crimes made, as we now see, against a majority of the participants in the 17th Party Congress. (*Indignation in the hall.*)

We should recall that the 17th Party Congress is historically known as the Congress of Victors. Delegates to the Congress were active participants in the building of our socialist state; many of them had suffered and fought for Party interests during the pre-revolutionary years in the underground and at the Civil War fronts; they fought their enemies valiantly and often nervelessly looked into the face of death. How then can we believe that such people could prove to be 'two-faced' and had joined the camp of the enemies of socialism during the era after the political liquidation of the Zinovievites, Trotskyites and rightists and after the great accomplishments of socialist construction?

An example of vile provocation, of odious falsification and of criminal violation of revolutionary legality is the case of the former candidate member of the Central Committee Political Bureau, one of the most eminent workers of the Party and of the Soviet government, Comrade Robert I. Eikhe, who had been a Party member since 1905. (*Commotion in the hall.*)

Comrade Eikhe was arrested 29 April 1938, on the basis of

slanderous materials, without the sanction of the Prosecutor of the USSR, which was finally received 15 months after the arrest.

Investigation of Eikhe's case was made in a manner which most brutally violated Soviet legality and was accompanied by wilfulness and falsification.

Eikhe was forced under torture to sign ahead of time a protocol of his confession prepared by the investigative judges, in which he and several other eminent Party workers were accused of anti-Soviet activity.

On 1 Oct. 1939, Eikhe sent his declaration to Stalin in which he categorically denied his guilt and asked for an examination of his case. In the declaration he wrote: 'There is no more bitter misery than to sit in the jail of a government for which I have always fought.'

On 2 Feb. 1940, Eikhe was brought before the court. Here he did not confess any guilt and said as follows:

'In all the so-called confessions of mine there is not one letter written by me with the exception of my signatures under the protocols, which were forced from me. I have made my confession under pressure from the investigative judge, who from the time of my arrest tormented me. After that I began to write all this nonsense. . . . . The most important thing for me is to tell the court, the Party and Stalin that I am not guilty. I have never been guilty of any conspiracy. I shall die believing in the truth of Party policy, as I have believed in it during my whole life.'

Eikhe was shot 4 Feb. (*Indignation in the hall.*) It has been definitely established now that Eikhe's case was fabricated; he has been posthumously rehabilitated.

(Many more cases were cited in the same vein.)

The speech was shattering enough. But it was notable also for what it did *not* say. The names of rehabilitated and innocent victims did not include any of the leaders of various oppositions: not Trotsky, Bukharin, Rykov, Zinoviev or Kamenev. There was almost exclusive reference to Party and military victims, hardly a word about peasants and other ordinary people, who also suffered severely. Furthermore, Stalin was presented as having been right up to 1934, and the *Party* as having been right all along. Khrushchev felt unable, it seems, to question the basic infallibility of the Party, which had just gone on doing the things that needed doing despite Stalin.

It was not a very convincing picture. It did not even begin to answer the question: how did it happen that the Party came under the supreme control of a cruel tyrant? How was it that his comrades, who included all the leaders on the congress platform, allowed such things to happen? Either they were willing helpers or dupes, or they were powerless executants of the Master's will. All this was the more embarrassing for a Marxist, who ought to seek explanations of major historical phenomena not in the evil of an individual but in economic-social circumstances. Khrushchev had no explanation at all, as Togliatti, the Italian Communist leader, among others pointed out.

An apocryphal story went like this. Khrushchev was addressing a meeting and speaking of Stalin's crimes. A member of the audience shouted: 'And what were *you* doing?' Khrushchev snapped back: 'Who said that?' Silence. 'Well,' he replied, 'that is what I was doing too, keeping silent.'

'Destalinisation' may have been, probably was, partly motivated by the desire to discredit Molotov, Kaganovich and Malenkov, and thereby to strengthen Khrushchev's political position. They were not attacked in Khrushchev's 'secret' speech to the Twentieth Congress. Indeed, Molotov was mentioned as one who suffered from Stalin in his last years. But they were clearly more vulnerable than Khrushchev, who could claim that his purging activities in the Ukraine were in obedience to central orders, while Molotov and Co. were right there at the centre of power. When, later on, they openly came to political blows with Khrushchev, he did not fail to blame them specifically for participation in various crimes of Stalin's.

Destalinisation ran its course, reaching a peak in 1961, at the Twenty-second Congress, where an old woman said that it came to her in a dream that Lenin was unhappy lying beside Stalin in the mausoleum: Stalin was removed and buried elsewhere. In the following year Solzhenitsyn's *One Day in the Life of Ivan Denisovich* was published after the editor of *Novyi mir*, Alexander Tvardovsky, succeeded in persuading Khrushchev himself to override the censors. For the first time, some details of the dreadful forced labour camps appeared, in powerful literary form, in a Soviet publication. But this is running ahead. For the moment it is sufficient to note the far-reaching effects of all these relaxations, and the extent to which they had the effect of untying tongues. While censorship remained very much there (albeit less strict than before), speech became very much

freer, as people gained confidence and learned that no one was
likely any more to be arrested for talking. Times were changing, and
optimism spread, about the possibility of what was called 'demo-
cratisation with the brakes on'. The brakes had to be on, because,
after so much blood and tyranny, an outburst could have catastrophic results. Here one saw yet again the age-old Russian fear of
anarchy lurking just beneath the surface.

In Russia proper the shock-waves of destalinisation could be
contained. But it was otherwise in Georgia, and in Poland and
Hungary.

Khrushchev could justifiably complain that people are ungrateful.
His nationalities policy, internally and externally, was more liberal
than Stalin's. Under Stalin's rule whole nations were deported, in
defiance of Marxist or any other socialist principle, for allegedly
being pro-German during the war. This fate attended the Volga
Germans, the Crimean Tartars, the Kalmyks, the Chechens, the
Ingushi and some other Caucasian groups. Their republics were
erased from the map. The survivors were rehabilitated under
Khrushchev, and all but the first two of the above list were allowed to
return to their reconstituted autonomous republics. (The Volga
Germans are still in Altai and Kazakhstan, and the Crimean Tartars
have recently been agitating in vain to be allowed back to the
Crimea from Central Asia.) Khrushchev relaxed cultural Russification and spoke out on the subject of the despot's national policies,
indicating that Stalin might even have deported the Ukrainians if
there had not been so many of them. Georgia had been the scene of
Stalin's oppressive actions towards the local Party in 1923 and this
had attracted Lenin's attention and indignation in his last lucid days.
In the great purge the Georgian Party and *intelligentsia* had been
massacred in great numbers. To call Stalin a friend of Georgian
nationalism would be the equivalent of confusing an Irish-born
member of the British establishment with de Valera or the IRA.

Yet it was a fact that he became a symbol of Georgian nationalism
after his death. I happened to be in Tbilisi in June 1956, a few weeks
after some major riots had occurred. Though unreported in any
Moscow newspaper, unmentioned even in Tbilisi's own publications,
they had necessitated the use of troops. I saw the half-torn notices
put up by the military commander declaring a state of emergency. I
saw also painted and chalked slogans glorifying Stalin, and spoke
with eye-witnesses (who, it must be said, disagreed widely with each
other. Both said that the troops opened fire, but one said it was in the

air, the other that there had been some killed and wounded). Georgians, who are certainly nationally very self-conscious, deeply resented some distant Muscovite telling them that the eminent local boy who made good was no good. While the agitation simmered down afterwards, it was one warning among many that relaxation can be dangerous to the regime.

The effect on Communists abroad was different, but even more disruptive. Brought up to believe that 'bourgeois' press stories on Stalinist despotism and terror were a pack of lies, many of them were deeply and sincerely shocked at the deception practised on them. There were other shocks to come. The Chinese attitude at first was ambivalent. It was only later that they came in aid of Stalin's memory against the 'revisionists' of the Kremlin. But the most disruptive effects proved to be in Poland and Hungary. Both countries, and especially Poland, were by tradition ill-disposed to Russia. Both had unpopular Communist governments imposed on an anti-Communist people. Both had seen many Communist leaders eliminated (in Hungary they were shot, in Poland merely placed in detention) for suspected National Communism or Titoism. The weakened party was still further weakened by the revelations about Stalin, with their corollary that their own repressions and trials (e.g. of Rajk in Hungary) has also been based on falsehoods. Khrushchev's apology to Tito for Stalin's attacks on him and the resultant reconciliation with Yugoslavia made past executions for Titoist heresy particularly monstrous.

Matters were made worse by economic discontent. In Hungary and in Poland the fall of Malenkov had led to a reassertion of the priority of heavy industry and neglect of consumer interest, in a sort of distorted reflection of what the leaders thought was the Moscow line they ought to be following. All this, plus frustrated and indignant nationalism, proved to be an uncontrollable mixture. Destalinisation contributed to the outburst by weakening the Party and the police. One could say that in the USSR (with exceptions in Georgia and a few other national areas) the cement of nationalism held the structure together, and there were strong objective reasons for relaxing the terror, but in Hungary or Poland the regime required terror to survive, and relaxation was very dangerous indeed.

Poland and Hungary erupted. In Poland there was a shift to a more 'national' Communism of Gomulka, but only after riots and demonstrations led to the collapse of the Party's 'Muscovite' leaders. Khrushchev had to recognise a change in relationships, symbolised by a payment to compensate for past deliveries of coal to Russia at abnormally low prices. In Hungary the 'national' Communists were led by Nagy, who replaced the hated Rakosi. Nagy endeavoured to establish a more popular Communist government, similar to that of Gomulka in Poland. But he was unable (or possibly unwilling) to control a powerful right-wing nationalist movement, which turned towards armed violence against the hated secret police and which was vehemently anti-Communist in inspiration. Cardinal Mindszenty had been tried and imprisoned under Rakosi. He was released, and became the symbol of the anti-Communist elements. It was then probably too late for the Soviet Union to expect positive results from a conciliatory policy; evidence accumulated that the leadership in Hungary was slipping away from the 'national' Communists, with whom some sort of deal might be made, as had been the case in Poland in the previous month. The last straw was the announcement that Hungary would withdraw from the Warsaw Pact, i.e. from the Soviet-led equivalent of NATO. This was too much. After some hesitation, the Soviet troops finally went in, Nagy was arrested and executed in highly dubious circumstances, and so was the commander of the Hungarian armed resistance, General Maleter. This bloody outcome contrasted with the relatively peaceful transition, with no Soviet armed incursion, in Poland. It is also very interesting and instructive to compare it with Brezhnev's action in Czechoslovakia twelve years later.

These events are not in themselves our subject. They are important for the light they throw on the evolution of the Soviet regime internally, and on the outlook of Khrushchev and his colleagues on their own situation and on the world. In my view, the intervention in Hungary was clearly forced, in the sense that without it the whole Soviet military-political position in the eastern half of Europe would have been in grave danger of collapse. Many Communists in the West left the Party in disgust, but they were thereby showing only their own misunderstanding and credulity. Had they understood the nature of the Soviet regime and of its satellites, the nature also of international relations and the cold war, they might well have found the Hungarian intervention to have been 'necessary'. But evidently they thought that the Hungarian Communist government had been supported by 'the workers and peasants' (or by most of them), and the realisation that this was not so upset them.

It is sometimes said that the Anglo-French adventure in Suez facilitated the Soviet military intervention in Hungary. If by 'facilitated' is meant that it gave a fine opportunity for counter-propaganda, then this was indeed so. But on the evidence it does seem that the arguments for sending in the army carried the day without reference to what the British or the French may have been doing.

Khrushchev Challenged and Triumphant

All these events in the second half of 1956 shook Khrushchev's position. The following is a probably sound reconstruction of what occurred.

His enemies could not attack him directly on the issue of destalinisation, or at least this would not be the open pretext of their attacks, though many must certainly have felt that he was rocking the boat dangerously on this issue. They chose to criticise his economic management. The Twentieth Party Congress in February had adopted a new (sixth) five-year plan. By December it was clear that it was unsound, and it was in fact announced that it would be amended; soon the whole plan was abandoned; it was replaced two years later by a new 'seven-year plan' to cover 1959–65. The Central Committee, or some group temporarily controlling it, used these difficulties to reorganise industrial planning. They were trying to cope with a real problem: the excessive autonomy of 'empire-building' industrial ministries *vis-à-vis* the co-ordinating organs. This, so it was said, led to the adoption of ill-balanced plans. But in coping with this real problem they strengthened governmental control by appointing a super-minister-overlord, M. G. Pervukhin, with powers over all the ministries (including, in the first version of the proposed reform, the Ministry of Agriculture). It was plain that this arrangement was not to Khrushchev's liking and was in fact designed to curtail his powers. This follows not only from the logic of the situation but also from the fact that Khrushchev scrapped this whole scheme within three months, when he was strong enough to do so.

It may be thought that many years later, with Khrushchev's opponents in power, a full account of the manoeuvres of the winter of 1956–57 must by now have appeared in some Soviet source. But this is not so. Partly this is because no description of recent factional struggles (or a truthful account of earlier ones) is likely to be published so long as present conventions continue; and partly the reason may be that the principal 'oppositionists' in the drama have all left the political stage and did not return to it after Khrushchev's fall. Neither Brezhnev (who was then a Secretary of the Central Committee and a candidate-member of the Politbureau) nor Kosygin (who was in charge of consumer goods industries) played any notable role. The opposition was later called the 'anti-Party' group. We know that they consisted of the old guard – Molotov, Malenkov, Kaganovich, plus Pervukhin and Saburov. Bulganin and Voroshilov voted with them in the confrontation which finally occurred in May 1957. But we will come to this in a moment.

Using the Party machine which he controlled, Khrushchev counter-attacked in February 1957. The pretext was again economic. He had a totally different solution to the problem of inadequate co-ordination between ministries: he proposed to abolish them, and to base planning on over 100 regional economic councils (*sovnarkhozy*), the regions being co-ordinated by the big republics (which contained several regions) and by the central planning agencies.

The 'anti-Party group' objected, on political and practical grounds. The name of the group was an invention of Khrushchev's after his victory over them, reminding us of the English sixteenth-century political-philosophic epigram:

> Treason doth never prosper. What's the reason?
> If it doth prosper, none dare call it treason.

In June 1957 Khrushchev was outvoted in the Politbureau by 7 votes to 4. Instead of admitting defeat, he established the precedent of appealing to a plenary session of the Central Committee. Marshal Zhukov, the prestigious war leader, is said to have helped to get the provincial members to Moscow quickly, and was rewarded with a seat on the Politbureau (though not for long). Khrushchev was victorious, and, so strong was the tradition of public unanimity, that no one in the session voted against and only one man abstained: Molotov did not vote for his own demotion.

The fact that Bulganin and Voroshilov had also sided with the opposition in the Politbureau was not made known at the time, and Bulganin remained Premier until 1958. The others, however, were removed from high office. None were ever to regain it. But none were the subject of any legal penalty. Molotov went as Ambassador to Mongólia, Malenkov to manage a power-station in Ust-Kamenogorsk, east of the Urals. Kaganovich also became a manager, and soon retired on pension. Pervukhin in due course became Ambassador to East Germany and then a divisional chief within Gosplan, where he still is (1975). Saburov faded from the public eye. Voroshilov was long overdue for retirement. When Bulganin was dropped, he became a regional economic official.

So one could act together to outvote the Party chief and suffer neither death nor imprisonment, though of course it did end one's political career. Times had altered.

What new men took the places of the fallen leaders? The minority in the Politbureau had been Khrushchev himself, Mikoyan, Suslov and Kirichenko. He brought Brezhnev into full membership in June 1957, together with Zhukov, Aristov, Belyaev, Ignatov, Kozlov, Kuusinen and Shvernik. (The last two, as well as Mikoyan, were very old war-horses.) It may be significant that they were all to be demoted well before Khrushchev's fall, with the exceptions of Suslov and Brezhnev, while Mikoyan faded into retirement. With their help he carried through the elimination of ministries and the creation of the regional economic councils, though, as will be shown, the measure was basically unsound and created unnecessary difficulties. He went ahead to weaken also the Ministry of Agriculture, ultimately dismissing the Minister, Matskevich. In every field he showed that he was the clear Number One.

The spring of 1957 also saw the launch of the world's first Sputnik, highlighting Soviet scientific achievement. Growth rates were impressive. Agriculture was doing better, though certainly not well enough. Foreign aid was politically effective, especially in the Middle East but also in India and Indonesia in particular. Alarmed Western writers exaggerated the nature and extent of 'Soviet economic warfare'. One example of 'Soviet penetration' reported at the time was that 'a consignment of Czech toothbrushes had arrived in Nigeria'. This nonsense shows the state of mind of some in the West. But Khrushchev himself was as infected by overoptimism, which suited his ebullient character.

When, in August 1958, he got rid of Bulganin and became Premier as well as First Secretary of the Party, he seemed to be all-powerful. The obedient press reported his lengthy speeches and praised his every action.

What sort of Russia was it over which Khruschev ruled? What did he want it to become? How far had it changed since the days of Stalin, who had died only five years before.

To some extent any answer to such questions must be speculative, but it is worth while to try an interpretation, if only to stimulate thought and, perhaps, dissent.

First, the elements of continuity. These were – and are – of fundamental importance. One party, hierarchically organised, keeping its discussions largely secret and presenting a unanimous face to the ordinary people. A party, true, which was rapidly increasing in numbers, soon to reach 12 million, but one in which ordinary members had little influence on those above them. The Party Secretariat controlled appointments, not only Party but state, social and trade union appointments. It dominated the government, and it was clearly Khrushchev's wish that it should do so. Local Secretaries were fully in command of their provinces and districts. At all levels this meant Party control over the press and the judiciary. Organisations not under Party control were not allowed to exist, at least in any sphere of the remotest political-social significance. Censorship of books, periodicals, even duplicated factory journals, and of course all newspapers, remained thoroughgoing. Though for the time being the censors were more lenient, Khrushchev himself reminded the writers that, were there to be any danger of a real intellectual dissident movement, his 'hand would not tremble' and he would suppress it firmly. So the basic structure erected by Stalinism was not greatly altered, whatever the attacks on Stalin himself. In many parts of the country obedient routine-bound Party Secretaries obediently made routine speeches criticising the 'cult of personality' to order, as previously they had sung hosannas to Stalin also to order, and they would brook no contradiction in either case. As a Georgian writer said to me once, when I suggested that the literary line had altered for the better: 'That is not the point, the essential point is that there is a line and that it is imposed on us from Moscow'. There is no sign that Khrushchev, brought up wholly within the system, had any intention of changing it in any of the above respects.

But change there was, not least in the party. There was more discussion, if only because it was no longer fatal to express disagreement. Party organs met regularly. The Central Committee met and talked, and a (no doubt edited) version of its proceedings was published. While naturally not including public attack on the top leadership, quite sharp criticism of ministers, mistakes in planning and also of expenditures did begin to appear, to an extent unknown for decades. Under Stalin criticism was either low-level ('in some parts of Siberia shoes on sale are not of high quality') or inspired from Stalin's entourage, in which case the man criticised trembled for his life and liberty and dared not reply. Under Khrushchev things became gradually more businesslike, and so did criticism. A Hungarian commentator (in private conversation) made the point this way. Under Stalin, a policy idea was associated with faction: that is, policy A was presented as being in the interests of the Party and policy B as being against these interests. Anyone advocating policy B was thus liable to repression. In just this spirit admirals were shot in the thirties for advocating cruisers rather than submarines. If they were wrong, their motives were suspected. Now (said the Hungarian) policies are rationally discussed in most instances: policy A has these advantages and those disadvantages, whereas policy B . . . Of course the careers of individuals could still be advanced or retarded by the adoption or rejection of policies with which they were personally associated, but this is so in every society. The effect of such changes was to widen greatly the area in which personal initiative could be safely shown.

Khrushchev clearly believed that this was good and repeatedly said so. Yet his whole background, and indeed the nature of the regime, made it impossible for him to be consistent. Be businesslike, put forward ideas boldly, advise us what best to do; he would say all this. But when his own pet ideas were at stake, he would force them through and demote or dismiss the objectors. We shall see what harm this caused to agriculture. Yet when in Kiev an agricultural research institute director defended certain technical recommendations on the grounds that they were in accord with the party line, Khrushchev exploded angrily: 'You are the experts, it is your job to tell us, and to be bold in saying what is wrong, not to take shelter behind the party line'. He was certainly being sincere. But the head of an institute in Kazakhstan, whose recommendations on fallow and grasses were uncongenial to Khrushchev, lost his job all the same. And although he first tolerated attacks on Lysenko, and allowed his surviving victims to revive genetics, Khrushchev in his last years chose to give political support to that pseudo-scientist.

What should be the limits of criticism, in agriculture, in literature, over economic policies? What precise meaning is to be attached to the Party's domination over society? How much disagreement is to be permitted within the Party itself? There could be no easy answer.

A major change, with substantial side-effects, was the obvious one: the end of mass terror. There were very few political arrests under Khrushchev, and no political executions. Fear greatly diminished. Personal feelings of security increased. The police's powers were cut, their great forced-labour economic empire dissolved. Dissident writers wrote poems about retired policemen living on their pensions by the uncontrollable Black Sea and dreaming that they had deported it to Siberia. Needless to say the police were still active. But this was a change which everyone felt, and which loosened many tongues. Khrushchev evidently thought this was desirable. The frozen fears of Stalinism were no good for a dynamic modern society, this was clear to him.

He was more concerned than many of his colleagues about ideology, indeed he felt that the future belonged to 'Communism', though he was unclear and perhaps naïve about what this meant. It did, however, have something to do with greater equality and with making things available to all without payment. Thus he acted to raise up the incomes of the lower paid and to improve their pensions, and he was concerned at the growth of educational privilege. To this end he not only eliminated tuition fees but also launched into a controversial educational reform, designed to introduce more work training ('polytechnisation') and to recruit the bulk of students in higher educational institutes from those with at least two years' work experience. This was clearly unpopular both with educationists and the upper strata of society, and the reform was very largely obstructed and then abandoned. The attempt, however, showed a sort of populist-egalitarian strand in Khrushchev's thinking, far removed from Stalinist privilege-creation. The privileged strata which arose under Stalin proved too strong in the end – though their resistance was fortified by the strength of the genuinely educational objections of having everyone work for the first years after leaving school (what of musicians, talented mathematicians, and so on? Soon exceptions were to multiply). His revised Communist programme, adopted at the Twenty-second Congress in 1961, contained promises to provide some goods and services free by 1980. It is an indication of his colleagues' disagreement with this undertaking that no word of it has been heard after his fall.

Indeed such ideas have an old-fashioned ring in an increasingly consumer-orientated society; the more prosperous citizens want to be free to buy a wider variety of better goods and services of their choice, not to receive a free issue.

He seemed to have been somewhat 'fundamentalist' also on religion. Stalin had persecuted the Church in the thirties, but became more tolerant during the war, when the Russian Orthodox Church took up a patriotic position. Many churches were also reopened under the German occupation. Therefore in the postwar years religious life was more active than it had been in the thirties. Under Khrushchev measures were taken to obstruct the Church's activities, many churches being again closed. Similar action against synagogues was linked with a more negative policy towards the Jews, after an initial period (1953-7) of relative relaxation. Khrushchev has sometimes been described as an anti-Semite. These words seem to me too strong. His actions are consistent with the sort of petty prejudice widespread among not-too-well-educated people in his part of Russia. But a real Ukrainian anti-Semite was one who joined the Nazis in killing and torturing, or who anticipated them under Simon Petlura in the civil war days. Such terms should be used sparingly. They do not apply to Khrushchev. But his impatience with organised religion, Christian as well as Jewish, was a noticeable feature of his period of rule.

So was a harsher policy towards crime. As already mentioned, *political* executions no longer occurred. However, the death penalty was introduced for criminal activities: not only murder in the first degree but also aggravated rape and a range of economic crimes: embezzlement, stealing large quantities of state property; in one instance a man was sentenced to death for adulterating sausage and selling off some of the meat for his own gain. In another, some state materials were being used for illegal private manufacture. Khrushchev also favoured the activities of non-judicial bodies, which were given powers to punish (e.g. by deportation) individuals alleged to be 'parasites'. He imagined this to be a step towards mass participation in a 'state of the whole people', a formulation dropped after his fall. The idea that crime needs to be severely punished is not in accord with early Bolshevik ideas, and the death penalty for offences other than treason was exceptional even under the Tsars. Stalin's executions were always ostensibly for real or alleged treasonable activities. However, a man of Khrushchev's 'folk' background does often have rather crude views on punishment, and not only in Russia.

He is also likely to have crude views on art. He seems genuinely to have favoured greater freedom for the painter, the composer, the writer, subject only to political censorship. But when some 'conservative' cultural officials showed him some modern abstract art, Khrushchev was horrified. 'Painted with a donkey's tail,' he shouted. One should not doubt his sincerity, nor yet the fact that his taste was not all that different from that of politicians in other countries.

Indeed, the *New Yorker* published a cartoon showing a couple of New Yorkers gazing at an abstract painting. Said one: 'Look, do we have to like it just because Khrushchev doesn't like it?' The difference is that politicians of other countries do not have the duty or power to decide what should be exhibited.

He was convinced that the deficiencies of public life and of the economy would be corrected without changing the basis of Party rule. He thought he could force through reforms, bully or replace slack or stupid officials, urge, harangue, stump the countryside and talk to the locals, and that results would follow quickly. His favourite phrase was . . . 'in the next two to three years'. Whether it is the supply of meat, or of fertiliser, or of feed grains, his time-horizon was short, his impatience great. Perhaps his age had something to do with it. Stalin had achieved total power before his fiftieth birthday. By 1958 Khrushchev was already 64.

He was certainly a product of his time. His experience was that of a Party Secretary under Stalin, plus the shock of war, when he was in the thick of the early disasters as well as the later triumphs. But while many colleagues in the leadership who had been of humble origin turned into grey bureaucrats, this never happened to Khrushchev. He was the last of a generation of uneducated leaders. The next one would consist of men who were, in the main, the products of technical higher education. Did this contribute to making them prone to greyness and bureaucratisation? Possibly. What is certain is that Khrushchev's style was quite different from theirs. In her fascinating memoirs, Nadezhda Mandelshtam distinguished between three generations of Party 'functionaries': the first could be a 'seminarist' given to passionate intellectual argument. Stalin shot almost all of them. The second was a much less well-educated, hail-fellow-well-met and rather crude 'doer', 'apt to wear embroidered Ukrainian shirts'. Many were also shot. The third category was the 'tight-lipped diplomat' species. Khrushchev was a survivor of the second category. It is puzzling that such a man should have been in Stalin's Politbureau. Evidently odd man out in character and manner, Khrushchev found himself increasingly frustrated and out of tune with his colleagues as the years went by, even though he exercised much power over the appointment, promotion and dismissal of the men around him. As we shall see, Khrushchev was finally ousted by men who, on 'Kremlinological' grounds, might appear to have been 'his'.

Chapter 6

The Fall of Khrushchev and the Rise of Brezhnev

Politically Khrushchev reached his apogee in 1958. He was First Secretary and Prime Minister. He had to his credit some popular and socially just legislation. Agricultural output had risen by more than 50 per cent over the depressed and depressing performance of 1953, and the 1958 harvest (aided by good weather) was a record. Industrial advance was satisfactory, and many Western commentators were deeply concerned about Soviet growth and the impact of Soviet aid. The sputnik was still news. Khrushchev's political enemies were scattered. The 'thaw' was limited and under control, the consequences of destalinisation having been safely contained.

Yet the last six years of Khrushchev's rule witnessed an accumulation of troubles. Some were not of his making, but, as the world's statesmen have always known, one gets blamed anyway if things go wrong.

In the field of foreign affairs, Khrushchev's attempt to secure a rapprochement with, or an impact on, America under Eisenhower was not an unqualified success. He visited America in the autumn of 1959, saw Hollywood, Disneyland, shook many hands. He seemed to make some impact on the inept Eisenhower. However, the 'spirit of Camp David' made very little difference to the pursuit of the cold war by either side. An unfortunate phrase, 'we will bury you', was held against him by Western propagandists. (He was often careless in his off-the-cuff statements, in and out of Russia, and must frequently have appalled his advisers and colleagues.) Then in May 1960 the U2 flight over Russia shattered any illusions he may have harboured about a change in us policy. The American high-level spy plane was shot down near Sverdlovsk deep in the Urals, while Khrushchev was meeting Eisenhower at a summit conference in Paris. Eisenhower lamely accepted responsibility and thereby appeared to be claiming that America had the right to overfly the

Soviet Union. Khrushchev walked out of the conference in righteous indignation. His outspoken confidence at the progress of Soviet military power caused Kennedy, before and after he became president, to speak of a 'missile gap': the USSR, on this interpretation, was forging ahead of the United States in modern weapons and the means of delivering them. This, as it turned out, was nonsense. America was still far ahead. But if it was Khrushchev's policy to reassure America and to lower the cold war temperature, he was evidently unsuccessful. Later in the same year he went to the United Nations, argued for an impracticable scheme of total disarmament, and banged his desk with his shoe, which did not help his image.

His meeting with President Kennedy in Vienna in June 1961 was a clear failure. Kennedy carried away the impression of blustering and bullying, which it could not have been Khrushchev's intention to convey. Then another crisis over access to Berlin, while not in itself very acute or dangerous, gratuitously strengthened the anti-Soviet lobbies in the Western alliance. Thus foreign policy was not making much headway, except that Soviet influence in the Middle East was consolidated. Then in the autumn of 1962 the Cuban crisis showed up the hollowness of Khrushchev's pretensions and dealt a blow to his domestic prestige.

His policy was understandable. In 1961 the Americans had sponsored the so-called 'Bay of Pigs' invasion of Cuba by Cuban exiles. This was defeated, but a nervous Castro appealed to Moscow for protection. It so happened that Soviet missile development was particularly far behind America's in the intercontinental category (i.e. Russia could not hit America), while America had more and better intercontinental missiles *and* had bases close to Soviet territory, plus Polaris submarines. The USSR had considerable numbers of missiles of shorter range, which could be targeted on Western Europe. If these could be placed in Cuba, then the USSR could achieve two objects at a blow; secure Cuba from American attack and, more important, establish a base near America which could counterbalance American superiority in long-range weapons (and her bases in Turkey, Iran and elsewhere). So Khrushchev took a calculated risk: he would secretly place these missiles in Cuba.

American intelligence discovered what was happening, while the missiles were being installed. Kennedy demanded their withdrawal under threat of nuclear war. (At this critical moment I happened to be in Washington and giving a lecture which was attended by some civil and military officers; I was surprised when members of my audience were called out one by one. I was not in on the secret, but Kennedy's ultimatum was due that evening.) His bluff called, what could Khrushchev do? He would point to American bases around Russia, but 'fairness' is irrelevant in love or cold war. He had no alternative but to withdraw the missiles, with Kennedy helpfully providing some face-saving formula to help him do it. He had to withdraw because of American superiority – and perhaps also because the Russians were more likely than the Americans to recoil at the thought of a nuclear holocaust. Khrushchev was left to explain to his colleagues why he decided to adopt so dangerous and unsuccessful a policy.

By then he had openly quarrelled with China. Just as the cold war problems had been inherited by Khrushchev, but he mishandled them, so trouble with China was highly probable whoever ruled in the Kremlin. Mao Tse-tung saw himself as the world's leading Communist revolutionary. Although he must have been well aware of Stalin's bureaucratic authoritarianism, he respected him as a revolutionary and a builder of socialism. Stalin's successors were inevitably men who were children or not born at the time of the Russian revolution, and the efforts these successors would make to modify Stalinism would inevitably be adapted to the needs of a post-revolutionary and developed society. China was at a quite different and earlier stage of development and its leaders were much closer to the revolution. Mao could scarcely have wished to treat a Malenkov or a Bulganin as an equal, let alone concede to them the leadership of the world Communist movement. As for Khrushchev, he seemed to Mao to be a bungling revisionist, and a Russian nationalist to boot. His manner was offensive to Mao. As polemics grew, Khrushchev decided in 1960 to withdraw Soviet technicians from China, causing grave difficulties to Chinese investment projects; China's 'great leap forward' was criticised as adventurism. By then the public slanging match was in full swing. The 'world Communist movement' had irredeemably split. Khrushchev could hardly have done much to prevent it, but his argumentative and rather crude style can be said to have made things worse. His lack of finesse, his shrewd but philosophically naïve arguments, failed to impress the more intellectual Communists in the West also; for instance, the Italian Communist Party felt more and more free of Moscow's tutelage and began cautiously to criticise the Soviet system. So came Communist 'polycentrism', a partial breakdown of Moscow control over Communists, which was at first denied by dedicated

Western cold-warriors but became increasingly evident as the years passed.

At home, Khrushchev made blunders, creating in the process several sets of enemies in the Party. He interfered too much in agriculture, he contributed to the troubles of industrial planning, and finally his methods were threatening intolerable administrative confusion. His handling of these matters convinced his comrades that it was time for a change, though all the problems which Khrushchev tackled were real enough, and would give trouble also to his successors.

Khrushchev's policies for agriculture up to 1958 were successful. This must have gone to his head, giving him faith in his methods and in the growth prospects of farming. The seven-year plan (1959–65) for agriculture envisaged impossible growth rates: given the quantity of machinery, fertiliser and irrigation works, the proposed increase of 70 per cent or so in output was beyond the bounds of reason. Khrushchev pressed his harassed officials to achieve what could not be achieved, and in doing so made things unnecessarily difficult. His agricultural 'campaigns' followed hard upon each other. There was the growing of maize. There was 'catch up the United States in production of meat and milk'. There was the plough-up-the-grass-lands campaign. There were imposed methods of cultivation: peat-compost pots, two-stage harvesting, reduction of fallowing. He even told the Uzbeks, who love lamb, that it did not matter if they bred sheep for wool, because the taste of meat depends on the cooking.

Nearly all his ideas had point. However, they were applied by petty officials accustomed to do Moscow's bidding. The *svodka* (report made to headquarters) was what mattered. Someone quipped: 'the trouble in our villages is due to *vodka* and *svodka*'. Take as a first example the virgin lands campaign, launched initially in 1954. It secured important quantities of wheat in favourable years. But, as the experts on the spot well knew (for they told me so when I visited Kazakhstan in 1955 with a British agricultural delegation), there is danger in monoculture in these marginal lands, danger of soil exhaustion, erosion, weed infestation. On similar soil in Saskatchewan great care is taken, with up to half the land left without crops in any one year. An excellent analysis, citing the Saskatchewan experience, in fact appeared in the literary journal *Novyi mir*. Yet Khrushchev insisted that the sown area could not be reduced, opposed expansion of fallow, refused to heed advice. Damage was done to soil and crops in consequence.

Maize became a 'political' crop. It had to be grown whatever the soil conditions or the availability of equipment or of labour. While certainly needed in much greater quantity, its imposition through Party orders on the whole country caused unnecessary losses in many areas. In one case cited in the Soviet press a farm manager was reprimanded for 'political underestimation of silage'. This was no way to run agriculture. Khrushchev of all people should have known the consequences of using Party-run campaigns to achieve results in agriculture. Thus a Party Secretary instructed a farm to plough up a field of growing clover, even though there were no other uses for that field. He was concerned that the *svodka* from his district should show a reduction in the area under grass, for that was what Moscow wanted to hear since Khrushchev was known to be against grasses. Now obviously this actual piece of nonsense was not due to any order by Khrushchev personally. He would not do so silly a thing. But the orders he *did* issue led Party Secretaries in the localities to act in this way, and he should have anticipated this. Just so, to take a very different example, a general order by Stalin to remove certain categories of suspects eventually translated itself into a quantitative arrest plan which local police officials tried to fulfil in individually ludicrous as well as tragic ways.

Similar kinds of nonsense followed from the 'meat and milk' campaign. More meat was – and is – certainly needed. But to expand output two or even threefold takes time and much increased supplies of fodder. Otherwise local comrades would either order excessive slaughtering to fulfil short-term plans, or breed more animals than could be fed properly. In fact both happened, at different times and in different places. The Party Secretary of Ryazan province, Larionov, became famous for trebling meat deliveries to the state in one year. How foolish was it of Khrushchev to praise him! How obvious that he will only have done this either by excessive slaughtering or by cheating. It was in fact cheating, as it later turned out: he bought livestock from neighbouring provinces and from peasants. Khrushchev expressed his disappointment when he heard this, and denounced false reporting. Yet his own actions had encouraged these excesses.

It was not so very different when he ordered the abolition of the Machine Tractor Stations (MTS) and the sale of tractors and combines to the collective farms. The measure, decreed in 1958, was soundly based. The MTS had been used simultaneously as political controllers and as suppliers of equipment to farms on hire. The two

functions coexisted uneasily. As early as 1951 two economists proposed the elimination of the MTS, but Stalin rejected this on
principle. It would mean selling state-owned machines to collective
(co-operative) farms, which was an ideologically retrograde step.
Khrushchev was not concerned about this aspect, and he saw no
danger to political control in the abolition of the MTS, since it could
be exercised in other ways, for instance through the Party groups in
the greatly enlarged collective farms. He saw the defects of the
system clearly: 'two masters in the fields', the farm management not
having the machinery they needed under their control. The MTS
were abolished.

Later I spoke with a Soviet farm manager who described the
measure as a mistake. Yes, he said, the old system had been wrong
because farms were *forbidden* to own tractors and were *compelled* to
hire them whether they wanted to or not. Now, however, they *had*
to buy them and could not hire them, even if they had no maintenance personnel or workshops. The correct solution would have been
to let the farms choose whether to buy or hire. Even in America
(he said, rightly) many farmers *hire* combine-harvesters.

Let the farms choose. This is what Khrushchev (and other party
administrators before him) would not do. Their whole training and
experience inclined them to the view that nothing would happen
unless ordered, and it was the Party's job to ensure that the right
things were done. Yet Khrushchev knew that more local initiative,
and flexible adaptation to the local conditions, were essential, and
frequently said so. Another contradiction, explicable by the past
experience of party officialdom, particularly in the agricultural
sector, where coercion had for so long replaced incentives.

Khrushchev also upset the peasants by taking fiscal and administrative measures against private livestock, and this after he himself
had reduced in 1953 the burdens imposed in Stalin's last years. His
motive seems to have been the usual one: to encourage collective
and to discourage private activity. But it so happened that peasants'
collective incomes ceased to rise, even fell slightly, in the years 1958–
63, and peasant irritation contributed to the poor showing of
agriculture in these years.

When, in 1963, the weather was bad, the crop was clearly inadequate to feed the humans and animals who needed it. Embarrassingly large imports of grain from the West were still insufficient to
maintain the inflated livestock population, and the number of pigs
dropped precipitately from 70 million to 40 million head. The

weather was not Khrushchev's fault, but there seemed to be hardly any reserves to cope with a bad year. The 1963 harvest proved a major factor in weakening his political position.

Industrial planning suffered less from Khrushchev's personal interference. 'Unfortunately he thinks he knows a lot about agriculture,' grumbled one expert whom I met. He had no such pretensions in respect of steel, heavy engineering or textiles. He did, however, cause two kinds of upsets. The first arose from his reorganisation of planning in 1957. The second concerned priorities.

We have already described the regionalisation measures, the *sovnarkhoz* reform. It contained one fatal flaw. In a system in which production is planned, in which there is no market, and which is industrially developed, it is not possible to give major powers to *regional* authorities. Every large factory draws many of its supplies from outside its own region (and let us recall that the number of regions exceeded 100). It is also bound to supply its products to numerous customers located in other regions. Consequently the region could not effectively control, or be informed about, either input or output requirements. The one thing it knew was the needs of the region itself. Consequently, either detailed orders were received from the centre about what was to be produced and for whom, or, in the absence of such orders, the regional authority produced for the region itself, frequently disrupting established supply arrangements with other regions. There were bitter complaints about this, with denunciations from Moscow of *mestnichestvo*, 'localism'. Local Party Secretaries were supposed to help impose national as against local interest, but in practice a regional Party Secretary is an integral part of his region's interest and pressure group, and is in any case judged largely by his region's plan fulfilment statistics.

To cope with these defects it proved necessary to set up a multitude of sectoral 'state committees', to take care of the common problems of major industries, a bewildering array of co-ordinating bodies, and finally co-ordinators of the co-ordinators. It may be said that the 'ministerial' system of centralised planning has many weaknesses, and this was (and is) indeed so. But the regionalisation led to chaos, to confused reorganisations and finally, after Khrushchev's downfall, to the restoration of the Central ministries.

It must be added that confusion reigned also in agricultural planning, following Khrushchev's deliberate destruction of the powers of the ministry of agriculture.

Economic priorities are, and must be, a source of conflict in all societies. That there were arguments on this topic in Khrushchev's years of power is a statement of the obvious. However, in his last years, Khrushchev offended some important groups, firstly by the extent of the stress on agriculture, secondly by his espousal of totally impractical plans for the chemical industry, part of which (i.e. fertiliser) also served agriculture. He seemed to the professionals to be dangerously unbalancing the economy: not enough steel, inadequate supplies of solid fuel, too little invested in building materials, and too much in chemicals. 'Too much' not because the industry was not in need of major expansion; it was indeed very backward. But it was being expanded too quickly, so that the machines, materials and trained manpower could not be provided in time. Chemical plans were very greatly underfulfilled, and the efforts to fulfil them had disruptive effects. Khrushchev counter-attacked the allegedly conservative planners, denounced 'metal-eaters' who demanded more and more steel. He probably also offended the military, who had been shocked by the Cuban fiasco and were anxious to achieve parity with the United States; they wanted more arms, and eventually got much more, under Brezhnev.

Errors of policy may have contributed to a slowing down in industrial growth, which was noticeable in the years after 1958. There were certainly other causes for this, and lower growth rates have persisted since Khrushchev's fall. But all this represented arguments against his methods and his management of the economy.

Finally, his administrative methods offended and disorganised. We have already referred to the planning chaos. It remains to dwell upon his reorganisation of the Party, which must have turned the bulk of the Party machine very much against him. He was dissatisfied with the way the local Party officials were working. They were not carrying out his intentions satisfactorily, there were too many cases of irresponsibility and failure to defend all-Union interests, in both industry and agriculture. Now it must be admitted that the weaknesses were real, but they arose out of a chronic and continuing ambiguity in the position of the Party official, especially in the economy: how far should he directly rule, thereby replacing the ministerial or local authorities? Repeatedly the Party officials were told to supervise without exercising 'petty tutelage' over those government officials who had formal responsibility for this or that sector of social, political and economic affairs. Khrushchev's policies seemed to have strengthened the party as against state organisation, but this led to difficulties. The point is that whereas a *state* official usually has direct responsibility for some one thing (say agricultural procurements in a province, or supplies of ball-bearings), a provincial Party Secretary is responsible for all things in his bailiwick, which meant he could be master of none, tending to concentrate attention on current campaigns. This situation needed to be improved, but Khrushchev's cure was worse than the disease. He divided the Party into two parts: one was to be concerned with industry, transport, construction, trade; the other with agriculture. With some exceptions, republican and local Party organisations were split along these lines, to the dismay of many comrades.

To make confusion worse confounded, Khrushchev also disrupted rural Party organs by setting up territorial Production Administrations in agriculture, whose boundaries did not coincide with the districts (*raiony*) which had been the basis of local Party organs. He also ordered the reduction in the number of *sovnarkhozy* (regional economic councils for industry) from over 100 to 47, so they no longer coincided with provincial borders. He also tried to organise larger regional units, combining several smaller republics. In Central Asia this was accompanied by the setting up of a party bureau covering Uzbekistan, Tadjikistan, Kirghizia and Turkmenistan, with a Russian at its head.

This was a truly remarkable exercise in losing friends and influence. Let us look at the consequences of these measures. Suppose that you were First Party Secretary in the province of Kaluga; you would then be responsible for the whole province. If it were divided between an industrial party and an agricultural Party committee, you must lose part of your functions and powers. Furthermore, some of these functions do not divide logically between 'agriculture' and 'industry'. Whose, for instance, is the task of worrying about supplies of locally made spare parts for farm machinery. There would be bound to be demarcation disputes. The whole thing smacked of thoughtless improvisation.

The *raion* (district) Secretaries protested semi-publicly; Khrushchev referred to their protest in a published speech. The Central Asian republican Secretaries' opinions can readily be imagined. How could Khrushchev have been so heedless of the effect on his own power-position of creating so many opponents, so much irritated frustration?

The last straw for some was personal diplomacy. In 1964 he tried to negotiate with West Germany. His aims were almost certainly

identical with those of his successors: to encourage a settlement that
included the recognition of the *status quo* in Europe and of East
Germany. But he sent his son-in-law, Adzhubei, editor of *Izvestiya*, to
negotiate. This was offensive both to the other Party leaders and to
the Foreign Office.

The man was wilful, crude, lacking in dignity, unpredictable, a
muddler. His fellow-members of the Politbureau must have reasoned,
quietly and in private, that he could rock the boat with excessive anti-
Stalinism. He allowed the publication of such works as the dangerous
exposure of labour camps by Solzhenitsyn. He interfered with
privilege by his abortive educational reforms. He was a muddler in
economic policy, in agriculture especially. He reorganised and disorganised the party. Therefore he must go.

These fellow-members were, moreover, changing, not always to
Khrushchev's advantage. Early in 1960 out went Kirichenko,
followed by Aristov, Belyaev and Mukhitdinov, all thought to be
favourable to him. Brezhnev, who at that time was considered a
Khrushchev man, was moved to the chairmanship of the Presidium
of the Supreme Soviet, certainly a temporary demotion.

Kozlov was promoted to a senior post in the Party Secretariat, and
he had the reputation of a conservative or neo-Stalinist; however, he
had to retire through illness in 1963, and Brezhnev then returned to
the Secretariat. It was also in 1960 that Kosygin returned to the
Politbureau. Despite all these manoeuvres, many of them still
obscure, a number of important leaders could be regarded as being
Khrushchev nominees: Podgorny, Polyanski, Voronov, Kirilenko,
Brezhnev.

On such grounds, Kremlinologists saw no danger to Khrushchev.
I attended a discussion at Oxford a week before his fall. No one
expected it. Nor, it must be said, did Khrushchev, who was resting
in the Black Sea resort of Sochi in October 1964 when the blow fell.
In his absence his comrades voted to oust him and called a meeting
of the Central Committee to confirm that he was indeed out.
Khrushchev, unsuspecting and unprepared, could only retire and
become a pensioner, 'on health grounds'. The fact that not a single
leader went to the wilderness with him, all of the Politbureau
retaining their seats, suggests that he had no support among them.

It is worth dwelling on the possible sources of error in the minds of
Kremlinologists. If a man owes his position to a stronger colleague,
it might mean that he is indeed his grateful supporter, but he may
also be harbouring jealous resentment. If two men worked together

for some years in the Ukraine or elsewhere, this could mean that they are political friends, but they could also have learnt to hate each other. If they came from the same district – well, as someone pointed out, Lenin and Kerensky were both born in the small town of Simbirsk. . . .

It must also be added that some traditional aids to Kremlinological analysis had vanished. A leader's absence from a formal occasion was not necessarily a sign that he was no longer a leader: he could be on holiday, or have a cold, or dislike opera. Also it became the practice (maintained until 1973) to print the names of the Politbureau in alphabetical order. True, other indices of relative importance remained: position on a photograph, or the number of organisations nominating a leader for Supreme Soviet elections. Nonetheless, the fixed conventions inherited from Stalinism were becoming less fixed.

Khrushchev became a private citizen. The change was peaceful. No one was arrested. Occasionally the deposed leader could be seen in Moscow. Then he died, a natural death, in 1971. The authorities did not know what to do. No *retired* First Secretary and Premier had ever died. Their solution was embarrassingly timid and evasive: they put out a four-line announcement of his death, without comment and with no obituary, no blame, no praise. He was buried at the Novodevichi cemetery with no official speech and none of his successors and erstwhile colleagues present. How typical this was of the spirit, and attitude to history, of the present leadership! Awkward questions are best unanswered. Even to attempt an official estimation of Khrushchev's achievements and deficiencies would be a very complex political task, and there are other and perhaps more important things to do. To allow an *unofficial* estimation of the services to his country of a major Party figure is contrary to Soviet political tradition and practice. So what remains is – silence. An undeserved epitaph for this most talkative of Soviet leaders.

The Brezhnev Regime

Leonid Ilyich Brezhnev was 58 in 1964. He had had a somewhat zig-zag career. Though of humble origin, he (like Kosygin and most others of this generation of leaders) had received a higher technological education. His first Party posts were in the Ukraine (he was Secretary of Dnepropetrovsk Provincial Committee just before the war). During the war he was a political officer, reaching in this capacity the rank of Major-General. He resumed the Secretaryship at Dnepropetrovsk in 1947, moving from there to the Party Secretaryship of the small republic of Moldavia. Just after Stalin's death, as we have seen, he became deputy chief of the political department of the armed forces, now as Lieutenant-General. He was then moved, in 1954, to Kazakhstan, as Second and then as First Secretary, of that republic's Party Committee, to carry out Khrushchev's virgin lands campaign. Khrushchev must have been satisfied, since in February 1956 he was brought into the Party Secretariat in Moscow and became candidate-member of the Politbureau, becoming a full member in June 1957. He also worked with Khrushchev in the Russian republic (RSFSR) bureau of the party. According to the Soviet encyclopaedia, his special responsibilities included heavy industry, supplies of the most modern weapons to the armed forces and 'cosmonautics'. As we have seen, in May 1960 he was suddenly given the more decorative post of Chairman of the Presidium of the Supreme Soviet (the job now held by Podgorny), but he was brought back to the Central Committee as a Secretary in June 1963, as one of Khrushchev's deputies. Now, with Khrushchev gone, he took over the Party First Secretaryship. Alexei Kosygin became Prime Minister. With Podgorny, who was Chairman of the Praesidium of the Supreme Soviet and formally the President of the Union, they formed another triumvirate, and with it came a reaffirmation of collective leadership. No senior Party official was removed. None of Khrushchev's political victims were restored to Politbureau membership. The formalities and decencies were carefully observed. Khrushchev was not criticised by name, but was accused (in a circumlocutory way) of hatching 'harebrained schemes' and making 'voluntarist' policy errors. ('Voluntarist' here means arbitrary placing personal ideas and preferences above a sober and objective analysis of the situation.) One can see what the new leaders most wanted altered by the steps they took to correct what they regarded as errors. The division of the Party into two parts was speedily eliminated. Agricultural policies and organisation were altered: the Ministry restored to power, and with it the former Minister, Matskevich; an end was promised to arbitrary interference from the centre with agricultural practices. The north and west of the Union would get a fairer share of available capital and fertiliser, having been neglected under Khrushchev. Tax measures hitting peasant private livestock were repealed. Farm prices were increased, and farm machinery output also. However, for reasons already explained, it was necessary to cut back on the impractically high projected levels of investment in fertiliser and in other chemicals.

It took a little longer to decide what to do about industry. The regionalisation had certainly been a fiasco, but to return to the old centralised ministries was also unsatisfactory. Khrushchev may have had the wrong remedy, but Stalinist centralisation did constitute a malady requiring a cure. Economists and planners had been engaged for years in a hard-hitting and fascinating discussion about how best to reform the economy; Khrushchev had tolerated this, though he did not adopt any of the far-reaching proposals. Some argued for a form of market socialism, with managers far freer to respond to consumer demand and to find their own suppliers, instead of having them designated by the planners. Others stressed the potentialities of the computer, of linear programming, of the 'mathematisation' of planning. Some of the mathematicians also supported a market, because their computers could not possibly cope with the millions of variables that occur if one tries to cope centrally with fully disaggregated detail. There was also a strong 'conservative' tendency, resistant to change, which partly reflected the vested interests of the controlling apparatus, whose jobs and career prospects were bound to be affected by rapid change, and partly genuine concern lest the advantages of central planning be lost. Needless to say, recent Western experience does not suggest that guided market economies can always achieve stability or avoid inflationary and balance of payments crises. So the problems were real.

It took until September 1965 to decide the next steps. The regional economic councils were abolished. A new and complex system of managerial incentives was introduced, with some cautious steps towards a bigger role for the profit motive and for commercial considerations. There would be bigger scope for scientific planning with wider use of computers. There would be no more 'voluntarism', and every effort would be made to achieve efficiency and technical progress. It seemed at first sight a moderately progressive document. The first year of the new leadership was very properly devoted to putting right the errors and distortions that marred Khrushchev's last years.

However, it soon became increasingly evident that domestic policy was veering in a conservative direction, that the group that overthrew Khrushchev included many who believed that he had been a dangerous experimenting radical – albeit an inconsistent one. On cultural matters they took several steps backwards. Khrushchev allowed Solzhenitsyn, and a few others, to mention forced-labour camps and prisons; biographies of rehabilitated victims of Stalinist terror could mention their fate: Tvardovsky, the courageous editor of the monthly *Novyi mir*, could use the journal as a vehicle for serious social and literary criticism. True, Khrushchev had his bad moments, as when he attacked modern art or particular writers who upset him, and he did put a stop to what he regarded as 'excessive' use of the concentration-camp theme. The censorship apparatus remained. Yet in retrospect the years 1956–64 must appear to be comparatively liberal. Gradually but inexorably, the 'conservative' and cautious line triumphed. Solzhenitsyn was silenced, criticised and then ignored: it has been credibly reported that it is forbidden to refer to him in any publication, except if an attack is specifically authorised from on high, as in September 1973. The bolder kind of writing was eliminated. Tvardovsky was dismissed as editor and died (a natural death) not long after. There was a reaffirmation of orthodoxy also in historical writing; no more lifting of the curtain on disagreeable episodes such as collectivisation. There was a strong reassertion of the correctness of the Party line, at all times and places, including renewed attacks on Trotsky, Bukharin and other non-rehabilitated old oppositionists. The chances of publishing an original novel, or historical work, receded. More and more authors turned to *samizdat*, or self-publishing, this being the circulation in typescript of unpublishable material. Some of this finds its way abroad, and almost every Soviet work of real social and literary interest since 1965 has been printed only abroad. This includes Solzhenitsyn's *Cancer Ward* (which was ready for publication in *Novyi mir* when the censors stopped it), *The First Circle* and *August 1914*, but also the works of many less well-known authors.

The one area where historical studies made some headway was in writing on the war. Here too there was an avoidance of awkward questions, this time about the disasters of 1941, which reflected or were thought to reflect on party infallibility. However, the flow of memoirs continued, and did at least give a more realistic picture of Stalin's role. Khrushchev went too far, blaming any failures on Stalin and attributing successes to the headquarters staff or particular generals (there were difficulties with the role of Zhukov after Khrushchev got rid of him in 1957). Now we had some more balanced accounts, of which Zhukov's own memoirs were an outstanding example.

Brezhnev and his comrades quickly altered the official attitude to Stalin and Stalinism. Attacks on him were stopped, or were limited to carefully drafted admissions that there were innocent victims of repressions. There was a petition circulating among the liberals to warn against a rehabilitation of Stalin, and this certainly suggests that this was proposed or considered. It did not occur in a formal sense; he was not re-promoted to the rank of demi-god. Instead the policy was followed of banning any public or printed discussion of Stalin or any part of his system, while he was quietly put back into the list of acceptable leaders, who had done many correct things and who led the Soviet Union in very difficult times with considerable success. His new status as a positive (but not divine) figure found expression in the erection of a statue to him behind the Mausoleum, by the Kremlin wall, alongside other important but secondary leaders. Much thought must have been devoted to this statue. He is shown in no Napoleonic pose, but gazing downwards modestly. This was partial reassertion of Stalin's historic role, but with no direct glorification and with an all-but-total ban on discussion of him, his role, his crimes, or his achievements, in public. The lowest common denominator of a way out, typical of the present leadership, and analogous to what was done in respect of Khrushchev's non-obituary. Intellectually neither courageous nor satisfactory.

The internal security policy of the Brezhnev group was and is somewhat more repressive than that of Khrushchev. There were repeated declarations against the alleged penetration of bourgeois ideology, and on the need to struggle against ideological deviations. Although political arrests were still a small fraction of what they had been under Stalin, they nonetheless increased, especially in the most recent years. The writers Sinyavsky and Daniel were sentenced in 1966 for sending critical works to be published in the West under a pseudonym. The distinguished poet Brodsky (who has since been allowed to leave Russia) was disgracefully treated, being deported from Leningrad to a remote northern farm for being a 'parasite', this offence being due to his not being a member of the Writers' Union and not making enough to live on by his writings (his poetry was almost all refused publication). There were arrests for real or alleged Zionism, for Ukrainian nationalism, and instances of the misuse of psychiatry to detain dissidents in asylums. Perhaps the authorities believed that anyone openly willing to oppose them must be mad. Cultural controls have been tightened, and the original

thinker is obstructed at every turn. These policies have attracted
adverse publicity in the West. Total secrecy makes it impossible to
make any estimate as to the numbers who may be arrested. In my
possibly incorrect judgement, Russia today has about as many
political prisoners as had Tsarist Russia in 1900. This is no cause for
congratulation, especially as their numbers probably exceed those of
1960. But even today's numbers are still a small fraction of those in
prison camps and exile in 1950 and 1938 when they must surely have
exceeded anything known to world history. Instead of Stalin's
millions there are Brezhnev's thousands.

The Brezhnev regime, then, from the standpoint of freedom of the
individual and of the human spirit, has been more consistent, less
flexible, less tolerant than Khrushchev, and its repressive tendencies
were strengthened by the shock effects of the Czechoslovak events of
1968. From the standpoint of developing Marxism (or any other)
ideas, progress was zero. No wonder that the distinguished old
scientist, Academician Kapitsa, pointed out that ideas flourish in
an atmosphere of fundamental argument and challenge, and that
Soviet Marxist philosophers have been notably absent from the
process of devising new adaptations of Marxism to the problems of
the contemporary world (Kapitsa's words were printed, though
probably in modified form). More succinctly the same thought was
expressed by an old literary critic: *sporit razuchilis*, 'we have forgotten how to argue'. Indeed, how can anyone keep their intellectual
powder dry when, for two generations, no one was allowed to
challenge the basic assumptions?

Symbolic of a return to a more negative policy was the re-labelling
of the Ministry for the Protection of Public Order (so called·under
Khrushchev) with its old and feared name: 'Ministry of the Interior'
(MVD), though internal security remained under the separate and
active Committee of State Security (KGB).

It is clear, from the experience of recent years, that the security of
the regime does not require either terror or mass arrests. Other forms
of control and persuasion, not excluding the threat of arrest, are
sufficient. The KGB is no longer a law unto itself, and its methods are
much less brutal and more intelligent than they were in Stalin's
time. The illegal circulation of uncensored materials continues.
Solzhenitsyn took up a critical stand, eventually challenging the
basic principles of the whole Soviet regime. He was abused, ostra-
cised, and in the end expelled. Some other dissidents were given exit
visas, or were compelled to emigrate. Sakharov, the physicist, has

publicly urged the West not to respond favourably to Soviet foreign-policy overtures, and has been attacked in the press, but not arrested. Of course, the world-wide fame of Sakharov and Solzhenitsyn did help to preserve them from prison. Lesser individuals who defy the authorities can get into very serious trouble. However, the regime is committed to legality and, although the legal principles which it has laid down are sometimes ignored or abused, it is sometimes possible to appeal to principles of justice. The KGB is not now as sure as it was in Stalin's time that it has the right to ignore human rights totally. The leadership likes to present itself as a group of reasonable men who conform to the country's laws, even while it cracks down on dissidents and firmly refuses to allow any organisation to exist outside the area of strict Party control.

A good example of the ambivalent attitude of the leadership is the case of the Jews. Under the Stalin terror it was clear that mere suspicion of a desire to go abroad was likely to lead to the suspect's disappearance. Some Jews wanted to leave but did not dare even to imagine the possibility. Restriction on Jewish activity continued after Stalin; under Khrushchev such activity consisted only of synagogues (some of which were closed down), occasional concerts of Yiddish songs and a periodical in Yiddish, *Sovietisch Heimland*, plus a newspaper in the remote 'Jewish autonomous area' on the borders of Manchuria. Connections with Israel were frowned upon, particularly as Soviet Middle East policy was pro-Arab. Complaints about educational and job discrimination were numerous. Criticism of this from abroad included some from foreign Communists, who were puzzled and irritated by the persistence of discriminatory practices.

This is not the place to go into the complex theme of the East European anti-Semitic tradition and its role in Communist-ruled countries. What concerns us now is the policy of Brezhnev and his comrades, faced with foreign criticism and the emergence of a demand from some Jews to be allowed to go. The demand was one result of the elimination of mass terror: the risks were now much smaller. At first the authorities reacted by arrests and threats. Then they decided that the principal 'agitators' could after all be allowed out, as that would take the steam out of the emigration campaign. The result surprised everyone; the news spread that there was a way out, that exit visas might be granted. Applications to go increased in number. Again there were detentions, threats, dismissals, refusals, financial penalties (such as the 'education tax', ostensibly to repay the state for the amount spent on educating the emigrants). But exit visas were granted in increasing numbers. Pressure from the West, especially America, was one factor, but in my view at least as important is a desire by the regime to avoid or evade awkward situations within the USSR. (Though the solution adopted is also an awkward one, since non-Jews find it much more difficult than Jews to obtain exit visas, which could well cause much annoyance to many non-Jews.)

Let us now look at the economic priorities of the new leadership. They inherited the same imperatives as Malenkov and Khrushchev did. More had to be done for the citizens, the housing programme had to be continued, more consumer goods and services were essential, of better quality. Khrushchev accepted the need for greater availability of consumer durables (and watches, radios, TV sets, refrigerators, washing machines became objects of mass consumption), but drew the line at cars. He thought that it was sufficient to have more taxis and car hire services. And indeed car ownership carries with it major consequences, social as well as economic, and ill accords with the image of a Communist country interested in world revolution. Brezhnev changed course, no doubt under the pressure of the upper strata of society, who were and are extremely interested in possessing a car. Of course, mass car ownership is still for the future, but output has risen greatly, with the erection of a Fiat factory bought from Italy, and more will come. Brezhnev is also personally identified with the priority of agriculture, and more resources have been devoted to it, though success was modest until 1973. The very first of the Brezhnev years, 1965, was one of poor weather, and while the 1968 and 1970 harvests were good, even they were below the planned requirements of the economy, while the bad weather of 1972 caused a sharp set back and again led to even more massive imports of grain from the West. However, 1973 was a record year. Meat remains short, though this is partly due to the policy of low retail prices, at which demand and supply cannot possibly balance. At the Twenty-fourth Congress (1971) much stress was laid on agriculture, consumer goods and services. The 'Malenkov' heresy was repeated: consumer goods were to grow faster than the output of producer goods: this pattern was adhered to in the years 1968–71, and was enshrined in the five-year plan of 1971–75. However, agricultural difficulties and an unbalanced investment plan (including shortages of building materials) led to a slowdown and to a reversal of priorities in 1972 and 1973.

One cause of the economic strains which have recently emerged has been the high priority of the arms programme. Soviet missile and naval expansion has been rapid, and it is the unanimous view of Western experts that, from being well behind America in 1964, the USSR has now achieved overall parity. It is significant that this was the sector for which Brezhnev had been responsible for several years when Khrushchev ruled. For a weaker Soviet industry to overtake the stronger Americans in the field of advanced military technology required, at least for a period, higher production of such technology than in America. This inevitably imposed a strain on this weaker economy, and must logically have affected the supply of civilian machinery and equipment, and therefore investment.

Why this great effort in the military field? This brings us to an assessment of the foreign policy of Brezhnev and his team. Let us begin with relations with other Communist-ruled states.

The quarrel with China continued, and even erupted for a time into border incidents. The Chinese repeatedly accuse the Soviets of concentrating large military forces on their borders, and on their side the Chinese invested much effort into making their own nuclear weapons. This could be part of the explanation of the high level of Soviet military expenditure: America *and* China have to be considered, and the possibility of the two coming to an agreement was in Soviet official minds several years before Nixon visited Peking. Mutual abuse between the two great Communist powers has continued and is continuing, but border incidents have ceased, or are not being publicised. There are many mysteries and uncertainties in Soviet-Chinese relations which could be the subject of a large book. The cultural revolution in China was sharply condemned by Moscow, but one of its principal architects, Lin Piao, was reported to have died in a plane crash fleeing to Russia. Some observers consider that a war between the USSR and China is probable, but evidence is lacking. However, the Chinese direct a stream of abuse at Moscow: 'new tsars', 'social imperialists', even 'Hitlers'. The USSR replies in kind. China urges the strengthening of NATO. But abuse is not war.

Brezhnev inherited an uncertain relationship with the European Communist states. They had acquired greater independence, and were undertaking experiments of their own. East Germany, vocally loyal to Moscow, tried out a new industrial planning structure based on cartel-like industrial associations. Hungary, after the 1956 cataclysm, turned easy-going and tolerant under Kadar's skilful leadership, and Moscow tolerated Hungary's adoption of a far-reaching move towards a market-orientated economy, radically distinct from the Soviet model and the East German variant. Romania adopted a nationalistic pose, with anti-Russian overtones, taking an independent line both over China and over economic integration. In Poland an ageing and cantankerous Gomulka went gradually back on the liberal promises of 1956, until falling victim to riots by indignant workers in December 1970. These and other varieties of behaviour were tolerated by Brezhnev, or were handled quietly by pressure behind the scenes. The exception was Czechoslovakia.

The Czech leadership had been the most consistently Stalinist. In 1952 they had massacred numerous leading Communists at Moscow's bidding, and they were least affected by subsequent destalinisation. However, the end of terror loosened tongues, and economic failures in what was a relatively advanced industrial country caused widespread demoralisation. After the discredited Novotny was finally ousted as Party Secretary, the choice of the party hierarchy fell surprisingly upon the relatively unknown Alexander Dubček, and the Moscow leadership accepted this, not knowing that this would open the floodgates. The 'Prague spring' followed, with the emergence of democratic freedom and a model of 'socialism with a human face'.

The events in Prague are of interest in the present context in so far as they show us the nature and content of Soviet policy. We know that, after several warnings and two meetings with the Czech leaders, the Soviet Union sent in troops and destroyed the Czech reformers. The destruction was political, not personal. Dubček did not suffer the fate of Hungary's Nagy, though he was roughly treated, detained and threatened in the first days after the invasion. There was minimum bloodshed, because, though there were very widespread and bitter protests, there was no armed resistance in the face of overwhelming force.

Why did they invade? After all, Dubček was a Communist who had been a friend of the USSR, and who swore loyalty to the Warsaw Pact and the Soviet alliance. The contrast with Hungary in 1956, when the invasion was precipitated by Hungary leaving the Warsaw Pact and by open anti-Communist activities, springs to mind.

It is said, with no firm evidence to support this, that the final decision to intervene was taken by a narrow majority and on exaggerated information supplied by the Ukrainian Party Secretary, Shelest. Such, at least, was the inspired leak in Moscow, noted by several foreign correspondents, after Shelest himself had been demoted, i.e. in the winter of 1972–73. This may have been just a lame excuse for an embarrassing action which outraged many friends of the Soviet Union. Even some normally 'muscovite' Communist Parties in the West expressed dismay.

In the Soviet view the Czechs had gone too far. What *was* too far? Not, it seems, adopting economic reforms of the market type, since Hungary had done so (in 1967) without a single Soviet soldier being placed on alert. Not because of too much independence from Moscow, for Romania under Ceausescu had gone further and survived with no more than some veiled warnings. The answer must be that the claim to have a new model of 'human socialism', a free press, the abandonment of censorship, toleration of non-Party associations with claims to political influence, was a mixture which was felt to be disruptive of the political balance in Eastern Europe and perhaps in Russia herself. The domination of the Communist Party over society, the suppression of free expression, these turned out to be essential to the survival of Soviet Communism in the sixties and seventies. For Brezhnev or anyone like him, freedom to oppose the Party, or freedom to advocate such freedoms within the Party, is self-evidently dangerous as well as heretical. Infectious, too, so it had to be stamped out. But the real reasons could not be openly given or discussed. A scenario was worked out which would have enabled Brezhnev to pretend that the troops were called in by a group of Czech party leaders to defend Czechoslovakia against 'imperialism' and 'reaction'. The scenario went wrong, as the world knows. The 'danger threatening Czechoslovak socialism' could not be described, defined or identified. The dangers to the Soviet system were, however, felt to have been real, so much so that the negative effects to be expected from sending 600,000 armed men into an allied country were accepted as inevitable.

The Czech events of 1968 influenced the Soviet leadership in the direction of demanding stricter ideological conformity at home. It caused a setback for economic reform also, since the fact that Czechs had proposed it in 1968 would be used as an argument against. These same events led to greater consciousness of the need to set limits to the autonomy of the lesser countries in the Soviet sphere. ('We can't really blame them; they've got an empire,' said an East European official in private conversation.)

How much difference to these policies did Brezhnev and Kosygin make? Would Khrushchev also have sent troops to Prague and imposed greater conformity? Possibly. He would surely have received such advice from his military and ideological apparatus. He did himself initiate attempts to achieve greater economic integration among Communist states, though he did not succeed in making much progress in this direction. It may in fact be that Brezhnev's actions in invading Czechoslovakia made it easier for him to get integration proposals accepted, even by Romania, though progress towards effective joint planning remains slow to this day.

Relations with Cuba have been correct, but a little cool. Castro is greatly dependent on Soviet aid, but hardly conceals his critical attitude to Soviet policy, which does not appeal to a revolutionary spirit. Soviet aid to North Vietnam was continued, and propaganda exploitation of American involvement persisted until it was soft-pedalled in the new rapprochement stage which began in 1972.

It is arguable that Brezhnev was continuing his predecessor's policy, towards the United States, West Germany and Japan, and that the main change has been in *Western* policy. Let us again recall that the recognition of the *status quo* in Europe and the recognition of East Germany have been Soviet policy aims for a decade if not two decades. It was equally firmly the aim of American and West German policy, especially in the Adenauer-Dulles era, to prevent any such thing. American policy was opposed to any large increase in trade with or credits to the USSR, on the grounds that it would strengthen an enemy country. (An impressive book by a Swede, Gunnar Adler-Karlsson, has been written on *Western* economic warfare.) An episode typical of the outlook of America under President Johnson was the abortive German steel pipe deal. The point was that large-diameter steel pipe was needed for Soviet pipelines, and this item was not on the list of strategic goods whose export to the USSR was forbidden. The Soviet Union placed an order for it in West Germany. The Americans objected, because it was seen that to deny them pipe would impose economic loss, or alternatively that supplying the pipe would strengthen the Soviet economy 'too much'. The Germans complied, and the deal was cancelled. Contrast this with the trade-and-credits discussions conducted with Nixon in 1973. American influence was paramount in Japan in the sixties, and this also restrained the Japanese from making any major move to improve their political and trading relations with the USSR.

Soviet economic relations with some Western countries were quite satisfactory. Italy was buying large quantities of Soviet oil. France left NATO and pursued an independent policy, to the evident pleasure of the Kremlin. Relations with Britain remained cool, since British leaders took a sceptical view of Soviet policy, opposed the European security conference which the Russians had proposed repeatedly, and finally (in 1971) expelled a large number of Soviet diplomatic and trade personnel from London on spying charges.

The new elements in the Soviet attitude to America are doubtless explicable by the consequences of the quarrel with China, and the fear of the emergence of an American-Chinese line-up hostile to the USSR. Economic considerations also played some role: the arms race is a burden on the economy, hence the desirability of slowing it down. There would also be clear advantages to be gained from expansion of East-West trade, especially if modern technology can be obtained. Large-scale ideas have also emerged for developing Soviet raw material resources with the help of Western credits. However, the biggest changes have been in the West.

The German settlement is the most striking example of this. Soviet propaganda for many years cast West Germany in the role of devil-warmonger. While such propaganda was an unrecognisable carica-ture of reality, it was based not only on the memory of 1941 but also on the fact that the Adenauer-Erhard regime refused to recognise either East Germany (described in official German publications as *Die Sowjetzone* or as *Mitteldeutschland*) or the eastern frontiers of Germany. It was committed to alter the *status quo*. True, this was to be 'by peaceful means', but these would have included pressure exercised jointly with the powerful United States. A German devil was also useful to the USSR in its relations with Poland and Czecho-slovakia, who had every reason to fear a nationalist German revival.

Brandt changed all that. By agreeing to recognise East Germany and the eastern frontiers he provided a basis for agreement, on terms which, we may be sure, Khrushchev would gladly have accepted ten years earlier, but which the West would have rejected out of hand at that time. The West also accepted the proposal for a European security conference.

The USSR found political and economic advantage in détente, and relations with Nixon and Kissinger were better than those which developed in more recent years. Indeed, when Watergate toppled Nixon some Soviet observers thought he was being punished by the right wing for being too cordial to the USSR! For a while the Soviets soft-pedalled criticism of American policies. However, the Soviet arms build-up continued; the aim was still that of catching up, of achieving 'parity'. As Soviet military power drew closer to that of the United States voices were raised to sound the alarm, which undoubtedly contributed to the subsequent deterioration of relations.

Soviet policy in the Middle East, while outspokenly anti-Israel, tries to minimise risks. While succeeding in weakening the Western position in the area, which was originally based upon anti-Soviet alliances, the Soviet's own position in Egypt proved to be dependent upon active support for a campaign against Israel, and Egyptians resented Soviet military advisers when Soviet policy was against military action. When Egypt and Syria attacked in October 1973, the Soviet Union had supplied the bulk of the attackers' weapons, replaced losses and backed the Arab cause. Yet, despite the dangerous moment when the Americans declared a world-wide alert, Soviet policy was to avoid a confrontation with America, to preserve the détente and to devise a peaceful settlement, while at the same time maintaining a pro-Arab posture and, with it, political influence in the region. These aims are to some extent inconsistent. So is the Soviet attitude on the Arab use of the oil weapon against America and Western Europe. On the one hand, the economic troubles of the Western world are a source of satisfaction for Moscow. On the other, the economic and political advantages of détente are unlikely to be exploitable if the Western countries are hard hit by Arab oil embargoes if there is Soviet encouragement for such policies. The USSR is also embarrassed by the intransigence of the Arab extremists, indeed, it seems to be in the Soviet interest to keep Israel in being, so as to be able to exploit politically the Arab resentment at her existence. The unpredictable and volatile policies pursued by most of the Arab states are a source of risk, and they can at any time turn sharply anti-Soviet, as is the case with the Ghadaffi regime in Libya. Relations are better with Algeria and also with Iraq, and in 1972 the USSR for the first time bought appreciable quantities of oil in that country. As one of the two super-powers, the USSR can scarcely be indifferent to the Middle East and its immense strategic and economic importance, but she is also very anxious to avoid a confrontation with the United States. The pursuit of all these aims can cause some logical incongruities and upset statesmen in and out of the region, which remains dangerous because a conflagration can break out there beyond the control of either super-power.

The most successful Soviet policy in Asia has been in relations with India, where America is unpopular because of its backing of Pakistan, while the Chinese are a feared neighbour. It is an open question whether Soviet activities in India are directed more to block China than to oppose America.

In fact the whole Soviet posture in the Third World in recent years is ambiguous. On the one hand the large Soviet fleet has been showing the flag in all the seas and oceans, causing alarm in some Western quarters. On the other, Soviet economic aid has been modest, except to Egypt and India, and has not been increasing. Apart from supporting Cuba, Soviet policies in Latin America have been cautious to the point of inactivity, with minimal support (except in words) to Allende's socialist government in Chile, though maximum propaganda exploitation was made of his fall.

Relations with the United States have been soured by a number of circumstances, some not of Soviet making, but some a consequence of Soviet policies, including that towards weapon production and deployment. Internal change in America has been towards a harder line, with Carter exploiting the issue of human rights and the US Senate unwilling to ratify SALT II. The USSR's exploitation of the conflict over the US embassy hostages in Iran greatly annoyed the Americans, and there was alarm at Soviet gains in Africa, the setting-up of governments beholden to Moscow, and supported by Cuban troops, in Mozambique, Angola and Ethiopia. Finally there was the Soviet intervention in Afghanistan. Though, as seen in Moscow, the troops went in to prop up a regime which was already a Soviet satellite, the movement of Soviet armed forces into an area not previously held by them had a very negative effect on Western opinion, and on US–Soviet relations in particular. It contributed to the victory of Reagan and the hard-liners, who advocate greatly increased arms expenditure in the belief that the Soviet Union is engaged in a worldwide offensive and seeks superiority in order to win a nuclear war. My own view is that this is not so, if only because of the evident dangers that nuclear weapons pose for the survival of the human race. At the time of writing the horizon is darkening.

What Does Brezhnev Stand For?

The Soviet arms programme appears to aim at parity with the United States, and her foreign policy is concerned to establish super-power status and Brezhnev as equal to any American president in world influence. But influence for what? What are the long-term aims of Soviet policy? World revolution? Communism? Expansion of the USSR, or Russian aggrandisement, or what? Some Western observers, and also the Chinese, view recent Soviet policies as a dangerous manoeuvre, designed to persuade the West to lower its guard and to ensure Soviet predominance, in Europe and elsewhere. They say that no real détente is possible or desired. They point to the Soviet arms programme as evidence of duplicity, although the American arms programme is capable of an identical interpretation. In any event, a vague concept such as 'aims' of policy is almost meaningless as a basis for forecasting action. In a sense, I 'aim' to acquire a luxury yacht in the Mediterranean; I would like to have one, but no such possibility exists, and my wish for the yacht has no operational significance. To take a more serious example, the Pope 'aims' to convert all Chinese, and also Ulster Orangemen to Roman Catholicism, but neither Peking nor Belfast worries unduly about it. The Soviet leadership may well feel that the earth, in the nuclear age, is capable of self-destruction unless firmly governed from one place, and they would prefer that place to be Moscow rather than Washington. They would prefer Wilson, Giscard d'Estaing, Schmidt, to be replaced by obediently pro-Moscow Communists. Note that only this species of Communist is desired by any tenant of the Kremlin; an independent or dissident Communist state, if recent experience is anything to go by, is not of the slightest attraction to the Soviet leadership. 'Aims' or 'objectives', whether of countries or individuals, in any case have little meaning save in the context of the *cost* they are prepared to pay to achieve them, or the risks they are prepared to run. There is no sign at all that Brezhnev is willing to pay much of a price, or to take risks, to achieve 'world revolution', and many signs that he desires stability and the *status quo* and wishes to avoid the dangerous and the unpredictable. This unheroic posture can readily be reconciled with an important strand in the Marxist tradition: after all, revolutions are not for export, and the contradictions of capitalism will bring due reward to the faithful if allowed to work themselves out. It must be admitted that the West's present economic disarray may herald a deep crisis, and the Communist countries are notably better than we are at containing inflationary instability. Add the dangers inherent in nuclear weapons, which neither Marx nor Lenin could have foreseen, and a logical case can be made out for the Brezhnev policy. Critics from the left, or from China, stress the essentially conservative 'establishment' and great-power view of politics which now dominates the Kremlin, and link this with the social-political privileges of the Soviet ruling strata. This could well be so; they certainly have much to lose. But why should they take risks?

It is worth while turning Marxist class analysis onto the Soviet state itself. This the Russians themselves cannot do. '*Le Marxisme, c'est pour les autres.*' It seems right to regard the Soviet ruling stratum as a self-perpetuating oligarchy which co-opts able citizens into its own ranks, and which, after decades of blood, strife and terror, sets a high value on tranquillity. It controls the instruments of production, which the state owns. Its right to rule and to suppress others is based upon allegiance to 'Communism', which it must profess. Indeed, while some may be cynical careerists, it is perfectly possible that most of the leaders believe they are building a better world with the aid of the 'sure compass' of Marxism-Leninism, while (in their view) the Western world is run by clever but compass-less opportunists whose ship is unseaworthy. It is a common feature of all political and social systems that those who benefit most from their existence tend to identify the preservation of their privileges with the good of society. Nor are they always wrong. Some left-wing critics of the Soviet order adopt an unreal, utopian standard of judgement, as if society in the 1970s can be run with no bureaucracy, no police, no managers or officials who tell others what to do. True, Lenin's original vision included Utopian elements, but Brezhnev must cope with reality. One recalls Dostoevsky's brilliant parable, in *The Brothers Karamazov*, on the Grand Inquisitor, who was certain that Christ, who returned to earth, had to be burnt as a heretic, in the interests of good order, organisation and *Realpolitik*. The same would surely apply to Lenin. Given Russian political traditions, a Brezhnev or a Kosygin cannot envisage allowing Western-style freedom, not only because this might threaten them, but because it could lead to chaos. Indeed, as the Grand Inquisitor pointed out, freedom is a burden most men prefer to do without. Many Soviet citizens are so fearful of chaos that they are prepared to tolerate Brezhnev and Kosygin, whatever they think of them, lest worse befall.

On this interpretation of the attitude of the Brezhnev leadership and of their comrades in the full-time Party apparatus, it is clear why the policy of détente with the West can coexist, indeed coincide, with repression at home. While repression is facilitated and justified by external danger, it has its own internal logic. It becomes all the more necessary in the eyes of Brezhnev, when threats from outside recede, because then 'the penetration of alien ideas' can be more dangerous, more dissolving. The ideological struggle must continue.

Lenin's dream had to be drastically modified by Lenin himself in the midst of chaos, civil war, hunger, pestilence. 'Dictatorship of the proletariat' exercised by a centralised Party in a backward peasant society became institutionalised under Stalin, who deliberately created a privileged stratum, while also terrorising the individuals that composed it. A modern powerful industrial-military state was created, and called socialism. Its present rulers were, almost without exception, brought up politically under Stalin, where they served as junior or middle-grade functionaries at the worst period of his despotism. Party and state officialdom was formed at this time. A man like Brezhnev is a product of this school, and represents it well. It lacks originality and brilliance, is philosophically almost null and void, and is without revolutionary élan. It is made up of conscientious administrators. They like their people to live better, and show some concern over social services and poverty (another increase in minimum wages, and a system of family income supplements designed to overcome reluctance to have children, are in process of being introduced). They are also aware of the importance to their own political security of improvements of living standards; a huge subsidy keeps the retail prices of livestock products well below costs of production, because price rises are unpopular and therefore dangerous. Their outlook on the arts, on women, on the family, is entirely conventional. Nor should this surprise us. The original revolutionaries were mainly intellectuals who knew the world and had lived abroad. Such men as Trotsky and Bukharin were talented literary critics. Their successors, and the successors of their successors, have been selected for qualities such as administrative flair, the ability to organise people and to carry out decisions. In the present generation they are in a formal sense educated men: a high proportion of party functionaries at all levels have degrees. But very few come from an intellectual family background, and therefore they must be expected to reflect conventional ideas current among the people. The conservatism of many of them springs also from the fact that they are first-generation elite, i.e. their fathers were, as a rule, workers or peasants with little education. As a wise Polish professor observed, men of humble origin who move up the ladder are often resistant to change. The next generation may be different.

It may be objected that if Brezhnev and co. are not exactly

cultured or intellectual, nor are most other statesmen. Johnson, Nixon, Reagan, were or are at least as conventional and philistine (and just as capable of lying if political convenience requires it). But the point is that they are not concerned *ex officio* to change the world, do not claim to be inspired by a subtle revolutionary philosophy. Perhaps the lesson to be drawn is that if revolutions bring to power men of the people, there is no reason why they should not bring with them the attitudes of the people, and these are in fact, and everywhere, much more conventional and conservative than revolutionary intellectuals imagine them to be. This process cannot be prevented merely because the individuals concerned read *Das Kapital* or other selected passages from the works of Marx and Engels. If in addition their control over the state, and over the means of production which the state owns, gives them a dominating position in society and power over the allocation of resources, this must be expected to reinforce cautious conservatism. Revolutionaries 'have nothing to lose but their chains'; these men are interested in preserving the system as it is. To expect anything else to have happened is surely idealism rather than Marxist materialism. Marxism teaches that, with only individual exceptions, people will in general pursue their material interests and invent or adopt ideologies to show that this is right. Why should most holders of Communist Party cards, fifty-five years after the revolution, behave differently?

The intellectual opposition includes some admirable and courageous people, but is small and weak. Its links with the working classes are minimal, with the peasants even smaller. The ablest and more ambitious worker is often able to climb the educational ladder, or take pride in his children doing so, and the Party is able to utilise him and so avoid a situation where he can become a leader of discontent. Though official political slogans can be seen everywhere, there are few countries in the world today where political passivity is so great as in the Soviet Union, or the chances of political action from below so remote.

Not so the chances of political action from above. It remains to record the climb of Brezhnev to a power position as strong as Khrushchev's at his apogee. Formally this is not so, as he is not the Premier as well as Party Secretary. Yet by stages he has achieved clear dominance over his colleagues in the Politbureau. In April 1966 his job as First Secretary became recategorised as General Secretary, a designation last used by Stalin. More and more fulsome press references to him culminated in the award to him of the Lenin peace prize in April 1973, which was followed by a burst of orchestrated glorification in the press. Then, also in April, some changes were made in the Politbureau. Shelest and Voronov went out, Andropov (Security), Gromyko (Foreign Affairs) and Marshal Grechko (Defence) came in. One consequence is to bring these key sectors more directly under the General Secretary's eye. But it had one side-effect. As already noted, the old practice of publishing ranking lists of party leaders had been dropped, and for eighteen years the Politbureau's names appeared always in alphabetical order. Brezhnev's came first because his name began with B, but it had done so under Khrushchev too, after the demotion of Aristov and Belyaev. But now we had Andropov, who certainly had to head an alphabetical list. In May 1973, when the first such list appeared, Brezhnev's name came first, while everyone else was in alphabetical order. This is unprecedented. The rule was always *either* a ranking-list *or* alphabetical order. So in this way Brezhnev's dominance was asserted for all who know their *Pravda* to see. And, of course, it was Brezhnev who conducted negotiations with Nixon, with Brandt, with Pompidou. Khrushchev before he himself became Premier, took Bulganin, Brezhnev did not take Kosygin. Brezhnev finally 'regularised' his position by himself taking the job of Chairman of the Presidium, a position corresponding to head of state, previously held by Podgorny.

It may be said: so what? In all countries one statesman is dominant in the government. What difference does it make if it is Brezhnev? Suppose that tomorrow he is ousted by his comrades, who might blame him for economic difficulties, or over-reliance on détente. Suppose that we have instead a combination of Kirilenko, Suslov and Gorbachev. What would change? Possibly they may try this or that remedy for economic ills, or might be less vocally optimistic about relations with the United States. But Brezhnev is so typical a product of the present ruling stratum that any likely successor is almost bound to pursue similar policies and even to use similar style and language. Unless, of course, there is a major break-down or cataclysm. It is dangerous to prophesy, because, in the time-gap between writing and publication, predictions have a nasty habit of being falsified. I will take a risk, and assert that, though economic problems will persist, the system is still strong and stable enough to preserve itself for many years to come.

Threats to stability certainly exist, and one of these is non-Russian nationalism, exacerbated by the stress on *Russian* nationalism ('the elder brother', in effect dominating the rest). As already stressed, the encouragement of pride in Russian history and achievement is an important, even essential, cementing factor on which the regime must rely; but this can call forth negative responses among Ukrainians, Uzbeks, Georgians, Latvians. The second threat arises out of inadequate economic performance. Agriculture lags behind needs, necessitating large grain purchases abroad; shortages of goods in the shops are becoming very serious; industrial efficiency remains well behind the more advanced Western countries; the quality of consumer goods is better than it was, but is embarrassingly low far too often. Brezhnev calls for efficiency and 'intensification', but can the central planning system achieve these aims? A few years ago I would have written with confidence the following phrase: 'there is clear evidence that the Soviet planning system is incapable of coping effectively with the problems of a modern industrial economy'. The evidence is still clear, but confidence is shaken by the accumulating evidence that many Western countries are also showing themselves incapable of coping with these problems. Similarly, while one can deplore the excesses of Soviet censorship and all the indoctrination and moralising that goes on, it is possible that Soviet puritanism and moral education serves social stability better than Western permissiveness and pornography. But a proper discussion of such matters would need another book, or maybe two.

So here we have a regime very different from the original revolutionary vision, still preserving the structure created by and under Stalin, but without his pathological excesses and with rather more consideration for citizens' welfare than the despot ever showed. If the revolutionaries who fought in 1918 had known what Russia would look like in 1978, perhaps they would not have fought. But then if the French revolutionaries of 1792 had known what France would be like in 1842, they might also have given up. As Eric Hobsbawm pointed out, revolutions are usually made by men seeking to achieve the impossible, but they do achieve something, which inevitably falls short of their Utopian aspirations. It is not very helpful to pronounce the Russian revolution a failure because it did not realise the unrealisable. The original objectives could not be achieved. Stalin's despotic system may well have appeared to many to be the only alternative to anarchy, or to the 'permanent revolution' advocated by his chief enemy, Trotsky. Brezhnev's more prosaic rule, with all its undoubted defects, is likely to be tolerated because no political alternatives are in sight, and because the Russian masses feel that disorder would impose sufferings most of all on the masses. After half a century in which they have suffered enough, there is attraction in the prospect of acquiring consumer durables and an apartment, and who should blame them?

A colleague who is fond of denouncing the wickedness of the Soviet regime from an ultra-left standpoint has asserted that the regime can exist either on the basis of ideology or on the basis of force; since ideology is not an important factor today, the basis of Soviet rule must be the police, the KGB, coercion. In my opinion this is an impossibly *simpliste* view, and not only of Russia. No serious observer would deny the existence and importance of coercion; the KGB, the censorship, tight Party control over all aspects of social life, are facts. But so is the acceptance of the regime by the bulk of the citizens. Their motives may have nothing to do with Marxism or Leninism, they may simply be indifferent, or glad to get a wage increase, or hoping to be promoted, or they may take pride in their profession, or be motivated by straight Russian patriotism. It is simply not the case that, in any country, people are either convinced ('ideology') or coerced ('secret police'). There are many inter-mediate states of mind. I must stress that acceptance does not imply satisfaction with an existing situation. A British or American building worker may broadly accept the system under which he lives, i.e. he has no particular wish to overthrow it, but probably complains about prices, desires a 20 per cent wage increase and has other grumbles too. When I served in the British army, my fellow-soldiers grumbled incessantly about all sorts of things, but were loyal and obeyed orders all the same, and not primarily because they would have been punished if they did not (though, of course, they *would* have been punished if they did not!). Soviet citizens have a great deal to complain about, though the older generation doubtless contrasts the present with a past that was much harsher, in material and moral terms. In a cafeteria in Kiev I once collected a large bowl of soup, two hunks of bread and a glass of tea, a snack which cost me all of sixteen kopecks, or ten pence. A woman standing behind me said, to no one in particular: 'There was a time when we went hungry.' True, I recall also another cafeteria, this time in Moscow, close to three big railway stations: another woman was complaining bitterly about having to come to Moscow all the way from the town of Alexandrov, 100 miles or so, to get various groceries unobtainable in Alexandrov. It remains the case that elementary requirements are in short supply, or are unevenly distributed with preference given to the larger cities. It is still hard to find attractive and well-made clothes, or to get repairs done, to arrange a funeral, to find a room at any hotel without an official priority, to move to one of the favoured big cities, or to deal with a clumsy bureaucracy over permits or certificates of many kinds (*Krokodil* once printed a story about the need for a certificate certifying that a certificate was not needed!). How much of all this is due to the fact that this is Russia, how much to Communist rule? One must add: how Russian is Communist rule in Russia?

This might be a good note on which to end.

Or is it? Will not the reader feel a justified sense of dissatisfaction? Does all this not leave some key questions unanswered? Or answered partially, indirectly, by implication.

I plead guilty, but with extenuating circumstances. Let me try to clarify my own views, and, hopefully, the reader's mind.

Firstly, is the Soviet Union and its government influenced by Marxist-Leninist ideology? If so, to what extent? True, this ideology itself is in some important part a product of the Russian environment, for it is Lenin's adaptation to Russian conditions of the doctrines of Marx and Engels. However, whatever their origin, ideas can influence people's perception of reality and of their own interests too. There is no doubt that Brezhnev and co. conceive of themselves as Marxist, even as guardians of Marxian orthodoxy. They manipulate doctrine, they keep a card index of quotations to justify whatever they consider needs doing on practical grounds. Yet it is going too far to pronounce ideology as merely this card-index of justificatory quotations. It is also a philosophical world-view. This does not mean that Brezhnev knows all about the negation of the negation or can distinguish between alternative interpretations of the doctrine of the falling rate of profit. The idea that something called 'dialectics' gives him some especially clever or sinister insight into the world's laws of motion is a fantasy. But there is a world-view in which he was brought up, which includes the following elements, among others:

(1) Socialist planning, defined as state control over the economy exercised by the Communist Party, is the right way. Errors and distortions are known to exist, but for Brezhnev and his ilk they can be corrected by modifications *within* the system, the system Kosygin has labelled 'directive planning'. It is this attitude, and not only vested interest, which causes them to react negatively to proposals for radical reform in the direction of a market economy. Such reforms

might yet come as a result of pressure of necessity, arising out of the inherent inefficiency of centralised controls, but there is a strong ideological predisposition to resist such changes.

(2) Private trade for private gain is seen as wrong, and suggestions to improve the existing methods by enlarging the area of private enterprise were and will be resisted.

(3) Brezhnev probably believes sincerely in the proposition that the hierarchical one-party state, with full Party control over press, literature, judiciary, is also ideologically orthodox, although in fact no warrant for the suppression of all opposition and for tight censorship can be found in any works by Marx, Engels or even Lenin up to 1920 or so (the overcoming of resistance by the possessing classes, or repression during a civil war, are another matter).

(4) Doctrine as well as early Soviet experience predispose the leadership to regard the capitalist West as potentially if not actually hostile. Therefore, when Brezhnev carries out a policy of conciliation and détente, and talks of a new era in East-West relations, this can be expected to be greeted with suspicions by some of his comrades. He has to justify this policy, to himself and to others, by insisting that it must be combined by ideological struggle and inter-system competition. Khrushchev too declared that peaceful co-existence is a form of conflict. As well as for doctrinal reasons, Brezhnev needs conflict (albeit in not too dangerous a form) because it justifies the degree of repression needed for internal security. + the state it self(-

(5) That Brezhnev is cognisant of the real forces at work in Western countries is very doubtful. But he has inherited a belief, based in the ideology, that capitalism will one day founder through its internal contradictions. This, as we already pointed out, can justify an ultra-cautious foreign policy.

'Be strong to protect ourselves from imperialist powers; trade with them, offer them peace and collaboration, while keeping our powder dry and also avoiding ideological infection. Maintain Party rule and social controls, creating thereby a haven of stability in an unstable world. Let the West destroy itself, through its internal economic crises and through its increasingly strained relations with the third world. No need to take risks or dangerous initiatives. History is on our side.'

Recent disarray in the West lends colour to such a view. However, there is also some fear of rapid destabilisation, because of the dangers it might cause; hence, when conflagration threatens, the

USSR sometimes joins the fire brigade, in the Middle East and elsewhere.

(6) Doctrine is vital for the legitimation of the regime internally, and it also attracts some support for Soviet policy overseas. The Party is in command of all levers of authority so as to 'build Communism'. Khrushchev wanted this to mean that, at some set date, certain goods and services became free: Brezhnev has preferred to abandon any promised date. But he must claim to be leading the country into this kind of promised land. A sceptic like myself might echo an old thought of Bertrand Russell's, that 'full Communism' is a vision with the role (and operational significance) of the second coming of Christ, that it is religious rather than practical-political. Brezhnev probably does *not* agree with me, but even if he did he would take care not to say so. Instead we are told that the USSR has reached the stage of 'mature socialism'.

(7) Internationalism is a key element in the ideology, 'The Internationale unites the human race'. 'Workers of all lands, unite.' Repeated assertions in this spirit frequently conflict, however, with *de facto* nationalism. This could take the form of belief that the greater power of the Moscow-based Communist Party is the best way forward to world-wide Communism. There is, of course, no inherent contradiction between pride in one's own nation's achievements and a belief in internationalism. But few observers of the Soviet scene would be satisfied with this sort of interpretation. Intense nationalism, Russian and also anti-Russian, is a very important aspect of reality in the eastern half of Europe, and in other Communist-ruled states too, China among them.

It is also not out of place to cite the words of a political scientist, S. V. Utechin, on the topsy-turvy role of ideology and theory:

'There is little doubt that Stalin intended the people to be aware of the fictitious nature of the theory, for an attempt on the part of the population to treat it as truthful (e.g. to believe that they enjoyed freedom of speech) would undermine the whole of his system of rule. Therefore any action based on belief (genuine or pretended) in the truthfulness of the official theory was treated as a most serious political offence. A profession of belief was obligatory; action implying belief was severely punished.' (*Russian Political Thought*, p. 242.)

This must cause us to pause for a moment to consider what we mean by 'ideology'. I have in mind a set of formal and explicit ideas recognised by those who hold them – and by opponents too – as influencing the behaviour of a group of people. If this group is in power, then the influence is also on the direction, aims and methods of public policy. In practice, needless to say, people are affected also by ideas which do not form part of the formal 'ideology' which they profess, or which may contradict it. In Russia, as we have seen on many occasions, both the behaviour of Authority and its acceptance by the people are often conditioned by Russian national traditions and feelings. In other countries, including those whose leaders profess pragmatism and deny having any ideology, the prevailing climate of ideas influences action and is in turn influenced by governments and mass media. We must also beware of assuming that what we do is 'natural', while anything alien in our habits of thought is 'distorted by ideology'. Thus buying and selling for private gain is illegal and immoral according to the official Soviet code, and praiseworthy or acceptable in Western countries; these attitudes are both value-judgements, inspired by ideas which differ.

In the USSR much attention is paid to ideology, though what actually happens can conflict with it, requiring concealment of facts and the rewriting of history. In the West the situation is much vaguer and contradictory. Some analysts of both societies may be tempted to deduce 'the real ideology' from actions and from the interests of the political actors. However, if one derives ideology from what men actually do, and then assert that what men do is determined by their ideology, one is arguing in a not-very-helpful circle. Perhaps it is best to say just that practical issues are seen differently by men whose ideas, aims and interests are different. They must, as political men, deal with practical affairs, but the 'ideology' is a pair of coloured spectacles, so that reality takes on a distinct hue, or it is blinkers, which prevents the wearer from perceiving (or opting for) some of the possible solutions to the practical issues which he encounters. It is hard, in most cases, to identify the impact of ideology, since all decisions by political men are to do with practical affairs and so ideology never appears in pure form.

It seems, on balance, that revolutionary Communist doctrine has to a great extent withered away, that its weight in decision-making and in strategic thinking has diminished, and that the interest of the ruling stratum in its own preservation, plus a strong undercurrent of Russian nationalism, explain more than other hypotheses do. Stalin created this ruling stratum, but tyrannised over them. Brezhnev is their man, their leader. His successor is likely to be in the same mould. Not all the facts fit snugly into this picture, but then there are contradictions in most situations.

The Chinese denounce the present rulers of the Soviet Union vehemently, calling them 'revisionist social imperialists,' 'new tsars' and 'fascists'. They also regard the Soviet Union as a super power which threatens China. It seems to me that the Chinese tend to substitute abuse for analysis. Indeed, what chance have they to analyse the origins and basis of the present Soviet system if they continue to extol the virtues of Stalin? However, the Soviet Union is subject to criticism from much more moderate and tolerant quarters, partly as a result of the wave of internal repression and the exile of Sakharov. A foreign correspondent has described the situation as 'a cultural counter-revolution in which the forces of conformity and reaction have become triumphant once more. It may be decades before Soviet society can recover from the negative effects of this counter-revolution, which began soon after the ousting of Khrushchev'. (*Observer*, 9 September 1973). This seems to me to be fair comment, though perhaps slightly overstating the extent of the change since 1964. It is also worth citing the comment on the same events by the former British Ambassador in Moscow, Sir William Hayter. 'The Soviet rulers believe, and history provides little evidence to contradict this belief, that Russia can only be governed as an isolated autocracy' (*The Times*, 7 September 1973). To recognise that this may be so is neither to justify nor to apologise for the regime, but to recognise it for what it is, and to help us to understand the function which it performs in Soviet society.

So we seem to have a ruling group set in its ways, holding back major social or economic reforms, anxious to preserve the *status quo* at home and abroad, to play the role of super-power and be recognised as such, while formally committed to Red Flag and Revolution. It has so far been able easily to withstand challenges from liberalisers and intellectual dissidents, at a level of repression which is a small fraction of Stalin's brutalities. Economic and intellectual controls stultify the leadership's own efforts to achieve greater world impact and greater efficiency. Yet Brezhnev could, if he spoke honestly, answer us thus:

'You in the West are in an advanced state of decay and moral-political dissolution, your culture is in a mess, people are losing faith in your institutions. Economic confusion, inflation, high crime rates, drugs, all this is evidence that bourgeois democracy and capitalism are on the skids. Of course it is true that we also have social problems, and that our history has ugly features about it, the Stalin terror especially. We had to do nasty things in Hungary and Czechoslovakia to maintain control in our sphere, though the victims were but a fraction of those killed by the Americans trying to maintain control in their sphere. But it would never do for us to allow free discussion of such things. We must keep control. We are a country without democratic traditions. Your people are inoculated by centuries of exposure to conflicting ideas, ours are all too susceptible to oppositionist demagoguery. Then we have difficult problems with some nationalities: look what happened between the Croats and the Serbs in Yugoslavia when *they* foolishly allowed too much freedom of speech. Our international situation also presents potential dangers. You may say we are unimaginative, obsessed with security, ultra-cautious. I must admit that some of our censors overdo things, that our indoctrinators can bore the pants off any thinking man: I have to sit through excruciatingly dull speeches. As for our economic system, I know its weaknesses better than you, my critics. But what would you have me do? Our oligarchical and hierarchical system is not quite what our revered teacher Lenin had in mind, but at least it enables us to govern Russia. What if the only alternative is disintegration? If we relax and are hanged by an indignant mob, stirred up by those intellectual rebels whom you in the west foolishly tolerate in your midst, do you really think there would be freedom, democracy and prosperity in our country? I may not be a genius, but I am the best General Secretary we've got.'

Maybe he is, who knows?

Appendix 1

Biographical Data

The following are brief biographical details on the principal 'actors' in the Soviet political drama. Lenin and Stalin are omitted, since they are amply discussed in the text.

NOTE ON RUSSIAN NAMES
Russians have, apart from surnames, one first or Christian name and 'patronymic', the latter being derived from their father's first name. Thus if Ivan Smirnov's father was called Ivan, he would be known as Ivan Ivanovich Smirnov. Women also use the patronymic, but with a feminine ending, which also affects those surnames which end in the letters V and N. Thus his sister might be Vera Ivanovna Smirnova.

BERIA, Lavrenti Pavlovich (1899–1953). Georgian. Joined Party in 1917. Became a leading member of police in Caucasus. In 1931 First Secretary of Party in Georgia. Wrote book propagating myths about Stalin's revolutionary activities. In 1938 became head of NKVD (secret police) of USSR. Member of wartime State Defence Committee, also of Politbureau. In postwar years Deputy-Premier, and made Marshal of the Soviet Union. In ruling triumvirate at death of Stalin, but arrested in July 1953 and later shot. Unsavoury reputation, feared by his 'comrades', but apparently seeking relaxations after Stalin's death.

BREZHNEV, Leonid Ilyich (1906–   ). Career given in text. General Secretary and leader of the Party.

BUKHARIN, Nikolai Ivanovich (1888–1938). Son of a teacher. Arrested for Bolshevik revolutionary activities in 1909. Fled abroad in 1911. Attended economics courses in Vienna. Later went to USA. Returned to Russia in 1917. Prolific writer and journalist. Key moments of career described in text. Executed on false charges in 1938.

BULGANIN, Nikolai (1895–1975). Party member from 1917. Economic administrator in 1920s. Rose to be Chairman of Moscow

Soviet, 1936, and to Deputy Premier in 1938. Held high party-
military posts during war. Politbureau member, 1952–58. Marshal of
the Soviet Union, 1947. Minister of Defence, 1947–49, 1953–55.
Made Premier by Khrushchev after Malenkov's fall in 1955.
Supported 'anti-Party group' (i.e. Molotov and co.) in 1957, dismissed 1958. Became Chairman of State Bank and then demoted
into insignificance.

EIKHE, Robert Indrikovich (1890–1940). Latvian. Member of
Party from 1905. Party official in Latvia during revolution, then in
Moscow and Siberia. Became deputy-member of the Politbureau in
1936, and minister of Agriculture. Arrested in 1938 (?) and shot in
1940. Typical of upper stratum of Stalinist victims of Stalin's purges.

KAGANOVICH, Lazar Moiseyevich (1889–   ). Only Jew to retain
senior Party post after 1938. Joined Party in 1911. Active agitator
before 1917. After many Party jobs in the provinces, became
Secretary of Ukrainian Party in 1925. Member of Politbureau from
1930, also Secretary of Moscow Party Committee. In charge of
transport and Deputy-Premier in thirties. Held many other posts
during and after the war, including Aviation Industry and in
Ukraine. Joined Molotov and Malenkov in opposing Khrushchev in
1957. Lost all official positions. Now retired on a pension.

KAMENEV, Lev Borisovich (1883–1936). Real name ROSENFELD.
Jewish. Expelled from Moscow University, 1902. Arrested, emigrated, returned, re-arrested and sent to Siberia as a leading
Bolshevik. Returned in 1917. Opposed Lenin over timing of October
revolution. Held leading posts as a close associate of Zinoviev.
Supported him and Stalin against Trotsky, and then (1926–7)
supported Trotsky against Stalin. Short spell as Ambassador to Italy,
1927. Several times expelled from Party and re-admitted. Arrested
1935, tried and shot, 1936.

KHRUSHCHEV, Nikita Sergeyevich (1894–1971). Career given in
text. Played dominant role in 1954–64.

KIROV, Sergei Mironovich (1886–1934) (real name Kostrikov).
Joined Party in 1905. Revolutionary activities especially in Siberia
and Caucasus. Senior political officer in Civil war. Party Secretary
in Baku, then (1926) in Leningrad. Joined Politbureau after defeat of
Trotsky as a strong supporter of Stalin. Leading role in seventeenth
Congress (1934) may have caused Stalin's jealousy. Assassinated,
December 1934. Great purge followed.

KOLLONTAI, Alexandra Mikhailovna (1872–1952). Daughter of general, educated in Zurich university. Revolutionary activity in 1903–08, then emigrated. Returned to Russia in 1917. Member of Central Committee in 1917, in charge of work among women. In 1920–21 a leading member of the so-called 'workers' opposition' to the Party majority. Also advocated free love. Became diplomatist, mostly in Scandinavia, incl. Ambassador to Sweden. Later worked in Ministry of Foreign Affairs, Moscow. She abjured her oppositionist past and supported Stalin.

KRYLENKO, Nikolai Vasilyevich (1885–1938). Joined Party 1904, as a student in St Petersburg. Many times arrested. Served in army in war, and carried out propaganda among soldiers. In November 1917 appointed by Lenin as Commander-in-Chief of Russian army, in place of General Dukhonin, who was murdered. From 1918 worked in judicial organs. Acted as Prosecutor in many political cases, wrote books on socialist legality. Also leading organiser of chess and mountaineering. Arrested and shot, 1938.

LITVINOV, Maksim Maksimovich (real name Vallakh). (1876–1951). Jew. Joined Party in 1898. Remarkable record of illegal activities before revolution. Lived in Switzerland for some years. Diplomatic representative in Great Britain on behalf of Bolshevik Government, 1918. In 1921 Deputy-Commissar for Foreign Affairs, Commissar from 1930 to 1939, again briefly from 1941. Well known for speeches at the League of Nations in 1935–39 on collective security. Kept away from affairs after 1943.

LUNACHARSKY, Anatoly Vasilevich (1875–1935). Intellectual and Party pioneer. Arrested, emigrated. Parted company with Lenin in 1907, over philosophical differences, but returned to Bolsheviks in 1912. Commissar for Education after the Revolution. Author of works on art and literature. Political influence waned after middle twenties.

MIKOYAN, Anastas Ivanovich (1895–1978). Armenian. Religious education. Revolutionary activities in Caucasus, 1918–19. Then Party Secretary in North Caucasus. From 1926 to 1955 was Commissar (later Minister) for Internal and/or Foreign Trade for long periods, also for Food Industry (1934–38). While a member of the Politbureau for most years after 1939, his principal role was 'overlord' of trade and supplies. Supported Khrushchev in 1957. Gradually withdrew from political life.

MOLOTOV, Vyacheslav Mikhailovich (1890–   ). Real name SCRIABIN. Bolshevik student activities from 1906. Arrested and exiled, and escaped (1916). Rose to high Party position in 1917. From then onwards worked closely with Stalin in economic committee. Became Premier in 1930–41, Commissar for Foreign Affairs 1939–49 and Minister 1953–56. Member of the Politbureau from 1926 until 1957. Member of State Committee of Defence during war. Continued to play leading role after Stalin's death until his fall in 1957. Became Ambassador to Mongolia, and finally retired on pension.

ORDZHONIKIDZE, Grigori Konstantinovich (1886–1937). Georgian. Revolutionary activities in Caucasus from 1903. Active Bolshevik within Russia, arrested, imprisoned, exiled. Important role in Revolution and civil war in many functions. Then leader in Caucasus to 1930, when he became top economic functionary. Commissar for Heavy Industry from 1932. Politbureau member from 1930. Repeatedly opposed purges. Committed suicide 1937.

PERVUKHIN, Mikhail Georgievich (1904–1978). Party 'technocrat' who carried out important function in directing economic planning. Deputy Premier 1940 and again in 1950–3 and 1955–7. Also served as Minister of Chemical Industry and Electric Power. Rose high in Party in last years of Stalin's life. In December 1956 was nominated to be economic overlord, but was superseded when Khrushchev counter-attacked. Demoted 1957. After spell as Ambassador to East Germany, became an official in the State Planning Commission.

POKROVSKY, Mikhail Nikolaevich (1868–1932). Joined Party in 1905. Leading Marxist historian even before the Revolution. Emigrated 1908. Returned 1917. Held some official posts, but chiefly famous for his academic writings on history. These were denounced after his death.

PREOBRAZHENSKY, Evgeny Alexeyevich (1886–1937). Son of a Russian priest. Party work and arrests from 1901. During Revolution was a leader in Siberia and Urals. Member of Central Committee and of Politbureau in 1919–21. Supported Trotsky against Stalin, and produced theoretical works of importance (notably *The New Economics*). Prolific writer. Expelled from party in 1927, readmitted and expelled again. Arrested in 1936 (?) and shot in the following year, without any public trial.

PYATAKOV, Yuri Leonidovich (1890–1937). Student revolutionary activities in St Petersburg. Joined Bolsheviks in 1910. Arrested, escaped. Important role in Bolshevik seizure of power. Political work in armies during civil war. Thereafter senior planner and finance official. Sided with Trotsky, but later co-operated with dominant Stalin faction. Deputy-Commissar for Heavy Industry 1933. Tried and executed, 1937.

RYKOV, Alexei Ivanovich (1881–1938). Party activities began while student at Kazan in 1901. Repeatedly arrested, imprisoned, exiled. From 1918 played leading role in economic affairs, notably as head of Supreme Council of National Economy, Premier, 1924–9. Close associate of Bukharin. Dropped with him from Politbureau in 1929. Held minor posts until arrested, tried, condemned and shot in 1938.

SABUROV, Maksim Zakharovich (1900–1974). Rose to high position as Voznesensky's deputy when latter was chief planner (1938 and after). For many years head of State Planning Commission. Achieved Politbureau status in 1952. Demoted in 1957 when he formed part of so-called 'anti-Party group'. Insignificant thereafter.

SUSLOV, Mikhail Andreyevich (1902–   ). Party Secretary in Rostov and Stavropol before the war. Secretary of the Central Committee from 1947. Party theoretician. Promoted to Politbureau rank in 1955, and has remained there. Supported Khrushchev, then Brezhnev. Has played big role in relations with foreign Communist parties.

TOMSKY, Mikhail Pavlovich (1880–1936). Real name: YEFREMOV. Printing worker and trade unionist. Joined Party in 1904. Arrested and imprisoned. Active Bolshevik in 1917. Became trade union leader after revolution. Well known also in international trade union circles. Supported Bukharin in split with Stalin (1928–29) and dismissed from his union posts. Committed suicide to avoid arrest, 1936.

TROTSKY, Lev Davydovich (1879–1940). Real name Bronshtein. Jewish. Revolutionary activity from 1897. Chairman of Petrograd Soviet in 1905 revolution. Arrested, exiled, went abroad. Returned from America in 1917. Joined Bolsheviks in July 1917. Played important role in Bolshevik seizure of power. Commissar for Foreign Affairs, then War. Major role in organising Red Army. Ceased to be

Commissar for War in 1925, expelled from Politbureau 1926, exiled to Alma Ata 1928, deported from USSR in 1929, murdered in Mexico, 1940. Vilified by Stalin. Author of *History of Russian Revolution* and numerous other works. Founded anti-Stalinist 'Fourth' International when in exile. Still inspires 'Trotskyists' in many countries.

TUKHACHEVSKY, Mikhail Nikolaevich (1893–1937). Guards officer in Tsarist army. Rose rapidly to high command positions in Civil war. Commanded Soviet army against Poles at age of 27 (1920). Played leading part in organising modernisation of Red Army in thirties. Became First Deputy-Commissar for Defence and Marshal of the Soviet Union, but arrested and shot in 1937 on false charges. Rehabilitated after Stalin's death.

VOROSHILOV, Klimenti Efremovich (1881–1969). Joined Party in 1903 and worked at Lugansk, now Voroshilovgrad. Arrested repeatedly. Rose to senior military command in Civil War, as an associate of Stalin. Commissar of Defence from 1925. Unsuccessful commander in World War II. Close crony of Stalin's in the dictator's last years. Member of Politbureau from 1926 until removed by Khrushchev in 1958. Served as Chairman of Presidium of Supreme Soviet (nominal 'president') in his declining years.

VOZNESENSKY, Nikolai Alekseyevich (1903–1950). Joined Party in 1919. After holding official positions, notably in Leningrad, he was suddenly promoted after arrests of most senior planners to be head of State Planning Commission (December 1937). Deputy-Premier from 1939, member of wartime State Defence Committee, and of Politbureau (full member 1947). Wrote book on war economy. Fell from favour mysteriously in 1949, shot in 1950.

VYSHINSKY, Andrei Yanuarievich (1885–1954). Revolutionary activities from 1905. Studied law. Served in Red Army in civil war. Joined Bolsheviks in 1920 (previously Menshevik). Became leading professor of law. Prosecutor (*Prokuror*) in 1935, performed this task in the great purge trials. In 1939 became Deputy Foreign Minister. Minister 1953–4. Frequently appeared in United Nations and international conferences.

YAGODA, Genrikh Grigoryevich (1891–1938). Joined Party in 1907. Served as a political chief in civil war. Became a Deputy-head of Cheka/OGPU (Secret Police) in 1920. Became Commissar and Head of Police (renamed NKVD) in 1934. Prepared first purge trials. Then himself purged, tried and executed.

YAKIR, Yona Emmanuilovich (1896–1937). Jewish. Distinguished service in Red Army in civil war, commanded armies at age of 24. Played important part, along with Tukhachevsky, in modernising Red Army in thirties. Arrested January 1937, later shot.

YEZHOV, Nikolai Ivanovich (1895–1939?). Political duties with Red Army in civil war. Various party official posts until rapidly promoted to Commissar of Internal Affairs (NKVD, secret police) in September 1936. Arranged for arrest and execution of predecessor, Yagoda. Launched intense purge and blood-bath, on Stalin's orders (it is still known as the 'Yezhovshchina'). Politbureau, 1937. Publicly extolled as 'iron commissar'. Suddenly appointed Commissar of Water Transport in 1938 and then vanished. Fate unknown, presumably shot.

ZHDANOV, Andrei Aleksandrovich (1896–1948). Revolutionary activity in army in World War I. Political work in Red Army. Then various Party and official posts, Secretary at Gorky, 1925, at Leningrad 1934 (succeeding Kirov), Politbureau member from 1939. Chief political officer in Leningrad during siege. Took major part in cultural repression in 1946–8.

ZHUKOV, Georgi Konstantinovich (1896–1974). Marshal of the Soviet Union. Distinguished soldier. Served in Tsarist army in World War I, and in civil war as cavalryman. Rose rapidly to senior command. In 1939 commanded Soviet troops in 'unofficial' battle with Japanese in Mongolia. Distinguished record in war with Germany, on Moscow, Stalingrad and many other fronts. Often acted as Stalin's deputy. Demoted after war, but became Minister of Defence after Stalin's death. Helped Khrushchev in 1957, briefly held seat in Politbureau. Was then retired.

ZINOVIEV, Grigori Evseyevich (1883–1936). Real name RADO-MYSLSKY. Jewish. Joined Party in 1901. Emigrated. Worked closely with Lenin abroad, returned with him through Germany to Russia in 1917. Together with Kamenev, opposed Lenin over October rising. Leader in Petrograd (Leningrad), and Chairman of Comintern, until removed from both posts in 1926. Worked with Stalin against Trotsky, but joined Trotsky in 1926. Expelled and readmitted and expelled again from Party. Arrested 1935, tried, condemned and shot, 1936.

Appendix 2

Chronological List of Events, 1917–65

1917	7 November	Seizure of power by Bolsheviks
	7 December	Cheka (the future secret police) founded
1918	18–19 January	Constituent Assembly meets, and is dissolved
	3 March	Brest-Litovsk treaty ends war with Germany and Austria–Hungary. Civil war grows in intensity
	11 March	Soviet government moved from Petrograd (Leningrad) to Moscow
	28 June	Decree nationalising large-scale industry
1919	2–6 March	First Congress of Communist International, Moscow
	October–December	Defeat of General Denikin's 'White' armies in the south. Admiral Kolchak in retreat in Siberia. British and other foreign armies withdrawn from Russia
1920	January–February	Final defeat of Denikin and Kolchak
	April	Polish offensive in Ukraine, followed by successful Red Army counter-offensive
	July	Polish counterblow drives back Red Army
	October	Peace with Poland
	November	Baron Wrangel driven out of Crimea. End of Civil War
1921	January	Soviet troops overthrow Menshevik government in Georgia, which becomes a Soviet republic
	8–16 March	Tenth Congress of Communist Party; end of 'war communism'. Suppression of Kronstadt sailors' rebellion

1922	April	Stalin becomes General Secretary of Central Committee
	May	Lenin's first serious illness
	30 December	The several existing Soviet republics form the Union of Soviet Socialist Republics (USSR)
1923	March	Lenin's second stroke removes him from political life. Ruling triumvirate formed by Zinoviev, Kamenev, Stalin
1924	21 January	Lenin dies
	2 February	Diplomatic relations established with Great Britain
1925	December	Fourteenth Congress of Party. Zinoviev and Kamenev join Trotsky in opposing Stalin
1927	May	Great Britain breaks off diplomatic relations
	December	Fifteenth Congress of Party adopts plans for speedier industrialisation and collectivisation. Trotsky expelled from Party. Many supporters exiled
1928	January–February	Stalin uses coercion in grain collection crisis
	October	First month of first five-year plan
1929	February	Trotsky deported from USSR
	November	Bukharin removed from Politbureau
	November	Stalin's article in Pravda announced full-scale agricultural collectivisation
1930	5 January	Decree 'on tempos of collectivisation'
	14 March	Decree on 'distortions' in collectivising peasants
	17 June	Stalingrad tractor factory starts production
	November–December	Trial of alleged 'Industrial party'; prisoners confess to sabotage, etc.
1931	10 December	Giant Magnitogorsk metallurgical works completed
1932	December	First five-year plan completed, $4\frac{1}{4}$ years after launching
1933	Spring	Famine in the south. Hitler in power in Germany
	16 November	Diplomatic relations established with USA
1934	January–February	Seventeenth Party Congress; Stalin's post renamed 'Secretary'. 'Softer' policies expected

1934 18 September   USSR enters League of Nations

1 December   Assassination of Kirov heralds wave of repression

1935 July–August   Seventh Congress of Comintern adopts anti-Fascist Popular-Front policy

1936 August   Trial of Zinoviev, Kamenev, etc. Prisoners plead guilty and are shot

September   Yezhov appointed Commissar for Interior (head of NKVD) and speeds up the purge and intensifies terror

December   Adoption of new ('Stalin') Constitution

1937 January   Purges and terror reach their height under Yezhov

June   Marshal Tukhachevsky and other senior officers shot. Purge extends throughout armed forces

December   End of second five-year plan

1938 March   Bukharin, Rykov and others sentenced and shot

October   Munich agreement to dismember Czechoslovakia; Soviet Union ignored

December   Yezhov dismissed from NKVD, replaced by Beria

1939 May   Litvinov replaced by Molotov as Foreign Minister

23 August   Nazi-Soviet pact signed. Negotiations with Britain and France broken off

1 September   German attack on Poland

17 September   Soviet troops attack and occupy Eastern Poland by agreement with Hitler

29 November   Soviet attack on Finland

1940   Stalin becomes Chairman of Council of People's Commissars (Premier)

12 March   End of war with Finland

May–June   Hitler's armies overwhelm France

28 June   Bessarabia annexed from Romania

21 July   Latvia, Lithuania and Estonia become Soviet republics

October   Labour decrees impose severe discipline

November   Molotov visits Berlin, sees Hitler

1941 22 June   German attack. War

1941	30 June	State committee of defence created: Stalin, Molotov, Beria, Malenkov, Voroshilov
	September	Soviet disaster in Ukraine
	19 October	Critical days in Moscow. State of siege declared in city
	6 December	Successful Soviet counter-offensive drives Germans away from Moscow
1942	26 May	Treaty of alliance signed with Great Britain
	June–August	Soviet retreat in South, to Stalingrad and Caucasus mountains
	November	Soviet attacks cut off German 6th army at Stalingrad
1943	18 January	Leningrad relieved
	2 February	End of German resistance at Stalingrad. Rapid advances in south
	6 November	Kiev re-captured by Soviet troops
	28 November	Teheran conference opens (Stalin, Roosevelt, Churchill)
1944	6 June	American and British troops land in Normandy. Soviet advances along whole front
	31 August	Soviet troops in Bucharest
	16 September	Soviet troops in Sofia
	13 October	Soviet troops return to Riga (Latvia)
	20 October	Soviet and Yugoslav forces reach Belgrade
1945	17 January	Soviet troops occupy Warsaw
	February	Yalta conference (Stalin, Roosevelt, Churchill)
	17 February	Soviet troops in Budapest
	13 April	Soviet troops in Vienna
	2 May	End of German resistance in Berlin, after successful offensives by Marshals Zhukov and Konev
	9 May	End of war with Germany
	July–August	Potsdam conference (Stalin, Truman, Attlee)
	9 August	Soviet declaration of war on Japan; invasion of Manchuria
	2 September	End of war with Japan
1946	March	Fourth (first postwar) five-year plan adopted
	15 March	Peoples' Commissariats renamed Ministries
1947		Marshall plan prepared, Molotov rejects it at conference in Paris

1947	14 December	Monetary reforms and abolition of rationing
1948	April	Conference of Soviet composers hears attacks on musical 'formalism' by Zhdanov
	August	Zhdanov dies
1949	April	Voznesensky (Chief planner and deputy-premier) dismissed, later arrested (shot in 1950)
		Chinese Communists succeed in Civil War. Chiang Kai-shek flees to Taiwan
		'Stalin plan for transformation of nature' launched
1950	14 February	Treaty of friendship and advance signed with People's Republic of China
1952	31 May	Opening of Volga-Don ship canal
	October	Nineteenth Party Congress. Malenkov presents main report in Stalin's presence
1953	January	'Discovery' of the doctors' plot to kill Soviet leaders
	March	Death of Stalin
		Malenkov retains Prime Ministership, but relinquishes Party Secretaryship. Khrushchev senior of Party Secretaries
	September	Plenum of Central Committee decides on agricultural reforms in Khrushchev's report
		Announcement that USSR has H-bomb
1954	7 March	Virgin lands campaign launched
1955	February	Malenkov resigns as Premier; Bulganin succeeds him
1956	February	Twentieth Congress of Party. Khrushchev's 'secret speech' attacking Stalin
	June–July	Decrees abolishing fees for secondary and higher education, and increasing pensions
	October	Soviet troops intervene in Hungary
	December	Central Committee adopts economic reorganisation, establishing Pervukhin as overlord
1957	May	Economic reorganisation pushed through by Khrushchev; regional economic councils (*sovnarkhozy*) created
	June	'Anti-Party group' (Molotov, Malenkov, Kaganovich, etc.) defeated

1957	4 October	First sputnik circles the earth
1958	March	Bulganin resigns; Khrushchev Premier as well as First Secretary
	March	Measures to abolish Machine Tractor Stations and raise farm prices
1959	27 January–5 February	Party Congress (Twenty-first) adopt seven-year plan
	September	Khrushchev visits United States, sees Eisenhower. Addressed UN
1960	May	U2 plane over Soviet territory, denounced by Khrushchev at Paris summit conference
	November	Conference of Communist Parties. Quarrel with China discussed
1961	17 April	Gagarin makes first manned flight into space
	June	Khrushchev meets Kennedy in Vienna
	August and after	Tension over Berlin
	October	Twenty-second Party Congress: Stalin sharply attacked, new party programme adopted. Stalin removed from Mausoleum
1962	March	Khrushchev reorganises agricultural administration
	October	Cuban missile crisis
	November	Party divided into two parts
1963	September–October	Agreement on nuclear test ban treaty
	December	Speed-up in expansion of chemical industry
1964	14 October	Khrushchev out. Brezhnev becomes First Secretary, Kosygin Prime Minister
1965	March	Plenum of central committee adopt new agricultural policies
	September	Adoption of economic reform measures; regional councils abolished, industrial ministries reinstated

Appendix 3

Membership of the Party

April 1917	80,000
March 1918	300,000
March 1920	732,000
March 1922	532,000*
May 1924	863,600 (of which 127,700 probationary†)
December 1927	1,236,000 (of which 549,000 probationary)
January 1934	2,810,000 (of which 935,000 probationary)
March 1939	2,478,000‡ (of which 889,000 probationary)
February 1956	7,215,000 (of which 420,000 probationary)
March 1971	14,455,000 (of which 645,000 probationary)

*Reduction due to removal of real or alleged careerists and corrupt elements.
†Applicants for membership undergo a period as probationary ('candidate') members.
‡Reduction due to great purge.

Appendix 4

Notes for Further Reading

HISTORY

E. H. CARR, *A History of Soviet Russia*. A multi-volume magnum opus, irreplaceable for the specialist. Ends in 1929 (Macmillan, 1950–71 and Penguin, 1966–73).

R. HINGLEY, *A Concise History of Russia* (Thames & Hudson, 1972). Illustrated, lively and accurate.

L. KOCHAN, *The Making of Modern Russia* (Cape, 1962). A very useful general survey of Russian history.

A. NOVE, *Economic History of the USSR* (Penguin, 1972). Mercifully short.

L. B. SCHAPIRO, *The Communist Party of the Soviet Union* (Blackwell, 1960, 2nd edn Methuen, 1970). The one-volume history of the party.

STALIN AND STALINISM

R. CONQUEST, *The Great Terror* (Penguin, 1971). Full and well-documented account of terrible years.

I. DEUTSCHER, *Stalin* (Penguin, 1970), remains a first-rate political biography.

N. KHRUSHCHEV, the so-called 'secret speech', in (*inter alia*) T. P. Whitney (ed.), *Khrushchev Speaks* (Univ. of Michigan Press, 1963).

E. GINSBERG, *Into the Whirlwind* (Penguin, 1968). The terror of 1937 admirably described by a victim.

N. MANDELSHTAM, *Hope Against Hope* (Collins and Harvill, 1971). The outstanding picture of Stalinist rule as seen by the best of the literary intelligentsia

R. MEDVEDEV, *Let History Judge* (Macmillan, 1971). The only comprehensive account written in Russia – but not published there – of what Stalinism was.

A. SOLZHENITSYN, *One Day in the Life of Ivan Denisovich* (Penguin, 1970).

A. SOLZHENITSYN, *The First Circle* (Fontana, 1970). Fiction of high literary and social merit.

A. SOLZHENITSYN, *The Gulag Archipelago*, vol. 1 (Fontana, 1974). First-rate 'documentary', not yet complete.

R. C. TUCKER, *Stalin as Revolutionary 1879-1929* (Chatto & Windus, 1974).

R. TUCKER (ed.), *Stalinism* (New York, 1977).

A. ULAM, *Stalin: The man and his era* (Allen Lane, 1974). Imaginative and controversial.

B. WOLFE, *Three Who Made a Revolution* (Penguin, 1966). Deals critically and vividly with Lenin, Stalin and Trotsky.

KHRUSHCHEV

C. LINDEN, *Khrushchev and the Soviet Leadership* (Baltimore, 1966). Sensible and clear account of the period 1957–64.

THE SOVIET SYSTEM

M. KASER, *Soviet Economics* (Weidenfeld & Nicolson, 1970).

D. LANE, *Politics and Society in the USSR* (Weidenfeld & Nicolson, 1972).

M. MCAULEY, *Politics in the Soviet Union* (Penguin, 1977).

M. MATTHEWS, *Class and Society in Soviet Russia* (Penguin, 1972).

J. MILLER, *Life in Russia Today* (Batsford, 1969).

A. NOVE, *The Soviet Economic System* (Allen & Unwin, 1977).

L. B. SCHAPIRO, *The Government and Politics of the Soviet Union* (Hutchinson, 1965).

Index

Names of places and soldiers mentioned only in the chapter dealing with the war of 1941–45 are not indexed.

Stalinism and After

27·40
48-52
63-72

ARCTIC OCEAN

Baltic Sea

Murmansk

Tallin
Riga 1
Leningrad
Arkhangel'sk

3
2

4
Minsk
Lvov
4

RUSSIAN SOVIET FEDER

Moscow

5
Kiev
Gor'kiy
Kazan

R. Ob'

Khar'kov
6
Odessa
Dnepropetrovsk
5

R. Dnieper

Volga

R.

Kuybyshev

Rostov
Krasnodar
Stalingrad
(Volgograd)

Astrakhan

Omsk
Novosibir

R. Irtysh

Sea

7
Tbilisi

KAZAKH SSR

Karaganda

Yerevan
8
Baku

Caspian Sea

Aral Sea

Syr Darya

TURKMEN SSR
UZBEK SSR

Tashkent

Frunze
11

Ashkhabad
Samarkand

Stalinabad (Dushanbe)
10

+ + + International Boundaries

- - - Soviet Socialist Republic Boundaries

-·-·- Western Inter-War Boundary of 1918-39

0   640   1280 km

For Ivo, Maddie and Oliver

CONTENTS

★ 1 ★

DANNY POWELL

Until 20 May, no one had taken Danny Powell very seriously. They liked him and they kind of guessed that he was extra special because they all knew he could run so blisteringly fast. Wow, could he run fast! Everyone knew he had the quickest pair of feet in the school. In fact, they all knew that Danny could run faster than anyone in any school in the whole of the United Kingdom.

Every summer it seemed, Danny would go to the UK School Games and come back champion. Whenever those UK School Games came round, the following Monday morning you almost knew that your school email inbox at Newham Secondary would deliver the same news: that Danny Powell had won the 100 metres. Again. This meant that he was the best young sprinter in the country. Still. Indeed, pretty much everyone who had ever met Danny knew that, one day, he would be a professional athlete.

But where the whole Danny story got a bit ridiculous

was when he told them that in the summer holidays after his A levels, he was going to beat Usain Bolt.

Oh, yeah, Danny? No one beats Usain Bolt. Usain Bolt is the fastest human being of all time. Dream on, Danny.

Danny hated the idea of being a show-off and so he had not intended to let it slip. He loved to run and he loved to win. It was, by far, the best thing in his life. But he never bragged. Not around school. Nowhere. He never wanted other people to think that he was a show-off, a swank. And so his dream of beating Bolt was one that he kept completely to himself. And if it wasn't for a robbery, from right under his nose, then it would have remained there.

It happened one day during school lunchtime. He wished it hadn't. And it was the stupid thief's fault. Such a stupid, dozy, hopeless thief. Danny was hanging around the school gates, the place he and his mate, loudmouth Anthuan, and a bunch of their mates in the sixth form always hung out at lunchtime.

No one saw the thief coming. He was probably only twenty years old, average in height and average in looks. He wore dark jeans and a dark T-shirt, but they only realized all that afterwards. At the time, all anyone realized was that with one slightly nervous and aggressive sweep of his arm, he had ripped off the shoulder bag that Jess had hanging loosely from her shoulder. He did it with such force that Jess, yelping in shock more than pain, fell to the ground.

Danny knew that it was wrong to get involved. *Keep your nose out of trouble*. That's what his father always told him. So he stood and, for about two seconds, he watched as the bloke hotfooted it down the pavement. A series of thoughts flashed through Danny's mind: *Should I let him go? Should I stay out of trouble? Might I get hurt? And should I stay here and look after Jess?* And then, in that very split second that he had persuaded himself to be cautious and avoid trouble, the thief stopped running and turned, and it seemed that he was smiling. He may just have been panting, out of breath, but from where Danny was standing it seemed that he had a triumphant grin on his face. And that was that. Danny was off.

The sight of Danny Powell at full speed is astonishing. He has a long stride and a natural balance, which combine into a beautiful elegance. So, when he is sprinting, it doesn't look as though he is trying hard – it hardly seems as though his feet touch the ground; it is more as if he is gliding. But, boy, does he move fast.

He flashed like lightning down the road. It was about two seconds before the thief turned again and realized that he was being pursued and, at that stage, his smile disappeared for good. Danny started closing on him quick and as the distance between them was rapidly disappearing, passers-by moved out of the way and stopped and stared. As Danny got even nearer, the difference between his speed and the thief's was so great, it was almost funny. The thief's arms were pumping hard, flailing desperately from side to side but, compared to Danny, he was going so slowly it was like he was running in treacle.

Danny got closer and closer: thirty metres away, twenty-five metres, twenty . . . Suddenly, he was almost able to touch him when the thief turned round, saw that he was beaten and dropped the bag.

And that was when Danny stopped running. He didn't want to catch the thief. What would he have done to him? Fought him? He had never fought anyone; he wouldn't know what to do.

So he just stopped running and picked up Jess's bag. And that was that. End of episode. At least so he thought.

The next day at Newham Secondary, they had school assembly. School assembly was held every Thursday and it was usually pretty dull. During school assembly, Danny and Anthuan and most of their friends would have their mobile phones out and would be busy texting each other. If you got caught with your mobile phone during assembly, it would be confiscated for the rest of the day. But hardly anyone ever got caught, at least not Danny or Anthuan; they were far too smart for that.

Up on the school stage stood the headmaster, Mr McCaffrey. As teachers go, Mr McCaffrey was OK. But he loved the sound of his own voice – and so he loved Thursdays and school assembly because that was his chance to be centre stage and do lots of talking. Mr McCaffrey also had a greying goatee beard that he seemed rather fond of even if he was slightly too old for it. He would stand and talk and stroke his goatee at the same time. Danny often wondered if Mr McCaffrey had any idea that barely anyone ever listened to a word he said.

Danny scrolled down the inbox of his phone. He was hoping for a text from Ricky, his brother. He adored Ricky, but Ricky was a student, away at university, and he never got in touch. Danny hated that. He missed Ricky. But he thought he might get a text from him today.

It was then, suddenly, that Danny's attention to his phone was ripped away. Anthuan gave him a hefty nudge in the ribs with his elbow. 'Dan,' he whispered, out of the side of his mouth. 'Listen up, Dan, he's talking about you.'

Anthuan was right. Up on stage, Mr McCaffrey was babbling on, as ever, but he was now babbling on about a robbery incident the previous day. *Oh no, please no!* thought Danny. He hated the idea of being the centre of attention.

'. . . and this thief thought he had got away with it,' was what Mr McCaffrey was saying, 'but he hadn't accounted for the fact that at Newham Secondary, we happen to have the fastest young schoolboy in the country. So well done, Danny Powell.'

Mr McCaffrey then started clapping and there was a flutter of applause around the school hall. Danny looked down, trying to avoid everyone's stares. But then Mr McCaffrey carried on: 'And so I would like to ask Danny Powell to come up here for a minute.'

Oh no! You can't be serious! thought Danny. But the headmaster was. And it was on stage that the day really took a turn for the worse.

'Danny,' Mr McCaffrey said, turning to him, 'well done. You have made us all proud.'

'Thank you, sir,' Danny replied.

'And here we are, at the start of the athletics season. Have you got any big plans?'

Danny felt flustered. *What should I say?* he thought. So he decided he may as well be honest – and he just said: 'Yes.'

'Would you fancy running in the Olympics?' Mr McCaffrey asked.

'Of course,' Danny replied. 'Who wouldn't?'

6

'Exactly,' said Mr McCaffrey. 'Good luck, Danny.' And Danny had just started walking off the stage when Mr McCaffrey said: 'One other thing, Danny . . .' So Danny stopped. '. . . I don't suppose you could beat Usain Bolt, could you?'

Danny paused. *What should I say? What should I say?* And before he could stop himself, he told the truth. 'It's going to be tough, but that's certainly the plan, sir.'

The second that Danny had let that sentence fly from his mouth, he wanted to catch it and take it back again. The school hall erupted with squeals and whistles and quite a lot of laughter. And Danny couldn't stand people laughing at him.

Five minutes later, when assembly was over, the school hall had emptied and the students had piled out into the open air, he was made to feel even worse. 'Dream on, Danny!' was the first comment that was flung his way. 'Danny, I hear Usain Bolt's really scared.' 'Danny, Bolt could beat you on one leg.' And: 'Danny, what planet are you on? Come back down to earth, you might enjoy it down here.'

Ha! Ha! Very funny, the lot of you, thought Danny as he turned left out of the school hall towards the classrooms. He hated people thinking he was arrogant. But what he hated the most was the idea that people didn't believe in him, that they should laugh at the very idea that he was going to beat Usain Bolt. *I'll prove them all wrong*, he said to himself. 'Bolt could beat you on one leg,' they said. How he wanted to ram those comments down their precious little throats.

For the rest of the day, Danny was not allowed to forget it. Most people were too scared to say anything, but he could see them smirking to each other.

Some were brave enough to comment. 'Usain's got no chance!' was one sarcastic comment. He hated that.

'Good luck against Bolt!' were the words of one younger boy. And he probably meant it, but Danny didn't like that either.

At the end of the school day, feeling thoroughly dispirited, Dan sought out the company of Anthuan. But that didn't turn out to be a very good idea either.

'Are you coming out to the movies tomorrow night, Dan?' he asked.

'I can't,' Danny replied. 'I've got to train, haven't I?'

'We're *all* going,' Anthuan said, slightly pleadingly, as if trying to play on Danny's conscience.

'I just can't,' Danny replied, shrugging. 'You know that. Training. I've got to train. I've *always* got to train.'

Anthuan seemed disappointed and went quiet. They walked out of the school gates together. And then Anthuan asked him a question that really surprised him. And the way he asked it suggested that he was slightly uncomfortable about it himself.

'Dan,' he said, 'do you really think you could beat Usain Bolt?'

Danny stopped walking, paused for a second and then answered: 'Ant, I know it sounds crazy, and I know I sound stupid when I say it. But this is my dream. The Olympics are coming. I've got a one in a million chance of beating that guy. So yes, I do think I have a chance. It's a slim one, but it's still a chance. What do you think?'

Anthuan looked down at the ground and furrowed his brow as if he was thinking seriously. 'I think you're my best mate in the world, Dan,' he replied slowly. 'And I don't want to be hard on you. But I hate seeing people laugh at you like they did today, you know that. So come on, Dan. You're so young still and maybe you should remember that. You could be out having fun tomorrow night, but you don't want to. Do you really think you're ready to race Bolt? I just can't help feeling that if you raced Bolt now, he'd have time to finish the race and eat a cheese sandwich before you came through the line.'

Dan looked at Anthuan with disgust. He felt angry and let down. 'Oh, right, I see. So not even my best mate believes in me. See ya.' And with that, he trotted off down the road and jumped straight on the 215 bus, leaving Anthuan standing alone.

Danny was furious. But, more than that, he was really upset. *Not even Ant believes in me,* he thought to himself. *I'll just have to prove him wrong too.*

★ 2 ★

THE OLYMPICS

If you are an athlete like Danny, then you have one dream, one massive dream that spills from side to side in your head like water in a glass. It washes over you and it never washes out; it dominates your thoughts and it gets in the way of the rest of your life. It can be a disaster for your schoolwork because it makes it so hard to concentrate on anything else. The Olympics. You spend every spare second of your life dreaming about the Olympics.

Sometimes Danny's dad, Roy, would catch Danny daydreaming and he knew instinctively what Danny was thinking about. 'Get on with your studies, my boy,' he would say. 'Forget the Olympics.'

'Don't know what you're talking about!' Danny would reply. But he was lying and he knew his father knew he was lying and so he would smile cheekily too.

It was impossible to forget about the Olympics. How could you forget about the Olympics when they were right here on your doorstep?

The summer Olympics were only two and a half months away. The London Olympics. London 2012. The greatest show on earth. That was what they sometimes called the Olympic Games. 'The greatest show on earth.' And here they were, the Olympics, in his very own city.

But the Olympics were not only in Danny's very own city, they were in his very own neighbourhood. Danny lived in east London, in a neighbourhood called Stratford. And the Olympics? They were heading for Stratford too. The Olympic Stadium, the very stadium where Bolt would be running, was barely three kilometres from Danny's house.

In fact, Danny had lived with the whole project from beginning to end. Every school day for the last four years, he would turn left out of his house in Widdin Street and head 200 metres to Anthuan's house, and together they would walk to Newham Secondary, taking a short detour via Bridge Road where they would witness first-hand the Olympics coming to life.

Bridge Road was on the edge of what seemed like a monstrously large building site. This was the huge plot of land that would be built into the Olympic Park. In Danny's mind, the Olympic Park was going to be the biggest playground in the world: it would have athletics, swimming, hockey, cycling, basketball. You name it, pretty much the entire Olympic Games was going to happen here.

At first, Danny and Anthuan could see nothing from Bridge Road because the entire building project was going on behind a high, blue fence. All they could tell was that the building site made a deafening noise and threw a haze of dust up into the air. But, around three years ago, things started to change. One day, when they were walking to school, they got their first glimpse of one of the new buildings, covered in scaffolding, poking its head above the fence, as if it was finally saying hello to the world. And this building simply got taller and taller, and as it neared completion, it became increasingly obvious that this was the main Olympic Stadium, the stadium for athletics, the stadium where Usain Bolt would run.

'Imagine Usain in that place,' Danny and Anthuan would say to each other, laughing. They could not believe their luck: that this was all going to take place here. And soon they had renamed the Olympic Stadium 'Bolt's Second Home'.

But it wasn't just Bolt's Second Home they could see. If they took another route, which afforded a better view into the park, they could see a whole team of buildings all slowly rising out of the ground until they were huge, gleaming, beautiful. And they were so close you could almost touch them. The aquatic centre, which was where the Olympic swimming and diving would take place, looked really cool; it had a strange, undulating roof that was designed to make it look like a stingray. And then there was the velodrome for the cyclists, the arena for basketball and a whole lot more. With some of the buildings, the boys had no clue what sport would be taking place there. But no matter, it was just so tantalizing to imagine the best athletes on the planet all coming here, right to their doorstep.

And to think that Danny's dad expected him to forget about the Olympics! Danny knew his A levels were important. But he also had a feeling, as if it was something in his blood and in his bones, that the Olympics were important too. Danny felt drawn to that Olympic Park, as if he was caught by some kind of magnetic force. Sometimes, when he was on his own on the way back from school, he would stand and stare at the park and allow himself to drift off in a long Olympic daydream.

But Danny's dad could hardly pretend that the Olympics weren't important. Danny's dad loved the Olympics. Every four years when the Olympic Games came round, he always made the entire family sit round the TV and watch it. First and foremost, they would watch the athletics, but they seemed to watch absolutely everything: the swimming, the gymnastics, the boxing, the judo, the wrestling, the taekwondo – all these weird different forms of fighting that seemed to be banned in the house but for which you could win medals at the Olympics!

Danny's mother loved the gymnastics. Danny's

father loved cheering on the Africans in the long-distance running events. Danny's older brother, Ricky, pretended that he wasn't interested, but, whenever the weightlifting was on, he would sit there watching, absolutely entranced, cheering on the big men from Russia and Bulgaria. No one quite understood why he suddenly became Russian or Bulgarian over the period of the Olympics, but there was no talking him out of it!

And Danny? For him it was simple. His first memory of the Olympics was when he was six, although he could remember them four years later and four years after that too. But he had a very specific recollection of one specific moment in each of the Olympics that he had seen. It was as if he had a special place in his mind for storing away the memories of one race, one race every four years: the men's 100 metres, the race to be the fastest man on earth.

And that was why he felt he already knew Usain Bolt. He had never met Bolt, never even seen him in the flesh, but, when he watched Bolt win the Olympics in Beijing four years earlier, he had been absolutely entranced. He had recorded the race on the TV and he must have watched it a hundred times since. More like a thousand times. He was mesmerized by Bolt's long stride and by the speed with which his feet left the ground. And he could not believe that Bolt was so much better in Beijing than everyone else, so much better that he had started celebrating his victory long before he had even got to the finishing line.

The night that Bolt had won the 100 metres in Beijing, Danny had found it hard to sleep. He kept on replaying the race over and over in his mind. At two o'clock in the morning, when he had pretty much given up trying to sleep, he had sneaked downstairs, switched on the TV and watched the race again. He watched it in slow motion; he watched it fast; he watched it with the sound turned down and with the sound turned up.

How did Bolt do it? That was the question rattling through Danny's mind.

But really there were other questions that he wanted answering: *Could I do it too? Could I come to the Olympics, when they are in London, and run that fast too? Would it be possible, here in London, for me to beat Usain Bolt?*

★ 3 ★

STEVE THE SPIKE

Danny stepped off the 215 bus, turned off the road, into the car park and towards the broad building ahead. This was his training facility, the place where his dream was allowed to grow. In school, they could laugh at his dream, but here is where it was nurtured. This is where it seemed real.

Danny had a regimented life: he would get up in the morning and go to school; after school he would go to training, then back home, supper, homework and bed; school, training, home, homework, bed. Over and over again: school, training, home, homework, bed, pretty much every single day. If you want to be Olympic champion, you have no alternative, at least that is what Steve the Spike told him.

And Danny liked listening to Steve. Steve was possibly both the smartest and the meanest coach in the world. Maybe the best coach in the world too. But he was probably the only person on the planet who really believed in him. Danny was eighteen; he was still at school, he hadn't even taken his driving test, and yet Steve completely and utterly believed that Danny could win the Olympics.

So he believed and trusted Steve. It didn't help having Anthuan telling him the opposite: don't train, don't go home to bed, come out to the movies with your mates. There were so many times that Danny wanted to do exactly what Anthuan told him. He wanted to go out with Ant and the others; he knew how much fun they had and he wanted that for himself too.

But he had a dream, and he was determined to follow it. And he knew that was more important.

When Danny arrived at the Lee Valley Stadium to train, he also knew he had to clear out of his head everything that was supposed to be inside his head at school: A levels, history, business studies, sports science and all the rest of it. He had to turn off one switch and flick on another. Turn off school and turn on running. Running fast. Every single second of his time down here at Lee Valley had to be devoted to that one single goal: training his legs to get from the start of a 100-metres race to the finish line as quickly as they possibly could.

Steve the Spike called their training centre 'The home of speed'.

'Feel the need for speed, Danny!' he would say. And almost every day his greeting to Danny would be, 'Hello, Speedboy.' That was his nickname for

18

Danny, Speedboy, and Danny liked it. 'Hello, Speed-boy,' Steve would say, 'you brought your speed today?'

But today, as Danny pushed open the door into the stadium, he knew he wasn't in the right frame of mind. He mumbled a 'Hello' to Gladys, the nice lady who worked on the reception desk, but he was distracted. He wasn't thinking about speed. In fact, he had probably left his speed behind. He was think-ing instead about Ant and what he had said about Usain Bolt and the cheese sandwich. And he could feel a deep sense of anger within himself. Ant had said that Usain Bolt could finish the race and eat a cheese sandwich before Danny came through the line!

The cheek of it, he thought to himself. But he hated the fact that this was making him cross. *How can Ant and a cheese sandwich make me so angry?*

'Hey, Speedboy!' Danny heard Steve's voice almost the second he walked through the door. It was loud and excessively enthusiastic. 'There are now seventy-one days to the Games. Are you ready to train hard?'

Danny rolled his eyes. 'Yeah, Spike,' he said unconvincingly. Steve the Spike was like a walking countdown clock; every single day that Danny came to training, Steve would tell him how long to go until the Olympics.

'Good!' barked Steve. 'Get changed, and then I

want to see you down in my office in five minutes. We've got plans to make. And then I'm going to kill you.'

Steve the Spike always seemed to have two things on his mind.

One: he always wanted to kill Danny. Every day, he said, he wanted Danny to die. Danny knew what he meant: he wanted to train Danny so hard that Danny's whole body would ache because of the pain and Steve wanted the pain to be so bad that Danny couldn't run any more, so bad in fact that he felt he was about to die. That, for Steve the Spike, was the definition of death. He wanted Danny to die, and then to rise again from the dead – a bit like Jesus, Danny thought, except he was pretty confident he could have beaten Jesus over 100 metres. But Steve wanted Danny to die and rise again every day, today, tomorrow and then the day after that. That was another thing that Spike liked to bark at Danny every day: 'Yo, Speedboy! You ready to die today?'

Two: planning. Steve loved to make plans. But the important bit was this: they were always good plans. Genius plans for becoming the fastest man in the world. That was why Danny was able to put up with Steve the Spike forever trying to kill him.

The point about Steve was that you had to understand his background; you had to know what he had gone through and where his nickname had come from. Back in the 1970s, Steve had been one of the fastest young kids in the country, one of the fastest young kids in the world. In fact, Steve then was pretty much like Danny now. And, like Danny, Steve had one dream, and that was to be the Olympic 100-metres champion.

But Steve's dream had come crashing down around him and was broken in the worst way imaginable. In 1982, Steve was selected for the British senior team for the first time ever, to run in the European Championships in Athens. This was a great moment for him: to represent his country on the athletics track made him feel so proud. It felt like the greatest day of his life, and yet he was only twenty-one and people who knew anything about running would say to each other: 'This boy has got a great future ahead of him.' What they thought was that Steve would run in Athens and probably do *quite* well, but they thought that two years later, when he was older and more experienced, he would go to his first Olympics and probably do *really, really* well.

But Steve never talked to Danny about Athens. He never discussed what happened there. Danny knew why. Everyone knew.

Steve got to the final of the 100 metres in Athens. He had done brilliantly to reach that stage, but he didn't leave it at that. In the final, he ran the race of his life and won the bronze medal. Not bad for a twenty-one-year-old. And there were stories in the newspapers with headlines like 'Steve sprints to medal triumph', 'Britain's new speed machine' and 'Britain's boy wonder'.

Four days later though came the accident that would end it all for him, a horrible, bloody, freak accident that no one had ever seen on the track before. It was the relay race and Steve was the second to run for the British team. When he was handing over the baton to the third British runner, he had got Great Britain into first place, but his mistake was that, having handed over the baton, he fell over. He was so exhausted from the effort that he just crashed to the ground. It was a stupid thing to have done and that is one of the many reasons why Steve hardly ever spoke a word about it to anyone.

Because, as Steve crashed to the ground, he fell in front of the Italian runner next to him. Giovanni Bongiorni was the Italian man's name. Steve had never forgotten it. Bongiorni was running at full pelt and had not had the chance to check his stride. He had probably not even seen Steve's right leg on the ground in his very path. And Bongiorni's left foot had come down on the back of Steve's leg and the spikes in Bongiorni's shoe tore a great gash down Steve's calf and into his Achilles tendon.

And that was the end of Steve's running career. And that was also why Steve was now so intense, why he cared so much, why he was so stressed sometimes, why he shouted, why he wanted Danny to die every day on the track. Because he did not want Danny to miss out on the very opportunity that should have been his.

After Steve's leg had been gashed on the track in Athens, he was treated at the side of the track by a British team doctor who gave him an injection to dull the pain and recommended that he be taken away to hospital, straight away. Steve was carried away on a stretcher, but, as he went, he had seen the doctor shaking his head slowly, with a dark look on his face.

The problem for Steve, as he would learn over the next week in hospital, is that the Achilles tendon is about the most important piece of kit that a runner needs. The Achilles transfers power and strength and information from the muscles in your leg to your feet and back again. Basically, if your Achilles isn't working, then you are not going to be much of a runner.

And that was why Steve never ran competitively again. The doctors never made his Achilles completely better. They tried, but Steve found that whenever he trained hard, the pain would come back, and when the pain came back, he could never find quite the same speed. And so he trained harder and harder, desperate to overcome the problem, but the harder he trained, the fiercer the pain, and the fiercer the pain, the harder it was for him to hit the same phenomenal speeds that once made him one of the fastest kids in the world.

It got to the stage where Steve would die in training every day. He would run himself so hard his whole body ached and his Achilles seemed to cry out to him: 'Stop! Please stop!' And so Steve would limp off the track, and then he would limp home, and then he would find that he was limping the next day too. In fact, Steve soon realized that he was going to limp for the rest of his life. And you can't hope to be the fastest sprinter in the world if you have a limp. So, for Steve, that was the end. He quit the sport. His dream was over.

And that was how Steve got his nickname, Steve the Spike. Or just Spike for short. To Danny, it seemed like a bad joke, but everyone seemed to call him that.

And that was also why Steve the Spike cared so much about Danny. He knew what Danny had put into his life as a runner. He knew the sacrifices that Danny was making. He knew that eighteen-year-old boys wanted to go out, hang out with their friends, go to the movies. And he knew that Danny almost always managed to say no. So it wasn't just that he liked Danny, he also admired him. And he wanted

Danny to achieve what he himself had never managed. He wanted it so desperately for him. And so pretty much every day, he went out with the intention of killing Danny on the track.

★ 4 ★

HOW TO BEAT USAIN BOLT, PART 1

Spike scratched the back of his head impatiently. He studied Danny. Danny had just walked into his office and he didn't look right. Spike knew from the look on his face that Danny hadn't brought his 'Speed-head' with him.

So he asked Danny what was up and Danny told Spike about school and the cheese sandwich and Spike laughed. Danny hated Spike laughing at him, but Spike continued laughing nevertheless. 'So those kids at school think you're slower than a cheese sandwich, do they?' he said, guffawing.

'No, Spike,' Danny replied tersely. 'They didn't say that.'

'What sort of cheese?' asked Spike, still laughing merrily at his own joke. 'We talking cheddar here, soft cheese, Stilton, or something runny, a cheese that runs, like a Camembert?'

'Very funny, Spike!' Danny replied, making it clear that actually it wasn't funny at all.

'I think I've got a new name for you, Dan,' Spike

continued, laughing to himself. 'No longer Speedboy but "The Camembert Kid".'

'Spike! Don't you get it? Not funny!'

'OK.' Spike stopped laughing immediately, stood up and changed his tone of voice. It was clear now that he was taking this seriously. 'I'm sorry your mates had a laugh at you today. But we've talked about this before, haven't we, Dan?'

'Yes, Spike.'

'No one thinks you've got a chance of beating Usain Bolt, do they?'

'No, Spike.'

'How many people in the entire world actually think you can beat him?'

'Two, Spike.'

'And are they your schoolmates?'

'No, Spike.'

'Who are they then?'

'You and me, Spike.'

'Exactly,' said Spike. 'You and me. No one else knows, and no one else will know that you've got a chance of beating Bolt until May the twentieth. That's the plan, isn't it?'

'Yes, Spike. That's the plan.'

20 May. It was all down to 20 May. In Spike's office was a poster he had made entitled 'Sunday 20 May'. And underneath in big letters was written: '68 days until the Olympics. The Day Danny Powell Shocks the World.' Danny laughed at that because

27

20 May was the day of the 100-metres final in the UK School Games and Danny didn't think that anyone would take the blindest bit of notice of what went on there. But Spike did. Spike's big plans revolved heavily around 20 May. That would be Danny's first 100 metres of the year and he expected Danny to run faster than Carl and Jesse. That was the plan.

The fact that Carl was fifty years old and Jesse died over ten years before Danny was born was irrelevant. Spike was obsessed with Carl and Jesse. He talked about them so much that they soon became known as Uncle Carl and Uncle Jesse. The reason that Spike was obsessed with Danny being faster than Uncle Carl and Uncle Jesse was because he believed that if you could beat them, then you had a chance of beating Usain too. Because the real identity of Uncle Carl was Carl Lewis and the real identity of Uncle Jesse was Jesse Owens and they were two of the fastest runners of all time. And if you could beat these guys, then you had a chance of beating Bolt.

All this was written in large letters on the poster on Spike's office wall. Towards the bottom of the poster, under 'The Day Danny Powell Shocks the World', there were pictures of Carl Lewis and Jesse Owens and a series of numbers next to their names. These numbers were the fastest times they had ever run over 100 metres, but they were not just their all-time personal fastest times, but their progression, their fastest time when they were twenty-one years old, their fastest time when they were twenty and their fastest time when they were eighteen.

Spike thought it was important that Danny knew how fast Uncle Carl and Uncle Jesse were when they were eighteen because then Danny could compare himself, almost as if he was running against them. He wanted Danny to come away from the UK School Games believing that he was faster than the two greatest legends of the sport.

So these are the facts that stared out at Danny from the poster on Spike's wall:

- Jesse Owens, aged nineteen, personal best: 10.40 seconds.
- Carl Lewis, aged eighteen, personal best: 10.29 seconds.
- Danny Powell, aged seventeen, personal best: 10.41 seconds.

Personal bests, it was all about personal bests. Or PBs as everyone called them. Every sprinter knows his PB. Every sprinter is trying to better his PB. Every sprinter wants his PB to be better than everyone else's. Your PB tells you and everyone else how good you are. At least that is the way Spike told it.

'The thing is,' said Spike, 'that the ignorant cheese-sandwich brigade at your school don't know what we know.' He was now pointing to the poster, jabbing the numbers on it with his index finger. 'That cheese-sandwich brigade don't understand that when you were seventeen, your PB was almost as fast as the great Carl Lewis when he was eighteen, and not far off the great Jesse Owens when he was nineteen.

'May the twentieth will be your first run of the season, your first 100 metres as an eighteen-year-old and I know how fast you can go and how much more speed you've got in your legs since last year. If you run a new PB on May the twentieth the way I know you can, then you'll have Uncle Carl and Uncle Jesse on toast. You'll sail past them. And that, Speedboy, will shove the cheese sandwiches right back down the throats of your mates at school.'

Danny was quiet. He loved hearing Spike talking like this. Spike gave him the confidence he needed. Spike made him want to prove everyone wrong, to show them just how good he was and how wrong they were, to wipe the clever little smiles off their faces, to show everyone at Newham Secondary that his dream wasn't so stupid after all. When Spike talked like this, it made Danny feel angry, excited, determined and, best of all, confident: confident that he could have his two favourite uncles on toast.

'Come on then, Spike,' Danny said, rising to his feet. 'Let's go train.'

'Good lad,' Spike said, punching him affection-
ately on the shoulder. 'I hope you've brought your
speed with you today. Because I am about to kill
you.'

★ 5 ★

TWO UNCLES AND A BROTHER

Spike may have lost his chance to be a sprinter, but he still loved the sport. In fact, Danny wondered if maybe the very reason that Spike loved it so much was because he never actually got his own chance. Either way, the end result was that Spike insisted that Danny showed respect for sprinting.

Spike loved the sport so much that he couldn't stand it when he saw young athletes who did not. Spike hated the new breed of cocky young guns that had risen to the top level and behaved as though they were God's gift. 'The swaggerers,' Spike would call them because of the way they would strut around as if they ruled the world.

So Spike loved Danny – because he saw that Danny was different; he was modest, humble and respectful of the sport. Danny was the opposite of a swaggerer. 'Speed is special,' Spike would say. 'If you've been blessed with it, you have to honour it.'

And that is why Danny came to know Uncle Carl and Uncle Jesse as if they really were his relations.

1. UNCLE JESSE

This guy was probably the coolest athlete of all time. At least in Danny's opinion he was.

Some days, when training had gone well, Spike would take Danny back into his office and show him a YouTube film of Jesse Owens. There were only a few short clips and Danny noticed that Spike's eyes would sometimes moisten as he watched them. Spike loved and admired Uncle Jesse so much it almost made him cry.

The film was only black and white and there were only clips from the 1936 Olympics. Those were the Olympics when Owens shocked the world. They were held in Berlin, the capital of Germany, three years before the Second World War, at a time when the power of Adolf Hitler, the German dictator, was growing fast. Those Olympic Games were strange because of Hitler, who wanted to use the Olympics to try to prove to the rest of the world how powerful he was and how his German nation was the best. Hitler saw sport and the Olympics as a mini-version of war; he wanted Germany to rule the world.

So Hitler was desperate for the German athletes to win absolutely everything. However, he had not accounted for Uncle Jesse who would turn out to be the star of the show. The 'king of kings', as Spike would call him.

Jesse Owens was a black American kid whose family were poor and whose grandfather had been a slave. When he was only seven, Jesse himself had to work as a labourer picking cotton in the fields. But, at school, it soon became clear that Jesse was something very special. And, when Jesse went to the Berlin Olympics, it also became clear that, despite whatever Hitler had hoped for, Jesse would be the star of the Games.

His first gold medal was for the 100 metres. This was the one that Spike kept showing Danny on YouTube. When you watch the clip, you can see a look of nervousness on Jesse's face at the start as he waited for the gun to fire. You can even see him swallowing; in fact, he seems to swallow so hard that he suddenly looks more nervous than before. But then the gun goes off and he is ahead almost immediately, and no one comes close to catching him.

After that, Jesse won the long jump, then the 200 metres. 'And don't forget,' Spike would remind Danny, 'that he not only won the 200 metres, he broke the Olympic record at the same time.' And Jesse then finished by being part of the American team to win the sprint relay.

'Four gold medals for Uncle Jesse,' Spike told him. 'And Hitler hated every single one of them. You know, Hitler hated Uncle Jesse's gold medals so much that he refused to congratulate him afterwards. Everyone else in Berlin seemed to love Uncle Jesse.

Whenever he was out on the streets, he was surrounded by fans who wanted his autograph. Some of them even found out where his room was and they posted their autograph books through the letter box when he was asleep.

'He was a true hero, Speedboy. But think about how hard it was: he was working in the fields when he was seven! How do you go from that to being Olympic champion? And he had Hitler against him too. He had people forever making his life hard. But he wouldn't let that stop him or get him down. What a triumph, and if you can be as good as Uncle Jesse, as noble and true to yourself and as fast too, then you could be a hero one day too.'

2. UNCLE CARL

The thing about sprinting – at least, this was another of the many things about sprinting that Spike liked to tell Danny – is that you are always chasing or being chased. If you catch the guy in front of you, then you can guarantee that there will be someone on your tail trying to catch you.

'You can never relax,' Spike told him. 'You can never rest on your laurels. The minute you sit back and think that you rule the world, that's the minute that someone else will come and catch you.'

Uncle Carl was amazing because he kept on going

and going. And, when he did get caught, he simply redoubled his efforts and got to the front again.

Uncle Carl was another black American. He grew up knowing all about Jesse Owens and all he wanted to do was copy him. And the thing about Uncle Carl was that when he decided he wanted to do something he pretty much always managed it.

So at the Olympics in 1984, when Carl was twenty-three, he competed in four events. They were the same four events in which Uncle Jesse had competed forty-eight years earlier. And, like Uncle Jesse, Uncle Carl won every single one of them.

But Uncle Carl was not done there. He won two more gold medals at the next Olympics in 1988, two more after that in the 1992 Olympics, and, in 1996, when he was thirty-five and everyone was telling him that he was too old, he proved them all wrong by winning one more, in the long jump. In fact, Uncle Carl won the long jump for four Olympic Games running.

Uncle Carl was also pretty cool, but in a strange kind of way. He was cool because he didn't care what people thought about him. He once appeared in an advert for car tyres wearing a pair of ladies' red, high-heeled shoes. 'Everyone thought he was crazy,' Spike said. 'Everyone laughed at him. But that's what I liked about him, Dan: he simply didn't care.'

And this was the lesson for Danny: be like Carl, be strong in your mind. People thought Carl was strange because of the ladies' red shoes, but he didn't let that bother him. And people thought he was too old to win an Olympic medal in 1996, but he didn't care about that either. He simply believed in himself.

As Danny left the Lee Valley Stadium later that afternoon, Spike again talked to him about Uncle Carl. 'Imagine what it would be like if Uncle Carl was at your school, Dan,' Spike told him. 'Uncle Carl was a real show-off. Can you imagine what those idiots in your class would think of him?'

'Sure can, Spike,' Danny replied.

'And do you think he would care?' Spike asked.

'Nope.'

'Do you think he would believe them if they told him that he was slower than a cheese sandwich?'

'Nope.'

'Exactly,' Spike said, putting a hand on Danny's shoulder. 'Look, Speedboy, if Carl was you, he'd be looking at those school kids and laughing to himself. He'd be thinking: "I will prove them wrong. I will wipe the smug little smiles off their cheesy faces. Because I know how good I am and they haven't got the faintest clue." Wouldn't he, Dan?'

'Yes, Spike.'

'Good. Now go home. Eat. Do your homework and go to bed. And before you go to sleep, think about Uncle Carl. Because when you start to think

like him, that's when you might start running like
him too.'

Carl and Jesse were never Danny's real uncles and
they never would be. But, though Ricky was Danny's
real brother, there were times when Danny wondered
if they were really related at all. Ricky was three
years older, but he now seemed a brother from
another lifetime.

Back in the old days, they used to be so close.
Ricky, Danny and Anthuan were a tight-knit group,
a trio of superstar athletes, all being killed together
on a daily basis by Spike. They would train together,
sweat together, watch athletics on the TV together,
talk about athletics together and then they would go
to sleep thinking about athletics too.

But people always go their separate ways. Anthuan
gradually grew bored of the regime; he didn't want
to train all the time, every afternoon. He wanted to
be free to hang out with their other mates. He slowly
drifted away and then, one day, Spike asked him very
gently if he really wanted to be an athlete or if he
wanted to quit. And he chose to quit. It wasn't an
angry exchange, but Spike had seen that Anthuan
had lost his love for the track, and, if you are trying
to run as fast as Danny and Ricky and Anthuan, you

either love it or you don't bother. It's all or nothing. And, when pushed, Anthuan was happy to choose nothing.

But Ricky was different. Ricky was astonishingly fast, immensely talented, probably the most talented of all three of them. Danny grew up always wondering if he would ever be as fast as him. He felt absolutely certain that his brother would one day run in the Olympics. He looked up to him; he loved him and he loved it that Ricky looked after him and encouraged him so much. But then Ricky said he was quitting too.

Danny hated that day. Ricky explained over and over: 'I'm going to university in Liverpool. I need to pursue my life, my career, and I can't do that here with Spike and, if I can't have Spike, I can't be a runner any more.'

And so Ricky left for Liverpool, but it was strange. It didn't seem that he was just a couple of hundred miles away; it seemed instead as if he had gone to the other side of the world. Ricky rarely called home and he hardly ever texted. Their parents said they were proud of him: the first member of the family ever to go to university, and he was probably working too hard to call. But that wasn't quite good enough for Danny.

And, as Danny grew older and faster, the silences grew and the bond between Ricky and him just faded further. After every race, Danny would always text Ricky to tell him the result and his time. He thought that, if nothing else, they would always be bonded by their love for athletics. But rarely did he get a reply.

There were times when Danny just felt like giving up on his big brother. But he loved him too much and he wanted Ricky to love him back. So he resolved not to give up, never to stop. So he made it his own private rule: *after every race you ever run, always, always text Ricky*.

That was why he was hoping for a reply from Ricky today. *Always text Ricky*. So he had texted Ricky yesterday to tell him about his race with the thief. He thought Ricky might like that. But no, no reply.

Ricky may have gone quiet, but one day, maybe, he'd turn the volume up again.

★ 6 ★

FRIDAY NIGHT FEVER

Friday nights are meant for fun. That is what Ant told Danny. Ant was telling him this a lot these days. Maybe he was right.

These were Danny's thoughts as he sat at his desk in his bedroom with a pad full of history revision notes on his right and a book about Hitler's rise to power to his left. This was one of the subjects he enjoyed most because it helped him understand Uncle Jesse a little better, but still: history revision or the movies? He knew where he would rather be.

He looked at his phone and the last text from Ant, forty-five minutes ago:

> We're going to be meeting at the usual place if you change your mind.

'Love to,' Danny replied. 'Same old answer.'

The same old answer was this: I have two priorities, the two As: A levels and athletics. Unfortunately, nothing else gets a look-in.

After he left school, Danny's parents expected him

to go to university like Ricky. His father always wanted him to be like Ricky. Danny quite wanted to be like Ricky too, but give up running? Never.

Danny looked at the history book. When exams came round, he hoped he would get the chance to write about 1936 and Hitler's Olympics. Surprise, surprise, this was his specialist subject. He loved the story of Jesse Owens in the long jump: how Hitler looked down upon Owens's victory with disgust, but how the German who won the silver medal, Luz Long, came up to Owens and warmly congratulated him. That was a brave thing that Long did. Just briefly, Owens and Long then became friends – and, a few years later, Long would die in the Second World War. And, in the years that followed, Owens made an effort to stay in contact with Long's family. Amazing story.

Danny wondered about the Olympics. *If I go, will I have a story? Will I go? And what will Usain Bolt be like?*

Danny looked again at his revision notes. *Come on, get on with your work!*

But it's hard to work when you are running the biggest race of your life the next day. Spike was going to pick him up because his parents couldn't make it. Usually, they travelled all round England to watch him in action, but not on this occasion – because they had already gone up to Liverpool to see Ricky. It was Ricky's birthday.

Ricky's birthday versus the biggest race of your life – what's more important? *Unfair question*, thought Danny. *After all, it's not even as though Mum and Dad really know exactly what tomorrow is all about.*

Danny looked again at his revision notes. *Come on, get on with your work!*

★ 7 ★

20 MAY

No one else knew that 20 May was so important. No one had a clue. They certainly did not know that Danny Powell's coach had a poster of it on his wall.

The day before, the Saturday, Spike and Danny had driven up to Sheffield in Spike's rather uncool, blue Ford Focus. Danny was unusually quiet, though that wasn't because of the nerves but because of the texts he was getting from Anthuan.

> **You missed a great night last night.**

And:

> **Dead cool movie.**

And then a while later:

> **Good luck in Sheffield. I know how important it is to you.**

But Danny did start to feel nervous too. He became aware of himself whenever he swallowed – like Uncle Jesse. And then he told himself that he didn't care – like Uncle Carl. And afterwards he felt a little better.

The UK School Games was the biggest school sports event in the whole of the year. Danny thought it must be like a mini-Olympics. There were thousands of competitors and pretty much every single competitor seemed to have a coach or a parent with them, or two parents, or even the whole lot. And every single boy and girl there felt that this was the biggest day of their lives.

The Don Valley Stadium in Sheffield was an awesome venue for the athletics. It could seat 25,000 spectators. Danny found himself blinking in amazement as he and Spike walked in. And then he swallowed and felt that nervousness run through him again. But swallowing is all right – at least that is what he told himself. That is what Uncle Jesse did, and he was the king of kings.

The day before a race, the night before, even a few hours before it, Danny would feel nervous. And that was when he and Spike would play chess, whenever possible, about three hours before a race. They would go to the venue, sit down somewhere quiet and Spike would bring out the chessboard. This was Spike's way of helping Danny take his mind off the race, to kill the nerves a bit. And Danny liked this; he loved going head to head with Spike on the chessboard and watching Spike getting competitive, so desperate and determined to win. He had never, ever beaten Spike at chess. Not once. But defeat on the chessboard seemed to set him up perfectly for victory on the track.

Danny liked the routine and the way it helped him. It went like this: nerves, chess, less nerves, warm-up, no nerves.

As the race got close, Danny seemed to change. He liked this change; it was as if he was becoming a different person, as if he was changing from Danny Powell into Speedboy. He would feel less and less nervous and more and more confident. He felt belief sweeping through him. He felt sure he could win.

There were now about two minutes until the start of the race. When you stand at the startline of a race like this, the whole world seems to stand still. At least that is what Danny always felt. You know that the crowd is large and you know they are making a lot of noise, but you don't hear anything. All you hear is your heart beating.

Danny sat down on the ground to try and compose himself. There are eight people in a 100-metres final and Danny thought, when he looked hard at all the other seven, that he could detect an element of nervousness in all their faces, in the way they were behaving. *Good*, he thought, *because a nervous athlete is more likely to make mistakes.*

Danny knew five of the other seven already; he had raced them enough times before and he was pretty confident he could beat them. And his PB was better than all the other seven lined up here. He hadn't lost a race against other boys his own age for four years, so why start now?

He looked over to Jimmy Lewis, the Welsh kid. Jimmy was tying and untying his shoelaces. He tied them again, then untied them and then tied them again. Jimmy always did this; he said it was a nervous habit that helped him concentrate. But it made Danny laugh; Danny liked Jimmy, but he was also wary of him because he knew that Jimmy was good, probably his biggest threat. He knew that Jimmy, on a good day, could push him. But he also knew that he had one thing that Jimmy wanted: a brilliant start.

Jimmy was taller than Danny and had longer legs and a longer stride. Theoretically, Jimmy should have been brilliant. But if you are going to be a world-class sprinter, then your reactions have to be razor-sharp; the very millisecond that the gun goes to start the race, you have to be powering off, your legs pumping hard to try and build your speed.

But while Jimmy's start was good, Danny's was brilliant. It is vital to start explosively quickly and Danny always exploded like a rocket.

He knew the race routine so well he could do it with his eyes closed. At the start of a race, when they announce 'On your marks', you step forward to the line and put your feet into your blocks – the steel blocks screwed into the ground. Then you wait, rest your feet in the blocks, try to be calm, tense but calm, and get that feeling that you are a coiled spring. And then, when the gun goes for the start of the race, you unleash the spring; you push off from the blocks with all the power you can summon.

The power of Danny's spring was immense and he knew it. Today he would have to be as powerful as ever.

But here is why 20 May was so important. At least this was how Spike had explained it, over and over again. It wasn't about winning the race – though that would of course be nice. It was all about the time in which Danny could win it. It was about how fast he could be. Because Danny's PB over 100 metres was 10.41 seconds and today he needed to go under 10.20 seconds. Because if he got under 10.20 seconds, then he would qualify to run at the British Olympic trials. And if he finished first or second in the British Olympic trials, then he would get a place in the Great Britain team for the Olympics.

Simple. Or maybe not. But that was the plan.

As those final seconds before the race ticked away, Spike whispered in Danny's ear, 'Good luck, Speed-boy. Your Olympic dream starts here.' And Danny knew exactly what he meant.

My Olympic dream! That was the thought racing through Danny's head. *Bring it on!*

'On your marks.'

There was the loud announcement, interrupting Danny's thought pattern and bringing all the runners to the startline. Danny went to his lane, crouched down in the starting position, put his feet back into the blocks and looked ahead down the track.

'Set.'

This was the last call before the gun. Danny raised himself slightly, ready to burst out of his blocks.

Bang!

The gun went and all eight runners burst out of their starting positions.

Bang!

The gun went again.

Again? Not again! Please not again.

But it had. That was the second gun blast that every sprinter feared.

So Danny stopped running and the other seven runners around him stopped too. They all knew what happened next and they all feared it.

Someone was going to be disqualified.

That is the horrible, harsh reality of sprinting at this level. You have to have those razor-sharp reactions; you have got to move like lightning the very split-second that the gun has been fired. But a fast start is so hugely important that sometimes people just get it wrong. Almost every first-class sprinter that has ever lived has got it wrong once or twice in their career. It is called a 'false start' – which means that you have started running before the gun has gone off.

It's a horrible mistake, but so easy to make – you're there in your blocks, poised, the adrenalin is pumping;

you're nervous, excited, like a wound-up coil ready to be sprung. And so sometimes the springs go early – before the gun. You go and then the gun goes after you. And the new rules in Danny's sport are so unforgiving, that one false start means the end. Disqualification. You are not allowed to run the race. It is an excruciatingly horrible way to lose.

That is why the sport is so hard. Because you can train all year, you can make all those sacrifices – and then you can waste it all on one tiny mistake.

And so when Danny and the other seven in the 100-metres final in the Don Valley Stadium heard that second bang, they all thought: *Oh, please, please, let it not be me.* Danny was pretty sure that it wasn't him. But he also knew the facts of the matter: *If I have false-started, then that's my Olympic dream over here and now.*

He walked slowly back to the startline and, just before he got there, there was a stadium announcement: 'False start. The runner in Lane Two. Lenny Passmore is disqualified.'

Danny turned to watch Lenny. He had seen him a couple of times before. He seemed a decent guy. But he had never seen him like this: angry, disbelieving and crying. Big tears rolled down his face. He refused to leave the race. He shouted at one of the officials. He protested his innocence. But then, eventually, he was led away; his hopes and dreams left in tatters on the track.

And then there were seven. Back on the startline again. Trying to concentrate again. Trying to forget about Lenny Passmore and the fate of the false-starter. Trying to run the race of their lives.

'On your marks!'

'Set.'

Bang!

This time the gun went only once.

Danny felt confident and strong. A good, powerful start. But what he hadn't expected was that Jimmy's start would be even better.

Never look at your rivals. Never look to one side or the other. Always look ahead. That was one of the key rules that every young sprinter learns before they even become teenagers. But Danny didn't need to look at his rivals to know, thirty metres into the race, that Jimmy was ahead. Jimmy had got the best start of his life. *Jimmy's in front of me. What's Jimmy doing there?* The thought raced through Danny's mind.

But the 100 metres is so quick and so fast that you barely have time to think. You just have to concentrate. *Pump the knees high. Concentrate. Feel the speed.*

At the sixty-metre mark, Danny was neck and neck with Jimmy. He felt he was flying, as though his feet were barely touching the ground. *Come on, Dan, pump the knees, high and hard.* At eighty metres, he wasn't sure if he was ahead. He felt Jimmy right by him.

Danny powered on through the line. *I've got it*, he thought. *I've definitely got it.* By centimetres, he was the champion. Again.

But that hardly mattered. What mattered was the time on the big scoreboard clock. And the clock showed that he had just run the 100 metres in a time of 10.17 seconds. He had smashed his own PB. He had beaten both Uncle Carl and Uncle Jesse too. By quite some way. But, most importantly, he had run fast enough to qualify for the Olympic trials.

Danny collapsed on to the ground and looked up at the sky. *The Olympic dream was still alive!* And there was a massive smile on his face. He felt the warm rays of the sun upon him. Momentarily, he felt very, very happy. *The Olympics! Usain Bolt!* The thoughts started charging through his mind – until he was interrupted by a loud Welsh voice.

'Oy! You! Superstar! Get up, man!' It was Jimmy Lewis. 'Get up, man! You must be the fastest oaf on the planet!'

Jimmy held out his hand to Danny who grabbed it and Jimmy hauled Danny back up to his feet. 'Well done, Dan! Great run,' Jimmy said.

'I thought you had me there, Jim,' Danny replied.

'Yeah, best start of my life and I still couldn't beat you.'

Danny looked up at the scoreboard. Their times had vanished from the screen. 'What time did you do, Jimmy?' he asked.

'I did a personal best, a great big juicy PB,' he replied. 'Can you believe it? 10.19 seconds!'

Danny swivelled round and put his hands on Jimmy's shoulders so he could look him straight in the face. 'You know what that means?' Danny asked.

'Yeah,' Jimmy replied nonchalantly. 'It means you're still faster than me.'

'No, Jimmy, you nutter!' Danny said. 'Listen. 10.19 seconds. You've qualified for the Olympic trials. You and me, Jimmy, Olympic trials! We could be going to the Olympics!'

'And you call me a nutter!' Jimmy replied. 'Try looking in the mirror and saying that and you will realize how stupid it sounds.'

'I do say it,' Danny replied. 'Almost every day. And it doesn't sound stupid at all.'

★ 8 ★

SERIOUS SPIKE

By the time Spike had dropped Danny home, it was late. They had not hung around the Don Valley Stadium long because they knew they had a big drive ahead of them. They simply waited for Danny to collect his medal, grab a quick shower and then off they went, laughing and cheering down the motor-way for all of about twelve minutes.

Spike wasn't into celebrations. He didn't like the applause or all the patting on the back. But Danny didn't care. He got into Spike's Ford Focus and didn't stop talking. He talked about the start of the race, the middle of the race and the end of the race. He talked about the forthcoming Olympic trials and then he talked about the Olympics and then he talked about Usain Bolt. He was so excited he could hardly be bothered to notice that he was doing all the talking and it was Spike who kept his eyes glued to the road, barely registering the triumph that his Speedboy had just pulled off.

'Come on, Spike!' Danny said eventually – after

about twelve minutes of non-stop gassing. 'Enjoy the moment.'

'No,' Spike replied. 'You enjoy the moment because you're entitled to. But me? I can only think ahead. I'm pleased with the way you ran today, Dan. But I won't lie to you. I'm pleased, but only *quite* pleased. I'm a long way from being *very* pleased. You made a couple of mistakes out there today, Dan. Your start wasn't good. Jimmy Lewis nearly had you. In fact, your start was very average indeed. But you ran a good time; you got the time you needed. So that's why I'm pleased.'

'So can't we enjoy that for more than twelve minutes, Spike? What's the problem?' Danny asked, a bit confused.

'The problem is this, Dan. You've just done the easy bit. You've qualified for the Olympic trials. That's the easy bit. But you cannot afford to celebrate as if the job's been done. It hasn't. It just gets harder from here. The Olympic trials will be harder than today, much harder. And then the Olympics? Well, you haven't the faintest clue what that will be like. You ran well today, Dan, but you've got to get so, so, so, so much better.'

And that was Spike through and through. Danny wasn't surprised, just a bit miffed. *What more can I do?* he thought to himself. *Am I supposed to train any more? Because I can't. I do not have enough hours in my day. Must I make more sacrifices? I have no more to make.*

55

So they drove on in silence. Danny texted Ricky with his news: the victory, his new PB and the qualification for the Olympic trials. He wondered to himself, *What is the point?* but he sent the text nevertheless.

He received another text from his mum:

Come on, Dan! Tell us what happened. Your father and I are desperate to know.

'Home soon,' Danny replied. 'Will tell all then.' Danny laughed to himself; he loved his parents, but he also loved to tease them. And then he plugged himself into his iPod, sat back and tried to replay the race in his mind. He liked doing that.

But any remnants of joy that survived the three hours in Spike's Ford Focus would soon be stamped out altogether. At 10.45 p.m., Spike dropped Danny off, shook his hand meaningfully and said to him in a serious voice, 'Well done, Dan. Honestly, well done. The dream is still alive.'

But then Danny put his key into the door of his house and soon realized that he may as well not have bothered with the dream at all.

★ 9 ★

A LEVELS OR OLYMPICS?

Danny's parents had got back from Liverpool earlier and waited up for him. They were sitting in the front room having a cup of tea. They were all fidgety and excited because they didn't know the result of the race and the minute Danny walked in, they both got to their feet. Danny's mum rushed over to him and took his bag, his dad stood stock-still and they both said in unison: 'How did you go? How did you go?'

'Not bad,' Danny replied, nodding his head, the big smile back on his face, playing it slightly cool. 'Not bad!'

'Oh, come on,' said his mum frustratedly. 'Spill the beans. Your father and I have been dying to know. Why didn't you text me? You cruel boy!'

So Danny sat down on the sofa in the front room and talked them through his race from beginning to end. He told them about the nightmare false start, about Jimmy, the start, about how he chased Jimmy and caught him, and about his time. His personal best, his new PB, 10.17 seconds. And throughout neither his mum nor his dad said a single word.

And finally he knew it was time to tell them what this all meant. He had not dared tell them before because he never wanted to let them down. He never wanted to promise anything he couldn't deliver. So he had kept it to himself that he thought he could run in the Olympics. But now was his chance. Danny felt excited and proud. He paused and then started speaking.

'The dream goes on.'

'What do you mean, Dan?' his father replied.

'You know what's going to happen now?' he said, sitting forward in the sofa. 'You know that magnificent Olympic Park just a few hundred metres away from us? You know the big stadium? The one where they'll hold all the athletics in the Olympics? The one that Anthuan and I, when we're messing around, call "Bolt's Second Home"?'

'Yes,' his parents replied in unison.

'Well, I'm going to run there in three weeks' time.'

'How come?' they asked, still in unison and slightly overexcited.

And so Danny explained. He explained first about the Olympic trials and about the qualifying time that was needed to run in them. With 10.17 seconds, he would be able to run in the trials. In three weeks' time, right here in the Olympic Stadium. And if he came first or second in the trials, then he would qualify for the Olympics.

Danny's mum seemed thrilled. She stood up and sat down again. Then she stood up again. She didn't know what to do with herself. So she sat down next to Danny. 'You clever boy!' she said, kissing him on the forehead. 'I am so proud of you. So, so proud.'

But Danny's dad did not respond in the same way. Not at all. In fact, he just stayed seated and said nothing. When Danny's mum realized that he wasn't sharing her joy, she went quiet and both she and Danny looked at him as if waiting for an answer.

'What is it, Dad?' Danny asked. 'I'm going to run in the Olympic Stadium. That's kind of cool, isn't it?'

'I just need a bit more information,' said his dad.

'OK, what do you need to know?'

'Well,' his dad said, slowly and seriously. 'These Olympic trials are a big deal, right?'

'Right.'

'Are they the biggest deal of your whole life? Will this be the biggest and most important race you have ever run?'

'Oh yes, without a doubt.'

'And,' his dad paused and carried on, 'because you are proud and because you've worked hard for your success as a sprinter, I take it that you'll be training hard for these trials, yes?'

'Absolutely. Spike is going to be killing me in training pretty much every day.'

'Right.' His dad then stopped and shook his head as if something was wrong.

'What is it, Dad?' Danny asked. He was now completely confused.

His dad said nothing and the silence was so complete that you could hear the clock ticking on the mantelpiece. Then, eventually, he sat forward and continued: 'OK. A couple more questions. One: while you've been up in Sheffield winning running races this weekend, what have your mates been up to?'

'I don't know,' Danny replied. 'Revising, I guess.'

'Revising for what?' his dad asked.

'For A levels.'

'And, Danny, when are your A levels?'

Danny's heart began to sink. He could see where his father was taking this conversation and he didn't like it. 'They start in two weeks' time and they finish the week after the trials,' he replied.

'And you want to do the trials?' His dad stood up and looked out at the street. He was now talking to Danny with his back turned. 'I'm sorry, Danny, but I just don't get this. You have the biggest, most important exams in your life coming up and you want to go and run? You're facing a set of exams that may influence the future course of the whole of your life. If you do well – and you should do well, you deserve to do well – you'll go to university. And you want to spend your every spare minute up at Lee Valley being killed by Spike?'

Danny looked at his mother for help, but it was clear he wasn't going to get it. She gave him a weak and apologetic smile.

'Dad, I can do both,' Danny replied.

His dad sighed deeply, paused and then turned back to Danny. 'Dan, you know that we love you and you know that we support you and we have so much admiration for the work and love that you put into your running. You know that, don't you, Dan?'

'Yes, Dad.'

'But you know, and I know, that you cannot do both. If you do both, you'll do neither to your best. Do you want to run and not win? Do you want to sit your exams and not do your very, very best? I don't think you do, Dan. If you study hard for your exams, then you won't have time to train and you never win races like that. And, if you train hard, then you won't have time to study and you'll screw up the exams.'

There was another prolonged silence. Danny didn't know what to say. Eventually, his father started speaking again. 'I'm sorry, Dan, I'm really sorry. But your exams have got to come first.'

'And the Olympics?'

'I know you want to run in the Olympics. That's always been your dream. But not these Olympics!

The Olympic Games will come round again in four years' time.'

'But they won't be here. They won't be right on our doorstep.'

'I know, Dan. I know.'

'But Dad! I could do both. I promise I could do both. I swear I can.' There was now a slightly desperate tone to Danny's voice. 'I'll do nothing else for three weeks: train and study, train and study. Nothing else, Dad. Nothing else. That's all I do anyway.'

An awkward silence now filled the room.

Then his father spoke again. 'Look at your brother Ricky, Dan. Look at him, a successful young man studying at university. Do you think he would be where he is if he'd decided to go running during his A levels?'

'Ricky?' Dan couldn't believe that his father was using Ricky to make his point.

'Yes, Dan, you don't get where Ricky has got by being a part-time student.'

'But I don't want to be like Ricky. He gave up running. I can't give it up. I'm a runner. I can't change that.'

His father paused again. 'Danny, do you want to go to university?'

Dan sighed. He was in a corner and he could see there was no way out of it. 'Yes,' he said wearily.

'Well then . . .' his father said quietly. He knew his point had been made.

An awkward silence ensued. They could hear the mantelpiece clock ticking again and the noise of a car engine out on the street. And Danny didn't know what to say; he didn't know what to do. He had never considered this. Never had he ventured to think that his dad would take against him. He felt stupid. He felt as though his dad was ripping something important away from him and he felt really, really angry. This was his life, his dream. He knew his dad was right; he knew that his A levels were important. But he was absolutely, 100 per cent convinced that he could do both.

'You've got to give me a break on this, Dad,' he said quietly, pleadingly.

'I cannot tell you how much I would like to,' his dad said. 'But I can't.'

'Mum?' Danny asked, hopeful that she might take his side.

But his mother slowly shook her head. She had a sad look on her face and eventually spoke: 'I'm sorry, Dan. But you know your father's right.'

Danny looked at his father, as if he had one last hope, and then back to his mother, as if she might provide it instead. But he got the same negative reaction from both. At that point, Danny could keep calm no longer. He was furious and he leaped to his feet.

'Right!' he shouted at his parents. He even surprised himself with how loud and angry he sounded. 'Have it your way. It's over. The dream is finished. My life, my dream. Finished!'

'Come on, Dan!' said his mum, trying to reassure him. 'It's just one Olympics. There'll be more. You'll have another chance.'

'No!' he replied, louder even than before. 'You don't get it, do you? This is my chance. Now. Right now. I might never be this good again. I might be injured in four years' time. I might not be so fast. I might be fat and overweight. I don't know what I might be. All I know is that now I am ready. Now is my time. And you two are denying me the dream of my life. Thank you very much indeed!'

And, with that, he walked straight over to the front door, stepped outside and slammed it loudly behind him.

★ 10 ★

DREAM OR REALITY?

It was cold outside, but Danny didn't feel it. All he felt was anger and frustration. And confusion. He started walking down the street, but he didn't know where he was going. Then he started running and he still didn't know where he was going.

And all the time, round and round and round in his head, there kept spinning the same nagging questions. *What's more important: A levels or Olympics? Studies or sport? Going to university? Or going to the biggest and best athletics meetings in the world and earning a living from it?* And there then followed more questions: *If someone offered me a deal where I could beat Usain Bolt and be Olympic champion, but, at the same time, failed all my A levels – would I take that? Was that worth it?* And then came another question: *Am I just kidding myself? If Usain Bolt can finish the 100 metres and then eat a cheese sandwich ahead of me, then maybe this whole debate is a colossal waste of time and energy.*

But one thing was certain: to his father, there was no confusion. A levels came before Olympics. End of story. Simple. And that then led to the other thought bouncing round Danny's mind: *Maybe Dad is right . . .*

Danny's dad – Elroy, or Roy to most people – was the kind of guy that everyone respected. He had a few good friends, but more noticeable was the respect that he commanded. Whatever he talked about, he always spoke wisely. Sometimes he wouldn't say much, but, when he did speak, he had this presence and people would listen. He seemed to have authority. He was straightforward, logical, level-headed – in other words, he was everything that an eighteen-year-old boy with crazy Olympic dreams didn't need right now. He was so infuriatingly sensible, Danny felt he wanted to throttle him.

But Roy's authority was well earned. He had not had an easy life. He was born in Jamaica, the very same Caribbean island that Bolt himself came from. But Roy had no memories of Jamaica because, when he was three years old, his parents came to London in search of work and a new life. Except Roy's father found that he didn't like the work or the life and so, within a year, he went back home to Jamaica. And that was the end of his father. His father had said he would come back soon, but he never did. Not so much as a flying visit. His mother, Juanita, kept photographs of him for Roy to look at, to remind him where he came from. But neither Juanita nor Roy ever heard from him again.

So Roy was brought up by Juanita, and Juanita alone. She worked hard to give him the food and clothing and the love he required and it was through her that he learned the lessons that would forever guide him: that the skills required to build a good home and a happy life were hard work and honesty.

And, as Danny wandered through the streets that night, he began cursing Juanita. *Was it her fault that he had a father who was so completely and utterly and unswervingly sensible? Was it her fault that his father wanted to stop him going to the Olympics?* He smiled to himself at the thought of Juanita – his splendid, loving grandmother. She had died when he was ten, but he treasured her memory dearly. She would have loved to have seen him running in the Olympics, here on their doorstep. So he couldn't and wouldn't blame her. And, come to think of it, it was hard to blame his dad too.

It was now nearly midnight and, without really thinking about where he was going or what he was doing, Danny found himself on Bridge Road, the best spot in Stratford, where he and Anthuan would come to stand and gaze at the enormous Olympic Park. Danny stopped now and stared. There were a few lights on in the park and he found himself imagining what it would be like on 27 July when the Olympic Games finally started. *What would it be like to be there? Sixty-eight days to go. What would it be like to be in the main Olympic stadium running the final of the 100 metres? And would his father come to watch?*

His father had always loved watching him run. When they were small, his father used to take the two boys to West Ham Park and race them. They would set up mini-racetracks, from the cycle path to the tree, to the tree and back again. Ricky v. Dad, Danny v. Dad, Ricky v. Danny – that was the one that Danny really liked, the one he tried so hard in. Anything, anything to beat his brother, but he could never come close.

And sometimes his father would take off his watch and time the boys separately and then coo in admiration at how fast they had gone. 'One more time, Dad! One more time! Let us try and break the record,' would be his and Ricky's excitable cries to their father and he would laugh at their never-ending supply of energy. Danny loved those memories.

But they were too precious. His father would only take them running when work allowed him to. His father always put work first. He had worked all his life in the Royal Mail and he was proud of the way he had done it. He had started as a postman. And then, after a few years, he was offered a job in the sorting office. He was good in the sorting office – his boss noticed how hard he worked and how people around him liked to work with him – and so Roy got promoted again and put in charge of a team of workers. And, eventually, he became the boss of the whole branch. And now he had forty-five people working under him. They all liked and respected him. And Roy never wanted to work anywhere else; he liked being loyal to his job; he liked knowing that every month he was going to be able to provide his family with more than they needed. He liked safety, security and stability.

In other words, everything that Roy liked was the opposite to everything that Danny wanted to do with his life right now. Roy liked safe and sensible, but Danny wanted to take a chance, the chance of a lifetime. He knew that running in the Olympics wasn't sensible. He knew that his father's attitude was probably the correct one. But he didn't want to let the dream go. He couldn't. This was the Olympics. His Olympics. On his doorstep.

As Danny stood on Bridge Road, looking over at the Olympic Park, he made up his mind. There and then he decided. He couldn't and wouldn't let his father stop him running. He had to run. He had a dream and nothing was going to stop him pursuing it.

★ 11 ★
THE PLAN

Danny stood out in the cold dark of the night, throwing small pebbles up at Anthuan's bedroom window. It was now half past midnight and he didn't want to wake Ant's parents. He threw two, three, four stones and then a dim light came on in the room and a hand was shuffling around at the curtains, eventually drawing them back. Ant's face peered out and he saw Danny standing in the street. Twenty seconds later, the front door opened and Ant ushered Danny in.

'What on earth are you doing here, Dan?' he asked.

'It's a long, long story,' Danny replied. 'Can I come in?'

'Of course you can.'

'Can I stay the night?'

Ant looked concerned. 'Sure, no prob.'

'I need your help.'

'Come on then. But quiet though.'

So they crept upstairs. Ant had a spare mattress and a sleeping bag under his bed which Danny had slept on numerous times before. And, when Danny was finally tucked up, ready for bed, he told Ant that he needed his friendship now more than ever.

'You know I'd do anything for you, Dan,' Anthuan said. 'You're my mate and have been for as long as I can remember.'

'OK, thanks, dude. But will you lie for me?'

Anthuan paused. 'Why?'

'Because without your help, I'll never get to the Olympics. And I know you think my whole Olympic dream thing is crazy and that I'm slower than a cheese sandwich . . .'

'Hey, I'm so sorry about that.'

'Good. Then will you lie for me, Ant?'

'OK, I'm in.'

'Good man. That's agreed then,' Danny said. 'And if this all goes to plan, I'll get you two tickets to the Olympic 100-metres final. Which I'll be running in. Of course.'

'OK,' Anthuan said, still slightly perplexed. 'But what do I have to do?'

'You can start by going to school tomorrow and reporting that I'm off sick.'

'OK. And what will you be doing instead?'

'Training for the Olympics, of course.'

'Dan, you're crazy. You know that, don't you?'
'Maybe. But it feels great.'

The next morning, Anthuan began his career as Danny's lying accomplice. And Danny got on the bus for the Lee Valley Stadium. On the way, he checked his phone; right now, more than ever, he so badly wanted a text from Ricky. But no, nothing. He sighed and then resolved to forget about it; there were enough other issues on his mind already.

He knew it wasn't clever to miss school, but he had to. Otherwise there would be no Olympics. And he had to convince Spike that what he was planning was smart.

He paused outside the door of Spike's office and took a deep breath. He needed Spike on his side in this.

'What you doing here, Speedboy?' Spike asked, pulling the spectacles off his face in surprise, when Danny walked into his office.

'You told me, Spike, last night. Don't you remember?' Danny replied. 'You said that I have got to get "so, so, so much better". I think that's what you said. You might have said "so" four times, or maybe three. I don't know. But here I am.'

'Sorry, Dan.' Spike's voice sounded firm.

'What do you mean, sorry?'

'It's school time, Dan.'

'Yes, I know. That's why I'm here.'

'I don't get it. School comes first. And your A levels are round the corner. No debate.'

'I know. I know. But Spike, it's you who says I need to get so, so, so much better. And it's also you who always says we need a plan. And so, on this occasion, I've come up with a plan of my own.'

'Hmmm.' Spike sounded unconvinced.

'It's simple,' Danny replied. 'Today I'm missing school. I needed to see you. And I'm going to train harder today than you have ever seen before in your life. But from tomorrow I can't and I won't miss any more school. And I have to revise after school. So from tomorrow we're going to have to train first thing in the morning. Six thirty. And that's six thirty every morning.'

'You're crazy, Speedboy.'

'Funny that, Spike,' Danny said, laughing. 'Everyone seems to be saying that at the moment. Now, can we get down to work?'

'Sure thing, Speedboy. But first we have got some studying of our own to do.'

'What do you mean, Spike?'

'I'll show you.' And, with that, Spike swivelled round in his chair and started tapping on the keyboard of his PC. 'You may have beaten Uncle Carl and Uncle Jesse, but now you're going to have to beat the rest of the world. That's what I meant when I said you have got to get so, so much better. And I think I said "so" four times, not three. Anyway,

I've got two new targets for you to set your sights on. Come here, I'll show you.'

TARGET NUMBER ONE

As Danny sat down and looked over Spike's shoulder at his PC monitor, Spike explained himself. In Sheffield, Danny had got his PB down to 10.17 seconds. But the fastest British junior sprinter of all time was Dwain Chambers. When Chambers was a kid, he ran the 100 metres in 10.06 seconds. If Danny was to have any chance of running against seniors in the Olympics, then he would have to prove himself as the hottest junior first.

'Beat Chambers' junior record,' Spike said, 'and then people will sit up and take notice.'

TARGET NUMBER TWO

The mythical sub-10-second mark. Every good sprinter knew what the 10-second mark represented. If you wanted to be a world-class sprinter, you had to go under 10 seconds. If you hadn't run under 10 seconds – and Danny hadn't got close – then you just weren't in the running. Ten seconds. It was only a number, but, if you ran under 10 seconds, it meant that you were a contender; it meant that the other sprinters would respect you. It meant that you had a chance of winning one of the biggest prizes in the sport.

As Spike explained: every Olympic final since 1984 has been won in under 10 seconds. 'We haven't talked about it before, Danny, because I didn't think you were ready,' Spike said, 'but now's the time for you to break 10 seconds. I know you can do it. But here's what you've got to realize: if you can't go under 10 seconds, you might as well forget about the Olympics altogether.'

Danny frowned. He loved it when Spike got serious. And he loved the new challenges that Spike set him. But, though these were two awesome targets, he felt excited. He felt confident that he could do whatever Spike asked of him.

'Well, come on then, Spike,' he said, standing up. 'We better get down to work.'

'Too right, Speedboy!' Spike replied. 'You'd better be ready to die!'

Later that afternoon, Danny felt superb. Superb and exhausted at the same time. He felt well and truly, completely and utterly killed by Spike. They had worked and worked and worked. They had concentrated on Danny's start and they had not stopped practising it until they were convinced that Danny had improved it. In Sheffield the previous day, Danny's start had, by his own high standards, been poor. Even Jimmy Lewis had got a better start than he had. So he and Spike were intent on perfecting it. So they worked on that start, again and again. And then they did some general sprint work. And then they went back to work on his start again.

So Danny left the Lee Valley Stadium happy. Sixty-seven days to go. He wondered what Usain Bolt would have been doing in training that day. And he filled his mind with his Olympic dream all the way home.

'Hi, Dad,' he said as he walked in. He hadn't seen his father since he had walked out the previous night.

'Hi, son. Are you OK?' his father asked. 'You didn't come back last night. We were worried.'

'I'm sorry, Dad,' Danny answered. 'But I was in a foul mood. I went to stay at Ant's place. But I've had a long think about it all and you'll be pleased to hear that I've decided to put my A levels first.'

'Really?'

'Yes. Really. And I need you and Mum to know my new schedule. I'll be leaving at six every morning to do extra revision at Ant's house. So don't worry if you don't see much of me first thing.'

His father looked surprised but delighted. 'That's great, Dan,' he said.

And, every morning for the next two and a half

weeks, Danny intended to tell his parents that he was revising at Ant's house when actually he was training at Lee Valley.

This was the big lie. The biggest, fattest lie of Danny's life. And he never lied, he hated dishonesty and the last people in the world to whom Danny wanted to be dishonest were the parents he loved so much. Danny didn't like the arrangement, but it had to be done.

So this was his schedule: get up at 6 a.m. Training from 6.30–9 a.m. School at 9 a.m., revise for his exams and be home at 6 p.m. Then: work, bed, sleep. It was exhausting, totally draining and repeated every day.

At school, Danny resolved to hide away. He didn't want to lie to any more people than he had to. So he decided to do his best to talk to no one apart from Ant. Just train, work, bed, sleep. And lie every day. Every day was a lie, but it had to be.

But it was only for that short period of time. Because on 10 June Danny would run in the Olympic stadium in the British Olympic trials. And then his secret would be known to the whole world.

While Danny was busy training and working and lying, just one thing happened of note. A text came through from Ricky. It came totally out of the blue, totally unprompted, and it was just eight words long. Danny didn't really understand it or why it had come, but he didn't delete it and he started looking at it at night before he went to bed.

'Believe me, Dan,' it read, 'you must never stop running.'

★ 12 ★

COVER BLOWN

There were just sixty-three days to go when Danny left training in his usual rush. Train, bus, school – the schedule was tight and he would run from the track to the changing room, from the changing room to the bus and then from the bus stop to school. However, this time he left the changing room, school-bag over his shoulder, broke into a trot to get to the bus and then stopped. His mum was standing there. He felt embarrassed. *What on earth is she doing here?*

'Hi, Mum,' he said sheepishly.

'Hi, Dan,' she replied. She said it softly. There was no anger in her voice. He felt slightly relieved by that.

'How did you know, Mum?' he asked.

'It just didn't seem quite right,' she said, still in a soft, patient voice. 'I'd been thinking about it all week. I'd been worrying about you. I felt so sad for you after your dad and everything on Sunday, I barely slept that night. And I've been feeling sad for you ever since. But I still just didn't quite understand why you have to go to Ant's.'

'So did he tell you?'

'Ant? Of course not. He would never betray you. No, I just thought I'd find out for myself what was going on and so I got up early this morning and followed you.'

Danny didn't know what to do. He felt guilty, embarrassed. He didn't know what to say. He could hardly even look his mother in the eye. They stood there, the silence awkward, the only sound the traffic on the road.

'I'm sorry,' Danny said eventually, almost in a whisper. He could barely get the words out. He felt tears coming to his eyes. He never wanted to let his mother down. 'I'm so sorry.'

His mother opened her arms as if inviting Danny towards her and he accepted the invitation and hugged her tight. 'I'm so sorry,' he repeated.

'Don't be,' she said in a more sensible voice, pulling away.

'But what will Dad say?'

His mother smiled at him: 'He doesn't need to know.' Danny studied her face; he was bemused. 'Look,' she said, 'I understand your father's position. And I understand your position too. I think you're both right.' She paused and then started again. 'And I love you for your passion and the way you're pursuing your Olympic dream, and I want to support that. And I'm sure Ricky would agree.'

'Ricky?'

'I can't tell you for sure, but I suspect that Ricky would love to be where you are now.'

Danny stopped to take all this in. 'What if Dad finds out?'

'We'll deal with that if and when it's necessary.' She looked at her watch. 'Now, shouldn't you be getting off to school?'

Danny chuckled. 'It's not easy, all this.'

'I'm sure it isn't. Now that you've got me on your side, Dan, I need to know what I can do to help. Anything.'

'Oh, Mum!' Danny looked at her wide-eyed as if he couldn't believe his luck. 'You couldn't wash my running kit, could you?'

★ 13 ★

8 JUNE

Danny woke early. In fact, Danny had hardly been able to sleep. Today was the day, 8 June, the day of the British Olympic trials. Forty-nine days until the Games. Danny's legs felt twitchy in his bed. He looked at his clock. It was only half past five. He knew he needed to sleep. He knew that sleep would help. *But what can you do when you're lying in bed and all you can think about is the fact that later that day you're going to be running for your life in the new Olympic Stadium? Go back to sleep? No chance!*

He thought about Uncle Carl and Uncle Jesse and their achievements and what Spike always said about them. Be like Jesse Owens: noble and true to yourself. And be like Carl Lewis: strong, stronger than the others, don't care about the others or what they say because you are stronger than they are. And Danny thought to himself: *Wow! If I can achieve half of that, I'll be doing well.*

And then, when his clock showed that it was six o'clock, he slipped quietly out of his bed. Downstairs, his mother was waiting for him with a cup of coffee and the breakfast table all laid out. They were quiet and businesslike; she could sense Danny's nerves; she knew he didn't want to talk. Danny ate fast, kissed his mother on the cheek and left. It was quiet outside and already light. It would be a clear day; he liked that. And if it went well, it could be the greatest day of his life so far.

The Olympic trials are all about keeping your head. At least that was what Spike told Danny later that morning as they drove in his Ford Focus slowly through the traffic to the Olympic Stadium. After a race, Spike never tended to say that much; before it though, he couldn't stop talking.

'If you stay cool, Speedboy, you'll have the rest of them chasing you,' he said. Danny had that nervous feeling in his veins and said nothing. 'Got that, Dan?'

'Yup, got it, Spike.'

Spike then told him how the 100 metres would work. There would be four rounds of racing and eight runners in each heat. So, if Danny finished in the top four in his heat this morning, he would qualify for the quarter-finals in the afternoon. Then, again, if he finished in the top four in his quarter-final, he would be down to the last sixteen in the semi-finals early the following afternoon. And then, again, if he made it into the top four of his semi, he would be in the final that evening. There were three spots in the Olympic team and if you came first or second in the final, you were guaranteed one of the three places in the team.

OK, Spike, no problem, Danny thought to himself. *So you're telling me that the best sixty-four sprinters in the whole of the country have all come for this, and I've got to finish in the top two! It sounds impossible. It sounds like the hardest day of my life. It sounds as though my time would be best spent back at Newham Secondary working for my A levels. But I've come this far. No problem, Spike. I'll have a go.*

Danny was still mulling all this over as they drove in through the gates to the Olympic Park. Today was the biggest day of his running life, yet here he was, feeling like a tourist going on an adventure. Driving through those gates felt like he was walking through the front door to Buckingham Palace and sitting down to have tea with the Queen.

The funny thing was that he knew pretty much what it would all look like. He had spent long enough staring down at it all from his favourite spot in Bridge Road. He recognized perfectly well where he was. And yet, to see it all here and now, all glistening and new, it was like a huge, shiny Christmas present that had just been unwrapped.

They had to park the car and then get on a shuttle bus. The shuttle bus took them to the warm-up track. There was not just one track here in the Olympic Park but two: the one in the stadium for competition and the other outside for warming-up.

Danny could not hide a smile as he and Spike walked on to the track. It may only have been a place for the athletes to warm up, yet it was the newest, best track he had ever been on in his life. It was so new. The surface was so clean and so perfect.

He looked around. Some athletes were jogging round the track, some were practising their starts and some were running slowly, exaggerating their movements to stretch their muscles. And, on the side of the track, some were stretching and some were lying down having their muscles massaged. Everyone seemed serious. Not just the sprinters but the distance runners, the throwers and the jumpers too. Danny recognized some of them from having seen them on the television. For a moment, he just stood and stared, and then Spike interrupted his train of thought.

'Oi, Dan!' he said in a cold voice. 'You know what the one single difference between you and all the other athletes here is?'

'What's that, Spike?'

'Look at them. They're all concentrating; they're all totally focused on what they're doing. All they're thinking about is how to prepare for this race. And you? You're standing here as if you're sightseeing on holiday. Or watching animals in the zoo. C'mon, Dan. Sharpen up.'

That was exactly what Danny needed. *Pull yourself together, Dan*, he thought. There was an hour until his race. *Warm up slowly. Stretch. Listen to your iPod. Focus. Prepare.*

There were eight heats in the first round of the 100 metres and Danny was in the fifth. Runners would be called twenty minutes before their heat. He saw Jimmy Lewis walking out across the track, ready to run. Jimmy, he guessed, must have been in an earlier heat. Danny stretched some more. And then, finally, he heard the call: 'Heat Five, men's 100 metres. Please go through.'

Danny gathered his kit together. Spike was not allowed to accompany him any further. 'This is it, Speedboy!' Spike said. He put his hands on Danny's cheeks so Danny had to look him in the eye and take in his every word. 'Think of Carl and Jesse. Be strong and be true to yourself and then I'll meet you out here a little later and we can start thinking about the next race.'

Danny then followed the other runners out of the warm-up track and through a tunnel under the grandstands. Within minutes, they were walking out into the middle of the stadium. Danny stopped and gazed around him. It was beautiful. It was the biggest, most beautiful stadium he had ever seen. The stand towered high to his right. It was like being at the bottom of an enormous cereal bowl. There were not many spectators in the stands, but he looked around, imagining what it would be like in two months' time when the biggest show on earth, the Olympics, was here. It would be absolutely amazing.

He walked over to his lane and pulled off his track-suit bottoms. But he was still mesmerized. Here he was: in Bolt's Second Home. He looked over to the stand to see if he could spot Spike, but it was too big. He couldn't see him anywhere. Then he gazed to the side of the track, where he knew the medals would be presented during the Games. Then he looked up at the scoreboard; it looked like the biggest flat-screen TV he had seen in his life. He saw his name up there. It said: 'Daniel Powell, Lane Three'. *Pretty cool*, he thought. *Wouldn't mind a photograph of that.*

Around the startline, his fellow competitors were preparing themselves. Danny tried to catch their eye to see how they were, but they all avoided his gaze. So he looked out for Spike again and still couldn't see him. And then, suddenly, his thoughts were interrupted by the stadium announcer.

'On your marks.'

Danny rushed forward to the startline. He didn't feel quite ready. He crouched down, thrust his feet back into the blocks and prepared himself to go.

'Set!'

He looked down the track and focused on the finishing line.

Bang!

The gun went off and all eight runners burst

forward. Danny felt he had got a reasonable start but, as he hit full speed, he realized that he wasn't at the front. *There are four people ahead of me*, he thought. *Four! Dan, you have to hit the accelerator! You can't blow it now! Come on, Dan! This is not good. Pump! Pump your knees!*

At the halfway mark, it was tight. There was one man ahead and then Danny and four others, all side by side. *Pump it, Dan. Pump it!* He started to feel stronger. He started to feel good; he felt his knees pumping hard. But then they were through the line and, in the blur of the finish, he didn't have a clue where he had finished. Did he do enough? Was he in that top four?

He looked up at the scoreboard again. He was scared: scared that he hadn't done enough, scared that his Olympic dream was over.

The names then appeared in order. He wasn't first. He wasn't second. He was third. He was OK. He had qualified for the next round. *But that was too close*, he said to himself. *That was scarily close.*

He looked up at the scoreboard again to check his time. 10.19 seconds. *Not bad*, he thought. *But not nearly good enough*.

Outside, Danny met up with Spike again and they went together to get some lunch in the Athletes' Restaurant. But something was up. Spike didn't say anything. Not a word. Not 'well done' or 'that was close'. Nothing. He would hardly even look at Danny. He pushed some pasta round his plate with his fork as if he was lost in thought, but still said nothing.

Only when he had finished the last piece of pasta did he put down his knife and fork and look up at Danny. 'Right!' he said quietly and commandingly. 'Shall we go home now then?'

'What do you mean, Spike?' Danny asked. 'I've got the quarter-finals in three hours.'

'What I mean,' Spike said, and Danny could clearly hear the anger in his voice, 'is that it seems we're wasting our time.'

'Why?'

'Because I'd rather be at home digging my garden than sitting here in the stands watching you run like that.'

'You didn't think I ran well?'

'Look, Dan, get serious. This is the seniors. It's not school sports day. This is the big time. I thought you were ready for it, but now I'm not so sure.' Spike paused. He started to talk louder and faster and with more rage in his voice. He picked up his fork and was pointing it at Danny's chest as if he was going to spike him with it. 'You want to know why you didn't run well? Because you walked into that stadium as if you were on a school outing. I was watching you. You didn't concentrate, you weren't focused and you were staring around at the stadium as if you'd seen a naked woman for the first time in your life. Dan, I wanted to shake you. When the announcer said, "On your marks," I was surprised you even heard it.'

Spike paused again. Danny said nothing. He knew that Spike was right. Spike sighed and then said, 'Look, Dan, I sat in the stands just now watching you and asking myself a question that I now want you to answer: why have we been getting up at six in the morning these last three weeks? What was it for?'

'Because I want to win the Olympics,' Danny replied nervously.

'Exactly,' Spike said. 'And somehow you still have a chance. But you were lucky because, if you run like that ever again, it's over. End of Olympics. You won't get a second chance. Just now you forgot every lesson I've ever taught you. But you've now got an opportunity to put all that right. Come on, Speedboy. Concentrate, focus, be true to yourself!'

And, with that, Spike opened his rucksack and pulled out the chessboard. 'Come on,' he said. 'Let's prepare for this race properly.'

Nearly three hours later, when Danny was walking into the Olympic Stadium for his quarter-final, he still had Spike's words ringing in his ears. *Come on, Speedboy. Concentrate, focus, be true to yourself!*

And this time he was determined to get it right. He didn't even look at the crowd. He didn't notice where Spike was sitting. He certainly didn't realize that Anthuan was there in the crowd, sitting next to his mother. And in the back of his mind he felt further reassured. Just after Spike had beaten him at chess, Danny had received another text from Ricky. Again, it came totally out of the blue. It just said 'Good luck' and Danny loved it.

He was in Lane Seven and he went straight over to his lane and stared down the track. *Now is your time, Dan,* he thought to himself. *Now you have to get it right.*

He then glanced over at the other runners. *They look scared,* he thought. And he realized that he wasn't scared at all and he realized that he had a familiar feeling in his veins, as if he had had an injection of warm blood into his body: it was confidence. He had got the confidence back. *You can do this, Dan, you know you can.*

'On your marks.'

This time Dan was ready. He crouched down in the starting position.

'Set!'

Dan looked down the track. He felt like a caged tiger, ready to spring.

Bang!

He was off like a rocket. *Good start, Dan,* he thought, *there's no one with you. Concentrate. Pump the knees.* Danny was ahead of the other runners immediately. At the 30-metre mark, he had a clear lead. *Concentrate, Dan.* At 50 metres, the lead remained. *Push it, Dan. Pump the knees.* At 80 metres, it was clear he was going to win. *Don't let up, Dan. Keep it going to the finish.* And, as he sped through the finishing line, he tumbled to the ground in utter exhaustion. He knew he had run well, there could be no doubt. Surely.

Dan swivelled round to look at the scoreboard. His name came up first. But, when he saw the time, he sprang to his feet in astonishment, as if he could not believe it. He had run 10.03 seconds. *A PB! A beautiful PB! Faster than Dwain Chambers! Faster than any young Briton has ever gone before! You beauty!*

Danny felt brilliant. He couldn't believe what he had just done. He stopped and allowed himself a minute to look at the stadium in which he had just run his fastest-ever time. And then he followed the other runners out of the stadium and back to the warm-up track. He struggled to contain his joy. *This is brilliant*, he thought. *I am absolutely loving it!*

★ 14 ★

OVERNIGHT FAME

'Danny! Danny!'

As Danny left the stadium, he heard his name being called. He turned round and two people were running towards him. One was a woman, about thirty years old; the other was a slightly older man wearing a suit and an open-collar shirt.

'Can we have a word?' they said, slightly out of breath, in unison.

'We just watched you run,' said the man. 'You were fantastic.' He put out a hand to shake Danny's. 'Hi. I'm Pete O'Byrne. I'm the athletics correspondent of *The Times*.'

'Jenny Nicholas from the *Daily Express*,' said the lady.

Again, almost in unison, they both took notepads out of their pockets and smiled encouragingly at him. They then started firing questions and Danny was still so excited he was delighted to answer them. The pair of them seemed decent enough so Danny chatted away.

They asked him all sorts of questions. Some were about sprinting and technique and the Olympics. And some were totally bizarre, like: what did you have for breakfast this morning? And: what music do you listen to? And: where do you live? How far away from the stadium? And: are you still at school? And: what A levels are you doing? And Pete and Jenny seemed genuinely interested in all Danny's answers.

He was almost finished when another couple of men with a TV camera arrived and also asked for an interview and he said yes to that too. But first, he said, he just wanted to ask Pete and Jenny, the journalists, a question of his own.

'Are you going to write about me in your newspapers?' he asked.

'Absolutely,' replied Jenny, smiling encouragingly. 'Danny, you're a great story. You could be the star of the Olympics and here you are, living only five minutes away.'

'Hmmm.' Danny's mind started spinning. 'When will it go in the papers?'

'Tomorrow,' she said. 'And good luck tomorrow too.'

By the time he got back to the warm-up track, Danny had given two more interviews, one to Radio 5 Live and one to another group of newspaper writers, three of them. He was a bit taken aback by it all and so he was happy to find Spike there waiting for him. He knew he could rely on Spike for a dose of cold reality.

'Fastest British junior of all time!' Spike said. He almost seemed happy. 'Now I've got two things to say to you, young man. One: well done, you proved that you can do this. And two: go home, forget about what you've done and think about tomorrow. What you've done today is now irrelevant, Dan. If you don't run well tomorrow, today counts for nothing. Got it? Nothing. Nothing at all. It's all about tomorrow, remember. So go on now, go home.'

And so Danny did what Spike told him. Except he didn't go home. He met up with Anthuan and went back to his house instead. That had always been the plan and after what had just happened in the Olympic Stadium, there was no way he was going to change it.

Back at Anthuan's, Danny had jobs to do. First: he had to ring his mum. That was hard; he didn't want to get emotional. You only get emotional at the end of a race and Danny felt as though he was still in the middle of one. But he had to agree with his mum how to tackle the second job on his list.

He always knew this second job was going to be hard, but there was no escaping it. So he borrowed some paper, sat down and wrote a letter to his father.

Dear Dad,

I cannot tell you how sorry I am, but I hope and pray that you'll forgive me. I've lied to you and I hate that. I've always been honest with you. I never want to have to lie again.

Today I ran in the Olympic trials. I promised you that I wouldn't but I did.

And for the last three weeks, when I've been getting up at six o'clock, it wasn't to go and revise for my A levels as I said it was. It was to go and train for this race.

I'm sorry. I lied. But I've had this Olympic dream and I couldn't let it go.

But I haven't let my A levels slip down the pan. I've worked hard. Very hard. I was just convinced that I could keep my A levels and my Olympic dream going side by side. I ran well today and I feel I've done well in my A levels so far too.

Please forgive me, Dad.

I'll come home tomorrow night to face the music, but now I need to concentrate on the Olympics. Today I broke the British junior record. Tomorrow I need to run the two best races of my life and I might then get to the Olympics.

I understand that you may be disappointed with me. Please don't be.

Please join me in my dream. Mum is with me. I'll let her explain. And don't be cross with her. If you're cross with anyone, it has to be with me. But I don't want you to be angry at all.

I enclose two tickets for tomorrow at the Olympic

Stadium. There's nothing that could help me prepare better than knowing that you were there and supporting me.

Love,

Danny

Danny folded the letter and put two tickets in the envelope. Anthuan promised to deliver the letter first thing the next morning; he also insisted that Danny take the bed that night. 'You're the champ, man,' he said. 'I'll take the mattress on the floor.'

'Thanks, Ant, you're a great mate.'

'And you, Dan,' Anthuan said, laughing, 'are a lot faster than a cheese sandwich.'

Danny slept well that night, much better than the night before. By the time he woke up, Ant had already got up and gone downstairs. And, when Danny followed him down, it was to discover that life had changed somewhat. He was no longer just a kid with a dream. He was a kid who was famous.

'Your secret's out now, Dan,' Ant said, a huge grin on his face. 'I've already seen your face on Sky Sports News. Your hair looks dead weird. You should remember to do your hair before you go on the telly next time!'

'Very funny, Ant!'

'But here,' Ant said, 'look at these. I went out to drop off that letter earlier and I got these on the way back.'

Ant pointed to the newspapers on the kitchen table. He had bought every newspaper in the shop and as Dan started flicking through the back pages, it became clear that they had all written about him. Every single one. *The Times* had his picture on the back page with the caption: 'Could this be Danny, champion of the world?'

Danny's heart started beating fast. Wow! He picked up the *Daily Express*, flicked in six pages from the back and there he was again, the headline: 'Local boy done very good.' Then the *Sun*: 'Danny, the Olympic super-kid.' The *Daily Mirror*: 'New kid on the Olympic block.' The *Daily Telegraph*: 'Local boy living the Olympic dream.'

He went on through the papers, reading and rereading them. He noticed from the results that Jimmy Lewis had got through to the semi-finals as well, but Jimmy barely got a mention. Everything was about *him*. The stories all seemed to concentrate on the fact that he was so young, that he was the new British junior record-holder and the fact that he lived little more than a kilometre from the Olympic Park. Some said he lived 'a stone's throw' from the Olympic Park; he could never throw a stone that far, but he figured that that wasn't really the point. Some called him 'the kid from nowhere'. Some said he was 'about to shock the world'. He liked the sound of that in particular.

But there was one element that appeared in every

story. Every single newspaper made the point that he had taken time out of his A-level schedule to run in the Olympics. They called him the 'A-grade Olympic student'; they said that he had gone 'from the exam hall to the Olympic stadium' and that he had 'passed yesterday's exam on the track with flying colours'. They even named his school, Newham Secondary. And some named the headmaster, Vernon McCaffrey. *Oh no*, thought Danny, *Mr McCaffrey didn't even know I was running today.*

An hour later, as Danny left Ant's house to meet up with Spike again, he realized that he felt funny. Not sick or anything. Not nervous. He just had this empty feeling in the pit of his stomach. It came from reading all those newspapers and it was very, very uncomfortable.

★ 15 ★

THE TRIALS, PART 1

Spike could tell that something was up. The moment he saw Danny, he knew. On race days, Danny was normally full of chat and he would walk around with his head held high, as if he was ready to take on the world. Today he was quiet, he seemed distracted and he kept his head down. They played chess and Danny was rubbish. He wouldn't concentrate at all. He lost in less than fifteen minutes.

Down at the warm-up track, Danny was going through the motions, warming up and stretching, but it was hard for him to concentrate because so many other athletes seemed to be paying him so much attention. Some just stared; some came up and shook his hand and said 'Congratulations'. Some joked to him: 'G'morning, superstar!' or 'Good luck with the exams!' And the occasional comment here and there was just plain nasty: 'It's all over now, sonny! I should get back to your homework!' said one. Another said: 'Enjoy the fame, kid, because you'll be forgotten about tomorrow.'

Danny didn't exactly warm to the spiteful comments but, more than anything, it just felt weird to be the centre of attention. Who were all these people? He recognized a few faces, but he hadn't spoken to them before. The only one he knew was Jimmy Lewis. Thank goodness for Jimmy – a familiar face. He sat and talked to Jimmy briefly and even though they were in the same semi-final, they wished each other luck. And then it was back to being the centre of attention again.

About an hour before his race, Spike put an arm round Danny and led him out of the warm-up track for a walk.

'It feels different today, doesn't it, Dan?' he said, but he didn't wait for an answer. 'I remember when it felt different for me. I was twenty-one, it was the European Championships in Athens and I was all over the newspapers too.'

'But you'd won a bronze medal, Spike. I've won nothing.'

'That doesn't matter, Dan. What matters is that you understand why you feel the way you do. Do you feel as though you want to hide, or run away, or as if you want to be sick, or scream out loud? Is that how you feel, Dan?'

'Sure is.'

'Well, that's how I felt too.' Spike then stopped walking and turned to Danny, talking really seriously. 'So here's the important bit, Dan. The bit that you really must understand. Here's the truth. The simple reason for you feeling funny is because you are good, really good: the best kid Britain's ever had. That's official, right? The complicated reason is this. Suddenly, everyone knows you're good: the other athletes, the newspaper people, the people who read the newspapers. They all know it because you showed them yesterday. And they all expect you to be good now, so they're all going to stare at you and watch you. That's what happens when you're good, Dan. Everyone watches. Now you've got two choices. Choice one: you can follow your feelings, run away if you want to and hide. You want to do that?'

'Not really.'

'Good. Well, this is choice number two. Every time you see someone looking, every time they make a comment, or stare, or if they're rude to you, or whatever – every time that happens, you have to tell yourself this: it's because I'm good. Now that can be very powerful, Dan. How many people, do you think, stared at you today or spoke to you who have never stared or spoken to you before?'

Danny shrugged his shoulders. 'I don't know. Maybe fifty, maybe eighty.'

'Good. Now that's fifty or eighty people telling you "you're good". Wow, Dan! I'd love to have that many people tell me I'm good. When someone tells you you're good, Dan, how does that make you feel?'

'I like it. It makes me feel strong.'

'Exactly. Well, you should feel strong fifty or eighty times over. You can go into this semi-final feeling stronger than you've ever felt before. Got it?'

'So these are your choices, Dan. And I want to know which one it's going to be. Are you going to take choice one, and hide or run away? Or choice two, and feel eighty times stronger? And I tell you: this is what Uncle Carl and Uncle Jesse were all about. How strong are you? Because those two were more choice two than any other sprinters that ever lived. So which is it going to be, Speedboy?'

Danny was quiet for a moment and then a smile crept over his face. 'Come on, Spike. That's the easiest question I've ever had in my life. I'll take option two.'

'Good man, Dan,' Spike said. 'You're sounding more like your uncles every day.'

Fifty minutes later, Danny was inside the Olympic Stadium, staring down the track, focusing hard. The crowd was far bigger today, it was almost a fully packed stadium, but he didn't even notice. He thought about what Spike had said and he felt strong, fifty or eighty times over. He didn't feel nervous and he could no longer feel that uncomfortable emptiness in the pit of his stomach. Instead, he felt that reassuring warmth in his arms and in his legs, that fantastic feeling of confidence.

His was Lane Five. Jimmy Lewis was Lane Two.

He recognized two of the other runners, in Lanes Three and Four. Deon Francis, in Lane Four, had been to the last Olympics. Tyrone Small in Lane Three had run for Great Britain many times and Danny had watched him on the TV. But he didn't think they looked scary. Neither of them. They looked normal. They each glanced his way a couple of times. *Are they telling me I'm good?* Danny thought to himself. *Now concentrate. Hard. Work your start. Make this your best start ever. Finish in the top four in this race and you'll be in the final.*

Bang!

The gun blasted. Danny reacted dynamite fast: it was as if he had pulled the trigger of the gun himself. Legs pumping. *Stay low at the start, pump the legs, drive hard in those first few strides. I'm ahead,* Danny thought. *I've got the start of my life. Concentrate. Keep your eyes fixed down your lane as if you're staring down a tunnel.*

At 50 metres, Danny was ahead. Clearly so. He felt that brilliant, flying, weightless sensation, as if his feet were barely having to make contact with the ground. Jimmy Lewis was back, hardly in the race. But Francis and Small were fast, clawing back Danny's lead. He could almost feel Francis next to him. *High knees, focus, straight ahead.*

At 80 metres, Danny was still ahead. Just. *Keep strong. Don't stop. Time your dip.* It's crucial in tight races to dip at the right time, to stretch forward your head and shoulders just as you're breaking the line. It was the difference between success and failure. Danny dipped. The crowd seemed to roar as he broke the line. *I've got it*, he thought. *I'm sure I've got it.*

He let his body tumble to the ground. As he hit the ground, he felt a very slight twinge at the back of his right leg, just above the knee, but he was too caught up in the moment to stop to think about it. He turned to read the scoreboard. It read: 'ıst, Daniel Powell.' And then the time flashed up: 9.99 seconds.

9.99 seconds! 9.99! 9.99! Danny leaped immediately to his feet and punched the air. Once, twice, three times. *9.99 seconds! The mythical sub-10 club!* He could not believe it. He rubbed the back of his right leg. He hardly felt it, but it was as if he had brushed a stinging nettle.

And then Jimmy Lewis was at his side. Jimmy hugged him hard. 'How d'you go, Jimmy?' Danny asked.

'I didn't make it, Dan,' he replied. 'But forget about me. You were awesome. You were totally, completely awesome. Congratulations!'

The other runners all shook his hand, one by one. It was as if he was royalty; he'd never felt like this before. Tyrone Small clenched his hand tight and said, 'You're the man!'

Tyrone Small said that! Danny thought. *A guy I've watched and admired on TV!*

The last to shake his hand was Deon Francis.

'Sub-10, mate, well done!' he said. 'Welcome to the club.'

'Thanks,' Danny replied. But then another thought suddenly came into his head. *Is my dad here?* He scanned the crowd, but even if his parents were there, he didn't know where they would be sitting. And there were simply too many people in the crowd. It was impossible to tell. *Did they see me? Has Dad forgiven me?*

Danny waved to the crowd. But really he was waving to his mum and dad, whether they were there or not. *One more race*, he thought to himself. *Just go away now and focus on one more race.*

Danny walked away from the track. He felt great. He switched on his phone and there was a text, another one from Ricky. Just two words this time.

Nice one.

Danny liked that. He liked that a lot. Almost immediately, his phone beeped again. It was another text; another one from Ricky.

Now do it again.

★ 16 ★

THE TRIALS, PART 2

Between the semi-final and the final, there were three and a half hours to wait. But the story had changed even more. Yesterday he was a complete unknown; this morning he was the new kid on the block and now, suddenly, Danny Powell was the favourite to win. His time of 9.99 seconds was the fastest of the two semi-finals and up in the stand where the journalists were sitting, the discussion was all about him. Him and him alone: 'He's improving with every round!' 'How much faster can he go?' 'Can he keep it going?' 'Will the pressure get to him?' 'And what about Francis?' 'Francis nearly caught him!' 'Francis won't let that happen again!'

But Danny was not aware of any of this. Danny was with Spike, sitting in the Athletes' Restaurant playing chess.

First chess, then the iPod, then the warm-up track. Then the final. It was amazing how fast time could pass. Danny felt relaxed. He glanced around occasionally. He wanted to see: were people looking at him? They were. And now it made him feel strong. Just one more race, a top two finish and he would be going to the Olympics.

This time Danny was Lane Four. Francis was in Lane Five. And in Lane Three was the winner of the other semi-final, Max Donne. Donne was good. Danny knew Donne was good. But he didn't mind. He felt strong and he felt that warm blanket of confidence wrap itself round him.

He focused. He looked down the track and thought about his start, the power thrust, knees high, speed.

'On your marks.'

The stadium suddenly went silent.

'Set.'

Think of the start, Dan, then drive. Start and drive.

Bang!

Danny's reactions were lightning fast again. *Drive, drive the legs.* He had the lead early, but Francis was with him, and Donne too. *Focus, drive, pump high with the knees.* He felt Francis on his right; he knew Francis was edging ahead.

Pump, come on, pump it, pump it! And then suddenly, he felt a shooting pain down the back of his right leg. 'Aaaah!' He heard a scream of pain and realized it was his own. It felt like he had been shot by a bullet. Suddenly, he was hopping on his left leg. The pain was excruciating. Like a heat rush charging through his thigh muscle. He couldn't run any more. He saw Francis and Donne disappear away from him. He clutched the back of his leg. It was throbbing with pain. He was halfway down the track. He fell to the floor. It was over. The Olympic dream. Gone.

And there had been no shooting; there was no bullet and no blood. Of course there wasn't. Danny knew the feeling. He realized immediately what had happened. His muscle had torn; the physical stress of the last race had been too great. The muscle at the back of his thigh: the hamstring. It was a straight-forward injury. And here he was, lying in the middle of the track in the Olympic Stadium. His dream over. It was too much and he couldn't stop the tears. They just came, streaming down his face. Too much. The Olympics. All over. He sobbed and sobbed and he couldn't stop himself.

Francis? Donne? He didn't know who had won. All he knew was that his right leg felt as though it was on fire. And that the dream – the dream was gone. And that he simply couldn't stop crying.

The tears wouldn't stop. But it wasn't the pain. The pain was bad, but he wasn't crying because he was hurt. He was crying because his life had been all about a dream and now that dream was over.

The next voice he heard was reassuring and famil-iar. 'It's all right, Dan!' it said. Dan looked up and saw his father. He had come to watch after all! He must have jumped over the fencing at the side of the stands to get to him. 'It's all right, Dan,' he repeated again and again.

Dan let his dad haul him back up to his feet. 'I'm sorry, Dad, I'm so sorry,' he said.

'Don't be, Dan, don't be,' he replied. 'I'm so proud of you. So very proud.'

His dad draped Dan's right arm round his neck so he could support him and then they started to walk. Slowly, with Dan hopping on his left leg, the tears still dripping from his face, they started to move. They went all the way down Lane Four and, as they reached the finish line, the crowd rose to their feet and applauded.

'Listen to that,' his dad said. He stopped momentarily with Danny still leaning heavily on him. 'Look around, Dan. Listen. Listen to the applause. That's for you.'

★ 17 ★

INJURED HERO

Two days later, Danny was back at Newham Secondary. His intention was to carry on with school life and A levels as normal, but normality, it seemed, was now officially impossible. Anyone who hadn't heard of Danny Powell before the weekend now knew his story. The teachers, the school kids, everyone.

They knew exactly who he was, how fast he had run, how he had missed school on Friday in order to compete in the trials and how he had cried in his father's arms on Saturday. They knew it because the Sunday morning newspapers had written even more about him than the papers the previous day. And for those very few students who had somehow missed the news through the papers, the TV, Facebook, Twitter, the radio or the endless round of phone text gossip, when they got to school on Monday morning to find a small band of journalists waiting at the gates, it was obvious that something pretty unusual had occurred.

When Danny had arrived for school that morning, hobbling along on crutches, the press cameras clicked away as if he was a film star. And a little later, Mr McCaffrey, the headmaster, was outside giving interviews. Mr McCaffrey, it seemed, was not remotely unhappy with Danny; in fact, Mr McCaffrey appeared to rather like the idea of getting his own name in the newspapers too.

The Sunday papers had already changed the story. On Saturday Danny had been written about as 'the Olympic super-kid', but on Sunday he had become instead the 'brave local hero'. Almost every newspaper commented on the fact that he had cried in his father's arms and Danny was a bit gutted about that. The *Mail on Sunday* and the *Sunday Mirror* had both said that the tears were 'the tears of a brave man', but nevertheless Danny couldn't help feeling that crying hadn't been the coolest part of the whole adventure.

He also wondered about Ricky. No word from him at all. He had got those texts after his semi-final, but nothing thereafter. Why not? He so wanted Ricky back, back home, back with him, back as a brother and a friend. But this was just peculiar. He thought about texting Ricky the result of that final race, the same way that he always texted him his results, but that would simply have been strange. Ricky had surely watched it. *What on earth*, he wondered, *would Ricky think if I texted him the result of a race that has been plastered over every single national newspaper?*

Pretty much whenever he was around the school gates now, Danny was surrounded by other boys and girls in the school, some of whom he hardly knew, all of them wanting to ask questions about the Olympics. And the funny thing was this. Only four weeks ago, when Danny had said he wanted to run in the Olympics, he had been made to feel that it was a preposterous idea, stupid. 'Dream on, Danny!' was the general reaction. But now that he was hobbling around on crutches and the whole dream was officially over, no one seemed to think it was so stupid any more. In fact, most people seemed to think it was a great idea and they told him so.

'You'll be fit for the Olympics, won't you, Dan?' was the kind of question he found himself answering twenty times a day. 'How long till the leg's better, Dan?' 'You can do it, Dan.' 'Can we come and watch you in the Olympics, Dan?'

It was all very supportive, but a little frustrating as he found himself having to explain, over and over again, the sad circumstances. He was injured and it would take the hamstring an estimated four weeks to heal. But, even if he was fit by the time the Olympics started, the point was that he had missed his chance. He needed to finish first or second in the trials to get into the British Olympic team and he hadn't. He had finished eighth. Deon Francis and Max Donne were going to run in the Olympics and he wasn't. It was as simple and annoying as that.

And it was strange, but, as Danny explained all this over and over again, he somehow felt that he couldn't just dole out a barrage of non-stop miserable news. Even though he himself was the victim in all this, he felt he needed to cheer people up. So he would finish by saying: 'Never mind, I'll be back in four years' time. Don't you worry.'

And that seemed to work for pretty much everyone apart from himself. Danny tried to put on a brave face. It was cool that the newspapers had written so many positive stories about him and he didn't mind the fact that everyone at school now wanted to talk to him, even if it was a little hard to concentrate on his A levels.

There had been other good things to come from the whole affair too: his father had forgiven him, completely and utterly. In fact, because of what had happened with his dad running on to the track, he had sort of shared the spotlight with Danny. The journalists had wanted to talk to his father too, so Danny had felt as if they were in it together. And his parents looked after him at home as if he was a young boy again. His mum brought him breakfast in bed. He liked that. He might have been eighteen years old, but what he felt he needed was a great, big, long cuddle and that was what he was getting.

Yet deep down, he couldn't stop feeling sorry for himself. During those endless hours of revision, his mind kept on wandering back to the Olympic Stadium. *9.99 seconds! Sub-10 seconds! Welcome to the club!*

And then he would start to wonder: what if? *What if I hadn't been injured? How fast could I have gone? How fast will they go when the Olympics are in town? And how fast will Usain Bolt be? Would I, could I have beaten Usain Bolt?* All these questions were totally useless, an utter waste of time, but Danny couldn't stop them coming, especially when he was sitting at a desk with a history book open in front of him.

Yet, as the week wore on, the drama of the previous weekend seemed to fade a little. Exams became his life, not the Olympics. And the other school kids stopped asking him when he would be fit and running again.

On Wednesday lunchtime, he walked out of the exam hall after a really horrible business studies exam, tossing over in his mind all the mistakes he had made and the answers he had got wrong, and the first person he saw was Jess. She was sitting outside waiting to go in.

'Politics,' she explained. 'I can't stand politics!'

'When do your exams finish?' he asked.

'Friday,' she said.

'Me too.' Danny paused. 'So, do you want to go to a party on Friday night to celebrate? A load of us are going round to Ant's house. Should be quite fun.'

Jess frowned and looked confused. 'But I didn't think you ever went out, Danny?'

Danny chuckled. 'Yeah, I guess you're right there. Normally I don't. But normally I'm not on crutches.

Normally I'm trying to be an athlete. Now I'm just trying to walk without my right leg killing me.'

Jess laughed. 'Ah, you brave soldier, you! But that's so sweet of you to ask. Friday night sounds great.'

Danny hobbled off. He liked the idea of Friday night: a normal life, relaxing, having fun with friends. And not having to be an Olympian any more.

Friday afternoon and the end of exams could not come fast enough. Danny had two exams left: business studies on Thursday morning and, after lunch on Friday, a sports science theory exam. And then he was free: A levels over, a night to celebrate.

Thursday came and went and it wasn't too stressful. *I did OK*, he thought, *not great, but OK*. And he was confident about the sports science. For Danny, that was probably the easiest exam of the lot.

At two o'clock on Friday after lunch, Danny stood outside the exam hall, waiting with the other students for their last exam. It felt to Danny as if he was reaching another finishing line. At 4.30 p.m., he would walk out of the exam hall for the last time in his life.

Just as they were about to go in though, his phone buzzed in his pocket. It was a text message from Spike:

Don't give up yet, Speedboy. There's still a chance. Ring me.

Danny couldn't ring before the exam; there simply wasn't time. And for the next two hours, while he sat there writing about sports science theory, he tried desperately not to think about Spike's text, forcing himself to concentrate on the exam in front of him. It wasn't easy. But, the minute it was over, he hobbled on his crutches to a quiet corner outside the exam hall and made the phone call.

'Spike, it's me. What's up?'

'There's still a chance, Dan. That's what's up.'

'I don't understand, Spike,' Danny replied, trying not to get overexcited. 'I'm injured and I didn't make the team. How can there be a chance?'

Spike then explained. He had been phoned that morning by Charles Perryman, the head coach at UK Athletics. It was Perryman's job to pick the Olympic team. Perryman had said that he didn't want to give up on Danny, that he thought Danny's performance at the weekend was so good that they had to try everything they could to get him in the team. There were three places in the team for the 100 metres: one would go to Deon Francis, one to Max Donne and the third was for Perryman to decide. Perryman could pick who he wanted and the man he wanted was Danny.

Danny's heart started pounding as Spike told him all this. 'But I still don't get it, Spike,' he said. 'I'm injured. I'm on crutches. I am, right now, undoubtedly slower than a cheese sandwich.'

'I know, I know,' Spike answered. 'It's not going to be easy. In fact, I don't want to get your hopes up at all. But this is the deal. A hamstring injury like yours should take four weeks to heal. It's already had a week so, three weeks from now, it should be OK. That will leave you just three and a half weeks until the first round of the Olympics 100 metres. Now three and a half weeks isn't going to be long enough to get you up to full speed. You need four weeks or a month. So this is what Perryman has told me. He said that he'll keep that third place in the team open for you. In two weeks' time, he wants to see you. He's going to come down to Lee Valley to watch you run. And, if you can convince him you're fit, you'll be in the team. How does that sound?'

'I don't get it,' Danny replied.

'What don't you get?'

'My hamstring needs another three weeks. But Perryman wants to see me running in two. How am I going to manage that?'

'Ah, yes. That's the other bit that needs explaining. This man Perryman, he really seems to like you, Dan. He's made some arrangements.'

'What arrangements?' Danny was getting more intrigued and more confused.

'Well, I first need to check. You've finished your exams now, haven't you?'

'Yes, Spike.'

'Good.'

'And I'm just about to go out celebrating.'

'No, you're not, Speedboy.'

'What do you mean?'

'Do you still want to run in the Olympics?'

'Come on, Spike, you know I do.'

'Good. Well, go straight home, pack your bag for the weekend and I'll be round to pick you up in an hour. Oh, and grab your passport as well. We're going to Sweden.'

★ 18 ★

CRAZY SCIENCE

By eight o'clock that night, Danny and Spike were sitting on a plane bound for Stockholm. By five past eight, on this, the forty-second day before the Games, Spike was snoring loudly and Danny was left to his own thoughts, trying to ignore the snorting coach next to him, peering out of the window at the country they were leaving behind and contemplating what now lay ahead.

They were going to see the most famous sports doctor in the world. For most injured sportsmen, that would be good news. Managing to get an appointment with Dr Kris Gerndt meant you had a pretty good chance of getting better pretty fast. His nickname was Kris the Cure. Sportsmen and women came from all over the world to see him and almost all of them seemed to say that he was a miracle-worker. For years, Kris the Cure had been healing the injuries of tennis players, golfers, rugby players, footballers, the lot. And Danny knew that he was very lucky to see Kris the Cure. This Charles

Perryman guy had done him a massive favour by arranging it.

But there was a small problem. Indeed, if Danny had been able to, he would have run a mile from Dr Gerndt. Because Dr Gerndt's technique involved needles and injections – lots of them. And Danny hated needles.

He had never forgotten the time that Ricky had a tetanus jab. When they were still young teenagers, they were training together one day in West Ham Park and, after beating Danny – as always – over a short sprint, Ricky had thrown himself on to the grass and spiked his hand on a rusty nail that was sticking out of the ground. It was not the bloody gash in Ricky's hand that Danny couldn't look at; he was fine with blood. It was the injection the doctor gave Ricky in his arm. Danny couldn't even watch, so how could Ricky just sit there and take it – without even flinching?

This was what was going through his mind as he listened to Spike snoring. In his sports science A level he had done a special project on sports injuries. He could for instance give you, off the top of his head, his Top Five Weirdest Sports Injuries.

1. Dave Beasant, who played goalkeeper for England, once dropped a bottle of salad cream on his foot, severed the tendon in his big toe and couldn't play for two months.
2. Sammy Sosa, a famous baseball player in

America, once pulled the muscles in his back when he sneezed.

3. Sam Torrance, a Scottish golfer, couldn't stop himself sleepwalking and, one night, he was sleepwalking in a hotel and injured himself when he walked into a flowerpot.

4. David James, another England goalkeeper, once pulled a muscle in his back when reaching for the TV controls.

5. Rio Ferdinand, the Manchester United and England player, once injured the tendon behind his knee merely by having his feet up on a coffee table to watch the TV.

There was also a fairly interesting list of weird medicines and therapies that sportspeople used and Danny had studied those for his A level project as well. He had heard of athletes in China drinking turtle blood! The trouble was that Dr Gerndt's methods seemed the weirdest of the lot. What Dr Gerndt did was inject people's injuries with some really strange substances. Some of the stuff he injected came from calves' blood! And some came from the comb on the head of a cockerel! How on earth Dr Gerndt ever came up with all these crazy substances Danny had no idea. And why did he need so many needles? That was weird.

All Danny knew for sure was that if he was to have any chance of getting fit for the Olympics, he needed Kris the Cure badly. He had been booked in for two days in Kris the Cure's clinic. Kris the Cure was to be his torturer and, hopefully, his saviour too.

The next morning, bright and early, Spike and Danny were sitting in the waiting room in Gerndt's clinic. Danny gasped in awe at the photographs on the wall. They each showed Dr Gerndt with the various famous sportspeople he had worked with. Danny didn't realize that he had treated so many!

So he was feeling a little better when the man in all the pictures came in. Dr Gerndt high-fived Danny and then Spike. He was oldish, probably about sixty-five, and his hair was grey and lank, but he seemed full of energy.

'So you are the new young superstar?' he said in English, but with a strong Swedish accent.

Danny liked that. 'Well, I was hoping to be,' he replied, gesturing at his right leg. 'Until *this* let me down.'

'Well, we must make you better,' the doctor said. He said it as if it would be easy. Danny liked that too. 'I have a ticket for the London Olympics, for the final of the men's 100 metres. That is always my favourite moment in the Games. And, when I spoke to my friend Mr Perryman yesterday, he said that I would very much enjoy watching young Mr Danny Powell running that day.'

Danny nodded. He was a bit embarrassed to hear that he had been talked about in this way.

'So come on, Mr Powell,' the doctor said, gesturing with his hands. 'We need to get to work on you.'

And that was where it began. They went into Dr Gerndt's office and Gerndt started asking Danny questions: how did the right leg feel when he injured it? Where exactly was the pain? Did it feel hot or cold? How did it feel now?

Then Danny was asked to lie down on a therapy table and Gerndt put his hands on his leg, poking it in certain places. At first he was gentle, but then not. Gerndt talked to himself as he was doing this, muttering away, but always in English, as if he was talking to Danny's injured hamstring: 'Interesting, interesting. Good. Oh yes, yes. How's that feel? Ah. OK. OK. Oh dear. Oh, poor you. Yes, yes. Now I understand. Right, well, off we go then.'

And, after that, he took Danny into another room that looked like a space-age science laboratory and was full of large electrical instruments and computer screens. 'This is where we really discover what has happened in your leg,' Gerndt said. 'We have to find out everything about it; we have to get to know it as if it is our best friend.'

What followed was baffling. Gerndt wanted to have as close a look as possible at the troublesome hamstring so he took pictures of it, three types of scanned photographs using three different pieces of his space-age apparatus. This involved shooting X-rays through Danny's body, then supersonic sound waves and then magnetic waves. Cool. At least that was how it sounded when Gerndt explained what he was doing. Danny, however, didn't feel a thing.

An hour later, Gerndt had studied the pictures and was sitting back down in front of Danny and Spike with a rather different expression on his face. He didn't look so confident now and he frowned.

'Look, Danny,' he said. 'I have some bad news and some good news. The bad news comes first. Your hamstring is not so good. It is worse than I had expected. The muscles are quite badly strained. Normally I would say, "Forget it". Normally I would tell you that you need to mend your body and you should not run again for two or three months. That is the bad news.'

Gerndt paused, as if he was thinking, and then he finally smiled. 'Ah, yes. You want the good news, yes? Yes. OK. *Now* is not normal. *Now* we have to think about the Olympics. I have my ticket to the 100 metres – remember? – and I want to see you run. And I think you want to run too, yes, Danny? OK, so we have to do something special, to give you some magic. And we have to hope the magic works. But what is good, Danny, is that you have a healthy young body, and healthy young bodies mend more quickly. So . . .' He paused again as if he had forgotten what he was going to say. 'In order to help the hamstring muscles with the healing process, I am going to inject . . .'

It was at that point that Danny fainted. He had been waiting nervously all morning to hear that word, or to see the flashing point of a syringe, and at the very mention of the word 'inject', he collapsed in his chair. He regained consciousness within a couple of seconds and opened his eyes to see Spike and Gerndt both laughing uproariously at him.

So there was to be no sympathy there. Danny would have to face two days of injections. Into his hamstring Gerndt would be injecting a liquid extracted from fourteen different plants, among them daisies, marigolds and deadly nightshade, a flower that got its name because the ancient Romans used it as a poison. But Gerndt didn't tell Danny that last bit. He felt Danny had heard enough already.

Indeed, Danny did feel like a punchbag. Suffering from Gerndt's injections was bad enough, but almost worse was the news on his phone which he had left switched off until the treatment was finished.

There were a series of texts from Anthuan and Jess:

Where are you?

We're waiting for you.

Come on!

What's happened to you?

Giving up on you now.

Hope you're still coming round to my house later.

As Danny read the texts, it was as though Gerndt had now injected him with guilt. *How could I be so stupid?* he asked himself. *How could I forget to tell them?*

Then finally, the next morning, Anthuan had written simply:

What happened to you last night? I thought we were mates . . .

★ 19 ★

THE LONG WAIT

Danny had always thought that there could be nothing better in the world than being an athlete. Now he had arrived at a different conclusion: there was nothing worse in the world than being an injured athlete.

Or maybe there was. Maybe there was nothing worse than being an injured athlete and having your father fuss all over you. Since the end of A levels, Danny's dad had completely changed his tune. While his mum was lovely and caring and always looking after him, his father seemed to become the Prime Minister of fitness. He was continually checking that Danny had done every exercise he was given, checking his nutrition was right, checking that the treatment and the care he was getting was spot on. Danny started getting five, six, sometimes seven texts a day from him, every one of them checking up on him.

And this actually made him laugh. It was lovely feeling that his dad was by his side, his number-one supporter. If only he got the same from Ricky who had become strangely silent again.

Since surviving his two days of torture in Stockholm, Danny now had a new occupation: waiting. Waiting for his hamstring to mend. Waiting for the two weeks to pass to see if his Olympic dream was dead or alive. And those two weeks took so long to pass; Danny sometimes found himself staring at the second hand of his watch and wondering why it wouldn't move a little faster.

He went on the Internet to see what other sportsmen did when they were injured. Michael Owen occupied his time by buying racehorses. *Nice idea, Michael,* Danny thought, *but I'm still dependent on my dad for pocket money! I can barely afford a goldfish, let alone a horse!* Jonny Wilkinson had filled his time by learning French and teaching himself the piano. *Nice idea, Jonny, but I've just done my A levels. There's no room in my head for any more learning right now.*

Yet it wasn't actually as if Danny was bored or had nothing to do. In fact, he discovered that being injured was a very busy, full-time affair. When he got home from Stockholm, he was told he could have a day to rest and that he was then expected to travel up to Sheffield where he would spend a week at the English Institute of Sport. This, it turned out, had also been arranged by Charles Perryman.

And after Sheffield, he was allowed home, but he was nevertheless expected to spend every day at the

Olympic Medical Institute in north London. And that had been organized by Charles Perryman too.

The English Institute of Sport was a massive, modern sports complex and it had hotel accommodation so Danny could sleep there too. The Olympic Medical Institute was not so massive, not so shiny and new, and was attached to a hospital. But the reason he was sent to both places was because some of the best sports doctors in the country worked inside them.

Every day, Danny was put through a different schedule. A lot of it involved heavy massage on his leg. Sometimes he was put in the 'recovery pool', a shallow swimming pool that he had to wade up and down in to strengthen the hamstring muscles. A lot of the time was spent in the gym keeping the other parts of his body fit. And at the end of every day, when Danny was utterly exhausted, one of the sports doctors would have to write a report and send it by email to Charles Perryman to tell him how well Danny was progressing.

The big question was this: was his injury mending fast enough? Would he pass his fitness test?

But Danny had other questions on his mind too, like: how had he been so stupid and selfish not to think about his friends? He knew and accepted that being a professional athlete required him to be very dedicated, but he had never considered that it would turn him into a selfish or thoughtless person.

He had rung Anthuan from Stockholm and explained what had happened. And Anthuan had called him an idiot and many names much worse than that, but Anthuan also understood what had happened and he said he was happy for Danny that the Olympic dream was suddenly alive again.

Jess seemed happy to forgive him too. 'Don't worry, Dan,' her text read. 'Keep chasing your Olympic dream. You so deserve it.'

He knew, too, that Jess was right: he had only one priority in his life right now and it was the hamstring. Could it mend fast enough?

The newspapers seemed to enjoy asking the same question too. Every two or three days, it seemed, there would be a small story about him. 'Danny back on track' was the headline one day in the *Daily Express*. The next day the *Daily Mail* had a story saying 'Powell stuck in slow recovery'. As the day of his fitness test approached, the newspapers seemed to write more about him. 'Big doubts for Danny deadline day' was one headline on the same day that another paper's headline was 'Perryman positive for Powell'.

Danny wondered where all these stories came from and which ones were true and which ones weren't. But what he knew for sure was that, as the fortnight wore on, his leg was slowly improving. He was delighted when the day came when he could throw his crutches away. And, a couple of days later, he felt he could walk without feeling any lingering pain from the injury. What a boost to his hopes that was! But, while he could clearly feel that his body was on the mend, the question remained: was it mending fast enough?

Eventually, the day arrived. The day of the test. Danny awoke early and he felt more nervous than he had before any of his A level exams. He felt sick, but only through nervousness, and that didn't matter. What mattered was his leg. In fact, what really mattered was Perryman.

★ 20 ★

THE TEST

Charles Perryman was an impressive man. He wore a suit and was fifty-three years old though he looked more like thirty-five. In fact, he looked as if he could probably pass the fitness test and run in the Olympics himself.

But he impressed Danny because of the way Spike was behaving. Spike was quiet, pleasant and polite around him – and Spike wasn't usually quiet or pleasant or polite at all. And Danny also noticed that Spike didn't swear once in front of Perryman – and Spike usually swore a lot. In fact, Spike offered to make Perryman a coffee and when Perryman said, 'No thanks,' he then offered to make him a cup of tea. And it was normally the case that Spike expected other people to make the coffee for him.

They were sitting in Spike's office at the Lee Valley Stadium, chatting. It was a dark, grey morning and cold, and rain was hammering down on the roof. Danny felt more nervous than he had ever done in his life. Perryman had come, as promised, to oversee

Danny's fitness test; Danny just wanted to get on with it all.

But Perryman just seemed content to chat. He talked about how excited he was that the Olympic Games were coming to London. He talked about the athletes in his team and who he thought might win medals for Great Britain. 'Just imagine winning an Olympic medal here, in London, at the London Olympics, in front of a British crowd,' he said dreamily. 'That would surely be the best thing any British athlete could ever hope to achieve.'

That didn't make all this standing around waiting any easier. *Can't we just get out there and get it done?* Danny thought.

'Now, Danny,' Perryman said, 'how much faster do you think you could run?'

Danny was slightly surprised by the question. 'I'm not really sure yet, Mr Perryman,' he replied. 'I've gone under ten seconds already, so I'm hoping to go a lot lower.'

'Good. What do you think of your chances of beating Usain Bolt?' he asked.

That question surprised Danny even more, but he could only give an honest answer. 'I don't wish to sound cocky, Mr Perryman,' he said. 'But I've been training all year to beat him. And I wouldn't have trained so hard if I didn't think there was a chance.'

Perryman narrowed his eyes, looking at Danny as

if he was studying him closely. 'Good. Good,' he said. 'And would you like that chance, Danny?'

'Yes, Mr Perryman, you know I would,' Danny replied.

'Good. Well, you've got it then.'

'Pardon?' said Danny, totally confused. 'What did you say?'

'I said, "You've got it then,"' Perryman said, smiling. 'You're in the team. You're going to the Olympics!'

Danny looked at Spike and then back at Perryman, and then at Spike and then at Perryman again. Spike looked shocked. Perryman was grinning broadly. *Was this some kind of a joke?* 'But Mr Perryman, I thought, I thought . . .' Danny was now stammering. 'What about the fitness test? I haven't done it. I thought that's what you'd come here for.'

'No, Danny,' Perryman replied. 'I came here to tell you that you've passed the test already. I've been checking your progress every day since you got back from Stockholm. I've been speaking to your doctors and sports scientists and physiotherapists every evening and I've now got more data and analysis in my laptop about you and your right hamstring than I have on anyone else in my entire squad. Danny, I know more about your hamstring than you will ever know. So I'm not going to make you kill yourself out on the track now. I'm not sure it'd do you any good and you don't need to anyway. Because, even though you didn't know it, you've been kind of taking this test every day for a fortnight now.

'The thing is, Danny, I've had to learn about you fast. To pick you for the Great Britain team in the Olympics, I needed to know what you were like. Were you worthy of a place in the team? Would you do your country proud? Could you, at eighteen years old, really come to the biggest sporting event on earth and do a good job? And not be too scared? And so I haven't just been speaking to all these doctors about your hamstring, Danny, I've been talk-ing to them about you. What are you like? And you know what? I now know how hard you have worked, Danny. I know that you have shown dedication. I know the answers to all the questions are yes. Yes, Danny, you would do your country proud. So I have been desperate to pick you for the team. I just needed your hamstring to come through the test too.

'And finally, last night, I spent another hour on the phone with the sports scientists at the Olympic Medi-cal Institute and up at Sheffield. And we all agree that your hamstring will hold up. In fact, you'll do better than that, much, much better than that. In fact, Danny, between you and me, you're not the only one who thinks you've got a chance against Usain Bolt. I do too.'

Perryman then held out his hand to Danny and added calmly: 'So, Danny Powell, welcome to the Great Britain Olympic team.'

Danny grabbed Perryman's hand and shook it hard. He was speechless, but not for long. 'Thank you, Mr Perryman,' he said. 'Thank you, thank you, thank you. Thank you so much.' He still hadn't let Perryman's hand go. 'I won't let you down,' he said breathlessly. 'You won't regret this, I promise you won't.' He then paused, finally let go of Perryman's hand and asked: 'But would you mind if I give my coach a hug?'

'I think you should do,' Perryman replied.

And so Spike and Danny hugged hard. And then they suddenly started screaming. In fact, together they screamed so loud that Gladys on reception heard it.

'Olympics!' they shouted. 'We're going to the Olympic Games! We're going to the Olympic Games!'

Five minutes later, Perryman had gone. Danny still felt as though he wanted to shout and scream. He wanted to tell the whole world. But instead, he sat quietly in Spike's office and fired off three quick texts and then a fourth, which was slightly longer.

Dear Dr Gerndt. Your magic worked. Thank you for being my magician. See you at the Games.

Ant. I passed. I'm going to the Games. Thank you for being my mate. When these Olympics are finally done, I hope to be able to show you the kind of friendship you've shown me.

Dad, Mum. I passed. I'm going to the Olympics. Thank you for your support. I hope so much to make you proud of me.

Ricky. Dunno how you are or what's going on in your life. But I've just made it into the British team for the Olympics. This is the dream we always talked about. I've got there. I hope you're happy. I'd love you to come down from Liverpool and share it with me.

★ 21 ★

FAME AGAIN

Here we go again. That was Danny's thought when he
woke the next morning to find that he was the big
story in all the papers again. It was just three weeks
until the Olympics opened and it seemed that excitement about the Games was growing by the day.
Olympic news and gossip dominated all the headlines and now Danny was back as the main story
again.

It was dead weird to be famous like this, all of a
sudden. When he walked down the street, people
would say 'Congratulations!' or 'Good luck!' or
'Bring us back a medal, Danny!' And he liked that.
That was fine.

He also liked being the local boy. Over the last few
years, he had heard so many people in Stratford
make funny comments about their borough, things
like: 'Nothing interesting has ever happened in Stratford before. And now we've got the Olympics!' And
now, just three weeks away, so many people seemed
so proud, so happy that they would be welcoming

the world right to their doorsteps. It seemed that the Olympics had made everyone feel like a group, a close community, because they all wanted the visitors from around the world who were coming to the Olympics to think that Stratford was a good place with good people.

And now these people had their own Olympian, Danny Powell, their own little superstar. Danny liked that. He liked the fact that he helped them feel that they had something to be proud of. Not only did they have their own Olympics, but they had their very own man to cheer for.

So that was the good bit about suddenly being famous. There were some funny parts to it too. Once a week since he collapsed injured during the trials, he had received a package through the post that was sent from the main offices in the Olympic Park. It contained letters, all of them sent to him. It seemed that people who wanted to write to him were putting his name on the envelope and then, below it, the address of the London Olympics – it was as if they thought he lived inside the Olympic Stadium!

That was strange enough. But these letters came from people from all over the country and some from other countries too, and they were all from people he had never met. They all said they were his fans and that he was their hero. Some letters came from girls who had put lots of kisses at the bottom of the letter. Some girls even included their photograph and phone number and asked him to give them a call.

Predictably, it was Anthuan who was most excited about all the fan mail. To be precise, Anthuan was excited about the female fan mail and he took it upon himself to write back to all Danny's female admirers on his behalf.

The bit that Danny didn't like about suddenly being famous were all the newspaper stories. That morning, after getting his place in the Olympic team, all the newspapers were discussing him. Almost every story about him said nice things – 'Well done, Danny', 'Three cheers for Danny!' That sort of thing. But they all went further than that.

They started asking questions about him and about what it would be like for him to be in the Olympic Games. Some newspapers said that there would be a lot of pressure on him to do well, maybe too much pressure. One newspaper wrote: 'The boy is only eighteen and his body has already broken down once on his brave march to the Olympics. Can we reasonably expect him to get to the finishing line still in one piece? Are we not asking too much of this courageous young man?'

Hmmm, Danny thought when he read that. *I'm not worried about that. Not worried at all.*

But there was something else, something that he did not find quite so easy to dismiss. On that first day of the trials, he had met those two journalists,

Pete O'Byrne, the guy from *The Times*, and Jenny Nicholas, from the *Daily Express*, and because he now knew their faces, he had started to read what they wrote. And today they both wrote about him and they both said pretty much the same thing.

In the *Daily Express* was:

Danny Powell is clearly the most exciting young athlete we have seen in this country for a number of years and his talent deserves admiration and support. However, it is a little crazy to believe that an eighteen-year-old is going to be an Olympic champion. It is plain and simple: he is too young. Yes, he is brilliant. Yes, he may become Olympic champion one day, in four years' time or eight perhaps. But not now. Boys of eighteen do not become Olympic sprint champions.

But what worried Danny even more was what he read in *The Times*. Pete O'Byrne had laid out lots of facts, all about the ages of sprinters at past Olympics, and they were not very friendly facts at all. Usain Bolt, when he won the 100 metres four years ago in the last Olympics, was five days short of his twenty-second birthday and the guys who finished second and third behind him were twenty-three and twenty-two years old. The guy who'd won the 100 metres in the previous Olympics, in Athens, had been twenty-two years old. And the guy who'd won four years before that, in Sydney, had been twenty-six.

When Carl Lewis first won the 100 metres, he was twenty-three.

This was what Pete O'Byrne wrote:

> The history of athletics tells us that sprinters do not hit full speed until their early twenties. Bolt was unusual to have gone so fast at the age of twenty-one. When you look back at years and years of athletic perform-ance, the evidence is not encouraging for the splendid Mr Powell. No one has been able to run faster than the rest of the world until they have reached their twenties. Certainly no one who is eighteen. Powell has already given us shocks and entertainment aplenty, but it would be the biggest shock of all if he was to push his eighteen-year-old body to achievements that no teenager has ever managed before. A teenage human body is not designed to do what Powell hopes to do. It sounds simplistic, but Powell is just not old enough to beat Usain Bolt.

Hmmm, Danny thought when he read it, *that wasn't really what I wanted to hear.*

★ 22 ★

HOW TO BEAT USAIN BOLT, PART 2

At training later that morning, Spike was in a furious mood. He was holding up a copy of *The Times*, shaking the newspaper in his hands and bawling at Danny. Danny had just made the mistake of telling Spike that he had seen the article and was slightly concerned about what he had read.

'You believe this?' Spike yelled. 'You mean to say you've read this and now you think you can't win? Danny! Come on!' Spike was shouting so loudly that Danny actually found himself edging backwards so that he was pinned against Spike's office wall. He could see the veins on the side of Spike's head bulging as the volume rose. 'Speedboy – what's happened to you? Yesterday you were singing and dancing because you'd been selected to run in the Olympics. And today you've read a couple of newspapers and you don't think you can win any more? Come on, Danny! Come on! Pull yourself together!'

Spike sat down in his chair and shook his head in dismay. Then he stood up again and then sat down.

Danny wasn't sure what to do, so he did the only thing he could think of and offered to get Spike a coffee.

Spike sighed loudly, shook his head again and then started talking, more slowly, more quietly, with his teeth closed, as if he was trying to contain his anger. 'No thanks, Dan. There is one thing you can do though. Leave the building now. Take a walk round the stadium and clear your head of the rubbish you've been reading. Just empty it all out so there's not a single word from *The Times* left infecting that sensitive little mind of yours. Walk once round the entire building and then come back here. I'll be waiting. And then we can get back to work. We've got a lot of work to do. We've got a man called Usain Bolt to beat, and it won't be easy.'

So Danny left Spike's office. He smiled to himself. He hadn't seen Spike in a rage like that for quite some time. When he saw that bulging vein on the side of his head, he thought Spike was about to explode. He knew that Spike would soon calm down – he always did. He just needed a bit of peace and quiet.

But Danny didn't walk round the building as Spike had instructed. That would have been absurd. He just went upstairs and said hello to Gladys on reception. He liked Gladys. She was always there, every day, always cheerful, always greeted Danny with a smile. They chatted for a while; Gladys told Danny about her son and daughter and how well they were doing at school. And, after five minutes, Danny excused himself, made Spike a coffee and took it downstairs to him.

Spike was staring at his computer screen and didn't look round at Danny. 'Enjoy your walk?' he asked.

'Yup. Just what I needed,' Danny replied. Spike couldn't see the smile on Danny's face. And the smile vanished the minute Spike swivelled round in his chair.

'Dan,' he said, quietly and seriously. 'I'm going to say this once and then we are moving on. Right?'

'Right.'

'You've forgotten about Uncle Carl. At least, that's how it seems to me. But you need to remember Uncle Carl now more than ever. If you worry about what other people are saying or thinking, you might as well not bother with the Olympics. Carl Lewis didn't care what the rest of the world said about him. In fact, he took great pleasure in ignoring them. He believed in himself and he loved proving everyone wrong. Again and again and again. Now it's your turn, Dan. Prove everyone wrong. Believe in yourself. Like Carl, Dan. Just like Uncle Carl.'

'I know, Spike. You're right.'

'Good,' Spike said. 'Because we've got work to do. There's less than a month until the Olympics

100-metres final. Now pull up a seat. I need to explain to you how you're going to win it.'

Spike started tapping the keys on his keyboard and Danny pulled his chair in closer so he could see. Up on the screen was a page entitled 'The Plan'. And under 'The Plan' was another headline: 'How to beat Usain Bolt'. Danny liked the sound of this. The next thirty minutes would be very important. Danny knew that and so he listened hard.

Usain Bolt, Spike explained, is the best 100-metres runner of all time. No argument about that. Everyone knows it. But he has a weakness. It's only a small weakness; in fact, it is so small that it has never bothered him in the past. But if anyone is going to beat him, they have to make the most of it. 'And,' Spike said slowly, 'it's all about reaction times.'

The ability of a sprinter to react to the starting gun in a 100-metres race is crucial. The quicker you react, the better. In other words, if you react fast to the bang of the gun, you'll get a fast start.

Technology is so advanced nowadays that, in top races, they sometimes use a recording device that can measure the sprinters' reaction times. In other words, it measures the time between the starting gun firing and the sprinters starting to move. Their reactions, obviously, are astonishingly fast. The quickest sprinters can react in not much more than a tenth of a second; the average reaction time of the best in the world is around one and a half tenths of a second.

'Now look at this,' Spike said as he tapped his keyboard again so that a new set of numbers appeared on the screen. 'These are the reaction times of the eight runners in the final of the men's 100 metres in the Beijing Olympics four years ago. What do you see?'

1. Richard Thompson, 0.133 seconds
2. Walter Dix, 0.133 seconds
3. Asafa Powell, 0.134 seconds
4. Darvis Patton, 0.142 seconds
5. Marc Burns, 0.145 seconds
6. Michael Frater, 0.147 seconds
7. Usain Bolt, 0.165 seconds
8. Churandy Martina, 0.169 seconds

Danny looked at the reaction times and focused particularly on Bolt's. *Very interesting, very surprising too.* Bolt's reaction time in the final was 0.165 seconds. That made him the second slowest in the race.

'You see what I'm saying?' Spike asked.

'I think I do,' Danny replied.

'Good. Well, you'd better look at this then, too.' Spike then pulled up some more numbers on to his screen. They were more reaction times from Beijing, this time from Bolt's 100-metres semi-final, and Danny leaned in to get a closer look. Bolt's reaction time in the semi was 0.161 seconds. That made him the third slowest starter in his semi-final.

Danny had never realized this before. *Bolt is a slow starter!* he thought. *Spike really does have a point. Bolt's reaction times are slow.*

Spike leaned back in his chair and raised his eyebrows at Danny. 'What do you think, Speedboy – interesting, eh?'

Danny paused. 'Yes,' he said. But the tone of his voice suggested that he clearly wasn't certain. 'The bit I don't get is this, Spike.' He paused again, as if he was trying to assemble his thoughts. 'I see what you're saying: he doesn't have the greatest of starts. And that should really hurt him. But it doesn't, does it? He may have had a bad start, but he still won the gold. He still broke the world record. If he's still going to destroy everyone else, what good is a slow start to us?'

'Good question, Dan,' said Spike. 'And here's your answer. Bolt always wins because he's so relaxed, so confident. These other guys – they might have a better start than him, but they lose it so quickly. He's always caught them by the 20-metre mark. And once he's passed them, they'll never catch him. But I wonder: what if you put Bolt under pressure? What if you can keep your lead a little longer? He's never been under pressure because he's always been ahead. So we don't know what he's like under pressure. For the last four years, he's never been scared; no one has worried him. What if you got him scared? What if he suddenly thought: this isn't quite so easy any more? What if he started to worry: I might not win?

'Here's a fact, Dan: some people like pressure and most people hate it. Obvious, I know. But what if Bolt is like most people? What if he hates it? Then someone else might win the Olympic 100 metres instead. And who's that going to be, Dan? Who?'

Danny never gave an answer to Spike's question. He didn't need to and Spike didn't need to hear it. But Danny understood loud and clear what Spike was saying and he thought it was brilliant. What a plan! What a coach!

The next two weeks were given over to Spike's plan. Danny spent his nights dreaming about the Olympics and his days at Lee Valley working on his start. He hardly saw anyone else or thought about anything else.

At the track, Spike worked his plan brilliantly. He went out and bought the newest and most expensive set of blocks he could find, which also contained a timing device to record the runner's reaction time. That way, Spike and Danny could work endlessly on Danny's reaction time. The first day Danny did fifty-five timed starts; the next day sixty-seven; the day after that forty-eight. And the thrill that Danny derived from this was huge because he saw his average reaction time get better and better and better.

Alongside the track, Spike had put up a large sign saying: 'Bolt's Beijing reaction time: 0.165 seconds'. And so for every recorded start that Danny did in training, the target was to beat 0.165 seconds. And then to get faster and faster and faster. And the ultimate goal was to have a reaction time faster than everyone in that Beijing final.

Danny was a fast starter anyway. His first start was 0.159 seconds. But after the first day of intense practice, he was down to 0.150 seconds. By the end of a week, his average reaction time was 0.142 seconds and, in the second week, it was coming down further.

On the last day of 'block work', Spike gave Danny a challenge. 'I want to see three starts under 0.135 seconds, OK, Dan? Three in a row,' he said. 'And once you've done that, I think you'll be ready for the Olympics.'

Immediately, Dan got to work. His first three start times were 0.133 seconds, then 0.134 seconds and then 0.129 seconds.

'OK, Speedboy,' Spike said. 'You now know.'

'I know what, Spike?' Danny replied, a little confused.

'You now know what it takes to beat Bolt. Now off you go. You're as ready now as you'll ever be.'

★ 23 ★

THE UNFORGETTABLE OLYMPICS

The Olympics are not just about running; they are not just about trying to get medals or trying to beat Usain Bolt. At least this was what Danny was quickly learning. As the days passed and the Olympic 100 metres got closer and closer, there were four episodes in Danny's life that he thought he would never forget.

UNFORGETTABLE OLYMPIC EPISODE ONE

Here is the weird thing about the Olympics: the amount of free stuff you get. A week before the Games, Danny was told to report to the British Olympic Association's headquarters in Central London to be given his team kit. He knew he needed a team suit and a team tracksuit and a couple of Team GB running vests, but he had no idea that he would be leaving with a pile of free clothes, shoes and stuff so big that even Santa would not get it all in his sack.

What Danny had never realized was that, by qualifying for Team GB for the Olympics, he had earned himself five pairs of free Team GB pants. And he didn't just get one Team GB tracksuit, he got three. He got two pairs of Team GB wrap-around sunglasses. He got four Team GB baseball caps. He got a pair of Team GB trainers and three pairs of Team GB shoelaces. That was to say nothing of his ten Team GB polo shirts, the seven pairs of Team GB shorts and a Team GB umbrella. He decided he would give his Team GB box of chocolates to his mum and his Team GB cufflinks to his dad. He was just about to ask why he would need a pair of Team GB gloves in the middle of summer when he was also given a Team GB dressing gown, two pairs of Team GB pyjamas, a Team GB toothbrush and some Team GB toothpaste.

Danny had been intending to take all this home with him on the London Underground, but he realized that he had so much stuff that he had to take a taxi. On the way home, he texted Ant excitedly:

> For being my mate, I've got a gift for you. I would like to present you with your very own pair of free Team GB slippers and a pot of Team GB hair wax.

UNFORGETTABLE OLYMPIC EPISODE TWO

The day before the Olympics were due to start, a week and a day before the athletics competition would begin, Danny moved into the Olympic Village. And he could not believe what he found there. In fact, the Olympic Village was so big that initially Danny found nothing; all he did was get lost.

The Olympic Village is where all the athletes and their coaches live during the Olympics. It can house around 5,000 people so it is less like a village and more like a small town. It is also a very exclusive place to go. Only Olympians are allowed in, no one else. There is a meeting zone near the entrance where friends and guests are allowed, but there is a limit. They cannot, for instance, go to the massive food hall where you can get everything from McDonald's to Norwegian pickled herring. And yes, to Danny's extreme delight, he realized that this was all free too, even the Norwegian herring.

Sometimes Danny had to pinch himself. Every day here, he felt partly like a kid and partly like a tourist. He wanted to say 'Hi' to everyone he recognized and at the same time he wanted to ask for their autograph. Instead, he kept on texting Anthuan:

In the food hall, Michael Phelps is sitting twenty metres away.

Or:

Just met Chris Hoy. What a great guy!

Or:

Did you know that the best-looking female athletes in
the Olympics all seem to do the pole vault?

It was only because of the flags that Danny stopped
getting lost. Almost every team from every country
had its own apartment block and they would drape
huge national flags out of their windows and over
the apartment block walls. So Danny soon worked
out that, to get to the Team GB apartment blocks,
he had to go left out of the food hall, down past the
Canadian block and then the Russian block, then
right at Brazil, past Egypt and New Zealand then
right at Morocco and there, on the apartment block
in front of him, would be a cascade of Union Jack
flags. He liked that; they made it feel like home.

Danny's room was in GB Block Two up on the
fifth floor with most of the athletes. The swimmers
were below him on the fourth floor and the cyclists
were up above on the sixth. Danny's room was next
to Deon Francis and Max Donne, all three of the
100-metre sprinters together in a mini-apartment,
Flat 32, with a shared sitting-room area. This was
great. Deon and Max were not his rivals any more
as they had been in the trials the previous month.
Now they were teammates, they supported each
other, they encouraged each other and, after a while,
they started joking around with each other.

Sometimes Planet Olympics seemed so weirdly

amazing that Danny had to pinch himself. *Remember why you're here*, he would say to himself. And then he would go to his room and reread the words on his bedroom wall. Because Spike, typical Spike, had printed off two pieces of paper and told Danny to stick them up and read them every day.

On one of them was a famous quote from Uncle Carl: 'My thoughts before a big race are usually pretty simple. I tell myself: "Get out of the blocks, run your race, stay relaxed. If you run your race, you'll win. Channel your energy. Focus."' Danny liked that and he kept replaying it in his mind. *Focus, Danny. Focus.*

The other quote was from Uncle Jesse and it was short but very sweet: 'One chance is all you need.' Deon and Max liked that one in particular, so much so that they started saying it themselves too. 'One chance, guys,' Deon would say in the mornings at training. 'That's all we need.'

There was something else that Deon said, something that Danny really liked. The three of them were relaxing in their flat one afternoon after training, chatting about the Games ahead, when Deon sat forward in his chair, as if he had just had an idea. 'I've got a good feeling about these Games,' he said. 'I really, truly believe that one of us three is going home with a medal.'

Max then looked at Danny and nodded his head in approval and, in turn, Danny looked at Deon. 'Sounds very good to me, Deon,' he said.

'Cool,' said Deon. 'Let's shake on it then.'

So the three of them clasped hands in a triple handshake. 'To us,' they said together. 'To a medal for Flat 32. To a beautiful shiny medal for a British sprinter.'

UNFORGETTABLE OLYMPIC EPISODE THREE

Like much of what happened at the Olympic Games, Danny had watched the Opening Ceremony on TV. He had seen it, thought it looked amazing. And here he was now, actually taking part in it.

At the Opening Ceremony of the Games, there are fireworks and dancing and singing. In fact, it is one long celebration. And, at the very end, the Olympians – the competitors in all the teams from all around the world – join in. They march into the stadium, team by team, in alphabetical order, led in by a member of their team carrying their Olympic flag. Thousands and thousands of them. But, because Great Britain were the hosts, they did not march in alphabetical order. Instead, they marched in last. And they got an astonishing reception from the crowd.

Danny walked into the stadium with Deon on his right and Max on his left, and the noise was so great he could barely hear himself think. As they waved to the crowd, the crowd waved back. In fact, the crowd shrieked back. And Danny could not stop smiling. He turned to Deon and started talking, but Deon couldn't hear so Danny shouted instead: 'I now understand why they call it the greatest show on earth!'

He also wondered what his parents would be thinking, watching on the television less than three kilometres away. He wondered what Ant would be thinking too so he texted him:

Feel like a rock star!

But there was one other thought that was playing on his mind. *Come on, Dan, enjoy it, enjoy it all you can. But remember, the next time you walk inside this stadium, it will be business. You're not here to wave, Dan, you're here to run.*

UNFORGETTABLE OLYMPIC EPISODE FOUR

As if Danny needed any reminder of why he was there, he got it four days later. He knew it was coming; he knew it would happen soon enough. In fact, he was a little surprised it hadn't happened earlier.

It was at breakfast in the Olympic Village. Half past nine. He was with Deon and Max as usual and they were walking over to a table to eat. And that was when Danny saw him, sitting at a table about thirty metres away; he was looking relaxed, chatting and laughing with his friends. In fact, he didn't look particularly different from anyone else in the breakfast room that morning. But it was him. Unmistakably him. Usain Bolt. The man himself. Here at the London 2012 Olympics.

Danny stood transfixed. He didn't want to move. He wanted to stand there and watch. There he was, the giant of Beijing. This was the man Danny had watched and admired. And now he was the man Danny had to beat.

The London Olympics, Danny knew, was the greatest experience of his life. But he also knew that no matter how great the experience, life still ticked on. He might be here at the Olympic Games, he might be running for his country, he might be in the same breakfast hall as his hero, Usain Bolt. Yet Ricky, his brother, was still nowhere to be seen, nowhere to be heard. Silent, absent, gone.

★ 24 ★

GOING FOR GOLD

As each day passed, the tension rose in GB Block Two, Flat 32. It grew little by little, so much so that Danny barely noticed. He knew that having Deon and Max with him was a godsend. They helped keep him calm. And, because they were each experiencing the same feelings of nervousness, they all understood how each other was feeling. But there was no doubt about it: as their big moment approached, the laughter started to die in Flat 32.

In fact, when they awoke on the morning of 4 August, they were all a little relieved. Here it was, their date with destiny. The moment they had been training all their lives for. The 100 metres of the London 2012 Olympics. The waiting was over.

The three of them breakfasted early, but they barely talked. They were serious, nervous; it was hard to make conversation. It was hard even to eat.

Danny saved his talking for his parents. He rang them at home, and he didn't know what to say, he just wanted to hear their voices. He just wanted to be reassured.

'You'll be brilliant,' his dad said. 'We are so proud of you. Whatever happens today and tomorrow, we are so proud.'

The three of them then headed to the warm-up track together to prepare. Danny was relieved to see Spike there waiting for him. Spike looked relaxed and that was what Danny needed. Because Danny still felt nervous and he didn't like that. Why hadn't the nerves gone? Where had that warm, reassuring confidence gone?

Danny tried to ignore the nerves. Instead, he got on with the job. He stretched, he jogged a little. He listened to his iPod. He tried to ignore the fact that, on the very same warm-up track, were another seventy-nine of the best sprinters in the whole of the world. Yes, Bolt was there. Bolt was pretty much the first man Danny saw when he arrived. Bolt looked huge, he looked awesome. *Stop it*, Danny thought to himself. *Ignore Bolt. Concentrate on yourself and not him.*

Just like in the trials, there would be three rounds of racing in order to reach the Olympic final and the competition would, of course, get harder and harder as you got through each round. The first round – the heats – they should be the easy ones. At least that is what Spike told him. 'Use the heats to find your feet,' he said. 'You feel nervous. Of course you do. It's the Olympics. Everyone feels nervous. You wouldn't be human if you didn't feel a bit like that. So go out into that stadium and get used to it. Get used to the crowd, get used to the tension. Focus, run well. And then come back here and we'll start talking about the next round – that's when the competition begins to get serious. But first – how about a game of chess?'

That sounded like a good plan to Danny.

There were ten heats and he would be going in Heat Three. He liked that: nice and early. Get it out of the way. And there was only one other name he recognized in his heat: Ryan van Zyl from South Africa, a powerful, tough runner who was brought up in safari country and told anyone who would listen that he only knew he was a decent runner when he was eighteen years old and successfully saved his life by running away from an angry, rampaging elephant.

Van Zyl was in Lane Six and Danny was in Lane Seven. And as Danny made his way to the stadium, he found himself thinking about that elephant; he also realized that he still felt nervous. And it was when he walked into the stadium that those nerves really hit him; he could feel his heart pumping. Every single seat in the entire stadium was full. And the crowd was shouting and screaming and cheering. And it was a noise like Danny had never heard before. Loud, ecstatic, excited.

Danny knew that, somewhere in here, his mother and father were watching him. And Ant was there too; he had come with Jess. But that didn't really help. Because there were so many thousands of people, Danny would never have seen them. And he shouldn't have been thinking about them anyway. He looked down at his vest; was his heart now beating so fast he could see his skin moving?

Come on, Dan, concentrate, he thought to himself. *Relax, remember what Spike said, this is the easy round.*

But it wasn't easy. They went down in their blocks, 'Set!', and then came the bang of the gun. But the bang was followed, within a split second, by a second bang. A false start.

Danny looked nervously around. *It wasn't me, was it?* He didn't think it was. What if it was? *I'm sure my start was good.*

There was a restlessness in the stadium as the runners and the crowd awaited the news. Who had false-started? Who was to have their entire Olympic dream wrecked by instant disqualification?

Next to him, Danny heard the throaty, hard tones of a South African. It was van Zyl, talking to him. 'You feeling scared, little boy?' he said. His accent was strong and sounded threatening, and Danny could see the flashing gold of his chain and, as if to match, the flashing gold of one of his canine teeth. Danny ignored him, but van Zyl didn't stop. 'Hey, little boy, I'm talking to you.'

Still Danny ignored him. He was not enjoying this. Not at all. 'Hey, little boy,' van Zyl said. 'I know you think it was you. You must be scared. Very scared. Do you want me to find your mummy?'

Still Danny ignored him. At least he tried to.

But van Zyl's creepy comments were interrupted by the stadium announcer. 'False start. Lane Four. Disqualification: Shinji Mirita of Japan.'

Danny stared at Mirita. He knew he shouldn't. He knew he was supposed to be concentrating on the race he was about to run. But Mirita looked as if his life had ended. He said nothing, did nothing, just looked around the stadium as if he was saying goodbye, and then walked backwards, a slow retreat from the Olympic Stadium, as if he couldn't bear to take his eyes off it.

But Danny was quickly shaken back to his senses. 'Lucky for you, little boy!' came the rasping whisper next to him.

He hated van Zyl. He wanted to win this race, but he was suddenly far more interested in beating the South African.

'On your marks.'

Danny went to his blocks. *Make sure you kick van Zyl's butt*, he said to himself.

'Set.'

He readied himself.

Bang!

Danny knew his start was poor. *But at least there was no false start.* He felt the runners on his left; he knew he was struggling; he knew van Zyl was comfortably ahead. *Come on, Dan!* Halfway and there was still some catching to do. Van Zyl was out of reach. *Come on, Dan. Stretch now.*

Danny dipped his head and shoulders forward at the finish. He knew he had run an appalling race. *Have I done it? Have I made the next round? Or have I blown it?* The whole race felt so close that he didn't have a clue.

He looked up at the scoreboard. Van Zyl had won in an easy 9.98 seconds. Then the scoreboard showed that the guy in Lane Two, from Ghana, was second. Danny waited for the third place result to come up. *Please let it be me! Please let it be me!*

And it was. Third place: Daniel Powell, 10.10 seconds. He was through to the next round.

'Hey, little boy!' Danny could hear van Zyl's throaty, South African voice behind him. 'You're too scared, little boy. These are the Olympic Games. You won't last another round.'

Once again, Danny didn't answer. But he couldn't help wondering if maybe van Zyl was right.

Spike was already at the warm-up track, waiting for him. *Thank God for Spike.* Danny felt he needed him more than ever. He knew that Spike would be furious.

He knew that Spike would tell him that he had run a lousy race. But he still needed some reassurance. He needed it badly.

But Spike wasn't furious. In fact, Spike wasn't angry at all. Spike was almost laughing. He was clearly chuckling to himself.

'What's so amusing, Spike?' Danny asked, completely mystified. 'I nearly screwed up the entire thing. I'm lucky to still be here in the Olympics. I was nervous, nervous as hell. And that van Zyl – what a lowlife! I let him get into my head. I let him bother me. Pretty much everything that could have gone wrong did go wrong, Spike, and you think that's funny?'

Spike paused to let Danny catch his breath and then he replied, slowly and warmly. 'Dan, I'm laughing because I'm glad. You're right. Everything you've just said is right. Yes, you did mess it up, big time. But you've also just told me why. You know perfectly well why. Because you were nervous. And because of that idiot van Zyl. I'm glad because if you understand why you messed it up, then you know perfectly well how to stop yourself doing it again.'

Danny looked at him perplexed.

'OK,' Spike said. 'Let's talk it through. How far did you run in there just now?'

'100 metres.'

'And is that any different to the distance you normally run?'

'No.'

'Good. So remember: it might be the Olympics, but everything else is the same. It's still 100 metres. You're still running in a straight line. There's nothing you are doing that is remotely different to anything you've done before. So forget that this is the Olympics. Just go out there and run the way you always have done. It's worked before and it'll work again.'

Danny nodded.

'And van Zyl?' Spike asked. 'C'mon, Speedboy! He was talking to you, right?'

'That's right, Spike.'

'And why? Why was he talking? Because he wanted to make friends? Why you and not the others?'

'I don't know, Spike,' Danny replied.

'Yes, you do, Dan. He's talking to you because he knows you're good. He's trying to unsettle you, Dan, because he's worried about you. Remember? But actually he's paying you a compliment. Bullies like van Zyl only target the competitors they're scared of. You need to remember that, Dan. Got it?' Danny nodded. 'Good. Now think about that and go out this afternoon and put it into action.'

And Danny then did exactly what Spike told him. In the second round in the afternoon, he ran a near-perfect race. He won in a time of 9.99 seconds. And he felt great.

And now he was in the Olympic semi-finals. The dream was still alive. More alive than ever.

And he also had a text on his phone. It was from Ricky.

> Keep going. Just keep on going. Two more races. I know you can do this. But whatever happens, I cannot tell you how proud of you I am.

★ 25 ★

THE CLIMAX

Today was the big day. Yesterday had been a huge test, but today was what really counted. Deon and Max had both passed yesterday's test too. They were both still in the race, but Flat 32 that morning was almost silent as they each contemplated what was ahead of them.

They had the whole day to get through. The semi-finals were not until seven o'clock in the evening. If they finished in the top four, then they would be in the final. At half past nine.

Danny felt horrible, nervous, as though he was waiting for his own execution. He could not wait for this evening, to get it over and done with. And yet he realized that he felt scared of it too. And the wait seemed so slow. He looked at his watch so often he began to wonder if it had broken. *Why wasn't that minute hand moving any faster?*

Just before lunchtime, Charles Perryman came to Flat 32. He said that the Team GB website had crashed because so many fans had been posting 'good luck' messages to Danny, Deon and Max. He also said that he had intended to carry up the bag of fan mail that had arrived for them, but that it was too heavy. 'But personally,' he said, 'I just wanted to wish you luck. And don't forget, this is the Olympics. It's special, boys. Try and enjoy it.'

Enjoy it? Was he having a laugh? Danny actually knew Perryman was right. He knew that relaxation and enjoyment would be the key to a good performance, though it didn't help that when he saw Usain Bolt in the food hall at lunchtime, he was smiling and laughing with a couple of others from the Jamaican team. *What's so funny, Usain?* Danny wondered. *How can you be so relaxed? And why can't I laugh and joke around like you?*

After lunch, Flat 32 decided they needed a distraction. A movie. That would help pass the day. So they watched *Rocky*, the film starring Sylvester Stallone as a heavyweight boxer. But, even during the film, Danny couldn't let his mind be distracted. He couldn't enjoy it. He still kept on looking at his watch. *How long to go? How long to go? How long to go?*

So he went into his room. He felt he needed to be with Uncle Carl and Uncle Jesse. He read their comments on his wall. Uncle Carl: 'If you run your race, you'll win.' And Uncle Jesse: 'One chance is all you need.' He read them and then reread them over and again. They made him feel a little stronger. He wished that Carl and Jesse could be here now, but he knew too that they had done what he was about to do, and they had been alone too. And it was all right to be nervous. Wasn't Jesse nervous? Did he not swallow hard as he crouched down, waiting for the *Bang!* of the gun, waiting to claim his gold medal?

But no words could make Danny feel better than the text from Ricky. Danny reread it and discovered that there were twenty-four other texts on his phone, from friends, family, from other sprinters, one from Jimmy Lewis, one from Kris the Cure, there was even one from Mr McCaffrey, his old headmaster. And they were all full of support. And he read and reread the one from his father:

> Danny, I never thought you could do this. But I was wrong. A lot of other people – your school, your competitors, the newspapers – they never thought you could do this either. You proved them wrong too. You proved us all wrong. Keep on believing in yourself. Keep on proving us all wrong. You had a dream. You can now make that dream come true.

That made Danny want to cry. And then he read and reread one from Ant:

> Bring me back gold, my friend. I hear Bolt is so scared of you he has cancelled his order of cheese sandwiches.

That almost made him laugh. In fact, that was the closest Danny came to finding anything funny all day.

*

To his great relief, Danny was in the easier semi-final, the second one, with Deon. Max was in the first and, in that race, he had both Bolt and van Zyl to contend with. Bolt was looking magnificent. Van Zyl was tipped as one of the very few who had a chance of beating him.

But the warm-up track was beginning to resemble a fast-moving reality TV show with contestants being voted off at a frightening rate. Yesterday morning, there had been eighty of them. Now they were down to sixteen. And forty-five minutes later, they were down to eight. And Max didn't make it. He finished fifth. His Olympic dream was over.

But Danny and Deon survived. Danny ran 9.99 seconds again and he felt better, confident. He finished third with Deon second. And their semi-final had only just finished when Deon wrapped Danny in a huge hug. 'Remember what we talked about?' he said, bouncing on his feet, the adrenalin and excitement shooting through him. 'We're in the final. Can you believe it? We're in the Olympic final! But we've done nothing yet. Remember what we said: there's going to be a medal from Flat 32. It's you or me, Dan, you or me!'

'Or both of us!'

★ 26 ★

THE OLYMPIC FINAL

Danny sat on the warm-up track, iPod plugged in, trying to focus. There wasn't time for chess. He thought about Kris the Cure, he thought about his father and mother and Juanita, his father's mother. He thought about Spike. And about Charles Perryman. And Ricky. And Ant. He thought about all these people who would be watching in the stadium. All these people who had supported him. He wanted to perform for them. He wanted the medal. He wanted to beat Bolt.

Focus, Dan, focus. He thought about Uncle Carl: *Be strong, don't be scared.* And he thought about Uncle Jesse: *Be true to yourself.*

And then Spike reminded him where his mind should be. On the start. On his reaction time. On beating Bolt at the gun.

'What was Bolt's reaction time in Beijing, Dan?' Spike asked.

'0.165 seconds,' Danny replied.

'Exactly. And tell me, Speedboy: what sort of reaction time can we expect from you?'

'I'll settle for 0.13.'

'Excellent. Start well, Speedboy. And then think of Uncle Carl: if you run your race, you'll win.'

It was just then that Danny's phone bleeped to signify a text. He liked these pre-race texts. They made him feel good.

But this one, he saw, to his horror, was from no friend. 'I know you're scared, little boy,' it read. 'Go home. You don't belong here any more.'

Danny deleted the text immediately. Then he looked across the warm-up track and on the other side he saw van Zyl, grinning back mischievously. *How did he get my number?* Van Zyl looked delighted with himself. He even started laughing.

That's all I need, Danny thought. But to make matters worse, as they started the walk over to the stadium for the final, van Zyl appeared by his side, so close that Danny could smell the sweat on his body. Danny moved to his left, but van Zyl followed him.

'You can't run away now, little boy,' van Zyl said in a quiet, threatening whisper. 'I can tell you're scared. You're scared, aren't you?'

Danny put his headphones back on to shut out van Zyl. But even then he saw the South African grinning at him cruelly.

Rise above it, Dan, he said to himself. But he was struggling and he knew it. All of a sudden, he felt nervous again. *Where's that warm confidence gone?*

When they walked into the Olympic stadium, they

were greeted by the loudest roar Danny had ever heard in his life. Danny took one look up at the crowd and then swallowed a big, lumpy swallow, just like Uncle Jesse's. And then he composed himself. *C'mon, Dan. Think of your start. Think of your reaction time. Think of 0.13 seconds out of the blocks. Think of Uncle Carl. Run your race and you'll win.*

He was in Lane Seven, Bolt was Lane Four, Deon was Lane Five and van Zyl was Lane Six. Van Zyl next to him – that was not what Danny needed. He still felt nervous. He felt more alive, more on edge than ever. But still nervous. *Where's my confidence?*

And then he heard that low, rasping, South African accent next to him again. 'Hey, little boy, you poor thing, you must be absolutely terrified.'

'On your marks!'

Danny stepped forward and crouched down, jamming his feet back into the blocks. A hush suddenly fell upon the whole crowd. You could hear a pin drop.

'Set!'

Now was the moment he had been waiting his whole life for.

Bang!

Bang!

Two bangs. A false start. Van Zyl rounded on Danny immediately. His face wore that same cruel grin, the gold tooth sparkling at the side of his mouth.

Was it me? Was it me? The whole crowd was suddenly murmuring, waiting for the stadium announcement. Who had gone early? Who had false-started? Who was about to be slung out of the Olympic final? *Was it me? Was it me?* Danny didn't know. He wanted to, but he wasn't sure. He thought he had got a good start. He had been trying so hard for a good start. But was it too good? Had he gone early? *Was it me?*

He looked at his seven rivals. No one seemed sure who it was. Deon shrugged. Bolt didn't seem to care.

There was no announcement. The stadium announcer seemed to be taking an age to discover who had transgressed. This was so painful. Again, Danny scanned his seven rivals. They were beginning to look impatient. Who was it? *Was it me? Was it me?*

And then at last: 'False start, Lane Seven, Daniel Powell.'

★ 27 ★

IT'S ALL OVER

Danny did not know what to do. Probably every single spectator in the whole stadium was watching him, watching how he behaved when faced with this horrible, horrible humiliation. Danny stood stock-still for a second, feeling the pounding in his chest, harder and harder, feeling the tear ducts of his eyes desperate to let go. He wanted to cry. But he knew he could not cry with the TV cameras of the world watching his every move. So, in a fleeting moment, he decided to run for it. He wanted away. He wanted to be as far from the Olympics as fast as he could go.

So he turned and ran. He ran back down the tunnel and out of the stadium. He was still in his running spikes, but he didn't care. He had left behind his kit, his iPod, his phone, his trainers, his tracksuit, everything. But he didn't care. He didn't care about anything.

Even though he didn't know where he was going, he knew the route. He had spent so long gazing down at the Olympic Park from Bridge Road he knew the fastest way out of the Olympics, out of the stadium, right up the slope, over the small bridge, then left, past the velodrome and the aquatic centre.

Danny was half-sprinting, half-crying. Some passers-by didn't even register him. Others stopped and stared. He heard others commenting, as if confused: 'Isn't that the young runner . . .'

But he didn't stop. Not for anyone. He couldn't stop until he was on his own. Completely and utterly alone.

He turned right again to the main gate out of the Olympic Park. He was supposed to stop at the security gates, but he didn't; he ran straight past and then just kept on going.

The furthest a sprinter normally runs in one go is 400 metres. That is their limit. But Danny just kept on going, away from the park, up towards Bridge Road and then round the corner until he had run nearly three kilometres and had ended up in Widdin Street. Back outside his own home.

No key. Of course he had no key. You don't carry your house keys on you when you're in the final of the Olympics 100 metres. So he started running again. Up the road, round the back of the houses and down the alley. He clambered over the wall at the back of the small garden behind his house, retrieved the spare key from where it was always kept beneath a flowerpot and let himself in.

Only when he got upstairs to his room did he kick off his spikes. He threw himself down on his bed and then he finally allowed himself to cry. In fact, he sobbed. He sobbed loudly. He pumped tears into his pillow.

His mind remained fixed on that split second, that moment in the stadium when every single spectator was looking at him.

'False start, Lane Seven, Daniel Powell.' And with that it was over.

'False start, Lane Seven, Daniel Powell.' His dream was finished.

'False start, Lane Seven, Daniel Powell.' All that work. The years of training. The effort. All wasted. All completely wasted. Buried. Over. The Olympic dream was snuffed out.

The tears kept pouring from Danny's eyes. He didn't know for how long. He didn't know whether they stopped when he eventually fell asleep, or whether they stopped purely because there were no tears left to pour out. But some time later, probably around midnight, an hour and a half after the Olympic 100-metres final, Danny's Olympic pain was brought to an end by pure exhaustion.

The Olympics had been so tiring. Danny had been either on edge, or on a high, or just hopelessly over-excited for over a week, nearly two. And he didn't realize the toll that took on his body which was suddenly crying out for the opportunity to rest and recover. The sleep he fell into was deep. So deep that when his parents and Ricky eventually got home from the Olympic Stadium, they couldn't stir him.

And if he was dreaming, it certainly wasn't an Olympic dream any more.

★ 28 ★

FALSE START, LANE SEVEN

Danny woke late the next morning. It was just before eleven o'clock. It seemed strange to wake up in his room because he was used to waking up in Flat 32, but he realized, within a millisecond, where he was and why. The whole of the previous night came flooding back into his mind, washing over him and knocking him over like a tidal wave.

'False start, Lane Seven, Daniel Powell.' The words started drumming through his mind immediately.

'False start, Lane Seven, Daniel Powell.' He buried his head under the pillow.

What happened to me? How could I have let that happen? Why? Why did I false-start?

He dragged the curtain gently back so he could see outside. It was a grey day. And then it struck him: he didn't even know what had happened in the final. *Did Bolt win? Did the awful van Zyl get a medal? How did his mate Deon do? Oh, Deon.*

Danny hoped Deon had won a medal. But he also

realized that he didn't care. He didn't want to know. He didn't want to be a part of the Olympics any more.

'False start, Lane Seven, Daniel Powell.' As far as he was concerned, that was the end of it.

At midday, there was a knock at the door. It was Ricky. Ricky! Really, really Ricky. He smiled at Danny and gestured to the cup of tea in his hand.

'I'm sorry, Ricky,' Danny said.

'What are *you* apologising for?' he whispered back. 'You don't have to be sorry for anything.'

There was silence. There was probably no one else in the world that Danny would rather have seen than his brother, but still he felt uncomfortable.

'What are *you* doing here anyway?' he asked.

'I'm glad you asked,' Ricky replied, sitting on the side of Danny's bed. 'I just wanted to explain.'

'Explain what?'

'Where I've been? Why I disappeared. Because it kind of seems important now.'

Danny frowned at him. There was a brief silence. Why was Ricky talking to him about this now? What did this have to do with the idiot in Lane Seven?

Ricky took a deep breath and then started talking. 'You don't know how brilliant you are, Danny,' he said. He seemed to breathe a sigh of relief as he said it. 'I know you feel like hell. I know you hate yourself for your false start. But I cannot tell you how proud

I am of you. And I can hardly explain how jealous I am too.'

'Jealous?'

'Yes, jealous.'

'Why?'

'Because you've done what I wanted to do. I wanted to become a runner and I didn't. You did. I wanted to run in the Olympics and I didn't. You did. I had the same dream as you and I didn't follow it. I wasn't as brave as you, Dan. I did the sensible thing. The right thing. But it wasn't the brave thing.'

'What d'you mean, Rick?' Danny asked. 'You're going to graduate from university in a year's time. You're a super-soaraway success.'

'Maybe,' said Ricky, rolling his eyes. 'But I cannot tell you how many times I've sat in the library at Liverpool University wishing I was down at the training track with you and Spike. And I cannot tell you how many times I've wondered: what might I have achieved? Could I have got to the Olympics? How good could I have been if I'd pursued my dream?'

'Pretty hot, if you ask me,' replied Danny.

'Maybe,' replied Ricky. He let the silence return and then started talking again. 'But I'll never know, will I? And if you want to know why I went so weird on you, never talking, never texting, never being your friend, your brother: it was because I was jealous of you, Dan. Every time I knew that you were running, it made me jealous. I was scared of you being successful because every time you won another race, it would make me think that I could have been successful too.'

'That's stupid, Rick!'

'I know. I'm not very proud of myself. But then, this summer, it got ridiculous. You started doing so well, I couldn't be jealous any more, just amazed at every astonishing step you took. So I went from being jealous to being your number-one fan.'

'Well, why didn't you tell me?'

'I didn't want to butt in. You had enough going on. I thought it best to leave you alone.' He stopped, paused and then started again. 'But I can't leave you alone now, Dan, because I've been desperate to talk to you, to tell you two things.'

'What's that then?' Danny looked confused.

'Well, firstly, that I'm sorry I've behaved like an idiot. And, secondly, that you may not have won the Olympics last night, but you've won admiration around the world. You might feel rubbish inside, but you shouldn't, Dan. What you've done is amazing.'

'Thanks, Ricky,' said Danny. He held out his hand. Ricky took it and shook it firmly.

After a moment's silence, Ricky asked: 'How are you feeling?'

'Still worse than I've ever felt in my life,' Danny replied, though he managed a chuckle.

'Can I get you anything?'

'No thank you.'

'Will you come down for lunch soon?'

'No thanks.'

'You've got queues of people hoping to see you. And the phone's been going mad with people wanting to ask if you're OK. Do you want to see them, speak to them?'

'No. Not yet.'

'Dad?'

'Not yet.'

'Mum? Spike?'

'Not yet.'

'Ant? A rather nice-looking girl called Jess?'

'No one yet. It's going to be a while before I can face the world again.'

Danny stayed in his bedroom for the rest of the day. He didn't eat or drink. He didn't talk to anyone. He slept a little. But most of all, he was replaying over and over in his mind the events of the night before. 'False start, Lane Seven, Daniel Powell.'

Only at around midnight, after he was sure that his family had all gone to bed, did Danny eventually get up. It was weird. He hated the Olympics and yet he still loved them. He never wanted to hear about the Olympics again, and yet he was desperate to find out what had happened in the 100-metres final. He knew that he couldn't avoid reality forever. So he went downstairs and made himself a sandwich. It was a cheese sandwich and he managed to chuckle to himself as he made it. Ant was right: Usain Bolt could indeed have eaten a cheese sandwich before Danny got to the finish. Because Danny never even got there.

Then Danny went through into the living room and turned on the TV. He had asked his father to record the 100-metres final – his final. And here it was.

He fast-forwarded through the beginning. He didn't want to watch himself being disqualified. He just wanted to watch the race.

So there they were: seven runners in the Olympic final when there should have been eight. And a gaping hole in Lane Seven. Bolt got a bad start. That made Danny smile. But then he caught the rest of the field. No surprises there. Bolt was brilliant, beautiful and strong with his trademark long strides. Again Bolt seemed strangely different from everyone else, as if the mechanics of his body had been put together differently.

The medals: gold to Bolt. It had to be, didn't it? Silver: Ryan van Zyl. Danny hated that. He despised van Zyl. Bronze: Deon Francis.

Deon! Bronze! For the first time in twenty-four hours, Danny felt a glimmer of real, genuine happiness. So Flat 32 did get its medal.

Danny knew he couldn't keep licking his wounds and feeling sorry for himself for very much longer.

The next day he was happy, though, to see Ant.

And he had a long chat with his father and mother. And Ricky kept close to him. Ricky seemed to understand best how he was feeling.

Everyone was lovely to him and full of support. And they all told him he had done so well. Danny himself still felt he was a failure and he would probably never stop feeling that way. But everyone else told him that they were proud, that it was a truly astonishing achievement for an eighteen-year-old to reach the Olympic final.

And then, midway through the afternoon, a package came for him. It was sent by Team GB and it contained all the items he had left behind when he ran away from the stadium. In particular, it contained his phone and, with it, over a hundred texts from friends and teammates.

The message from everyone was the same. 'Be proud!' Everyone said it. Deon, Max, Spike. Everyone he cared about.

Danny liked that. He liked that a lot. He read and reread them.

Eventually, he was forced to emerge briefly from his room. He had no choice, his mother told him. And late that night, there was a knock at the door. Ricky came to tell him that someone had come to see him and he insisted on seeing him and he would not go away until he had spoken to him. It was Charles Perryman.

When Danny got downstairs, Perryman was

sitting in the living room with a cup of tea in his hand, chatting to his father. His father quickly exited the room, leaving Danny and Perryman together on their own.

'How are you, Danny?' Perryman asked.

'Pretty low,' Danny replied. 'About as low as I've ever been.'

'OK, Danny, I understand. But you've got to stop feeling sorry for yourself now. You can't just run away like this. I didn't pick you for the team so you could disappear the minute something went wrong.'

'I'm sorry, Mr Perryman,' Danny said. 'I didn't mean to let you down. I didn't want to let anyone down. But my Olympics are over.'

'No, they're not, Danny. They most definitely are not over. We need you back.'

'I don't understand, Mr Perryman. My Olympics are gone.'

'No, Danny. We need you in the relay team. You joined the ranks so fast that I never thought of using you in the relay. You've never practised with the team. It seemed too much of a risk. But we've just had an injury. One of the boys is down. We need you, Danny. We have a chance of a medal, a good chance. But without you we've got no chance at all. What do you think?'

Danny sighed. He felt emotionally drained, exhausted, finished. But how could he possibly say no?

'OK, Mr Perryman,' he said. 'I'm in. And I swear to you that this time I will not let you down.'

And, somewhere within him, Danny suddenly became aware that actually he wanted to run again.

★ 29 ★

ONE LAST CHANCE

When he stormed out of the Olympic Park on Sunday night, Danny had no intention of coming back. None whatsoever. But on Tuesday evening he moved back into Flat 32; on Wednesday he started practising with the relay team; on Friday they came second in their heat to Usain Bolt and the Jamaicans; and on Saturday evening they were in the Olympic final.

The sprint relay is a four-man team race. Team GB would have Deon Francis running the first leg; he would hand over the baton to Tyrone Small, who had run in the 200 metres; Small would hand over to Max Donne; and then Max would hand over to Danny.

The strong favourites were the Jamaicans: Usain Bolt plus three other speed machines. Second favourites were South Africa, and behind them the United States and Great Britain.

An hour before the race, the British team practised together on the warm-up track. It felt funny for

Danny to be there. He had to stop his mind from wandering back to the last time. But that wasn't too hard. He liked being in a team. He liked Deon and the boys. And they were now looking after him like a kid brother. They especially looked out for van Zyl. They wanted to protect Danny from him; everyone knew he was a bully. Not only did they want to win themselves a medal, but they particularly wanted to beat van Zyl and the South Africans.

There was one man who Danny had not seen much of since the previous Sunday – Spike, the man who Danny truly believed was the best coach in the world. Spike loved speed and he loved Danny, but he hated the relay. It was running in the relay that ended his own career and he always found the relays hard to watch. So Danny was surprised when Spike came and joined them at the warm-up track.

'Didn't think I would see you here, Spike,' Danny said.

'I know, I know,' Spike replied. 'It wasn't easy. But I had to come. I'm sorry I haven't brought the chess-board, but I had to see you.' They moved away from the rest of the team and sat on the side of the track together. 'I just wanted to tell you, Dan, that today is the first time I will have watched a relay live since my own career ended. I cannot stand them. But, much as I cannot stand them, I'm more desperate to see you run in one. In the Olympic final. You deserve a medal, Speedboy. Have you brought your speed today, Speedboy?'

'I think so, Spike.'

'Good. Because you'll need it. You'll need nothing else. Because you're ready. Today is your day. I want you to know that. Van Zyl has been so busy boasting these last few days he thinks he's better than he really is. I don't think he'll have a chance of matching you today. Today is your day, Dan. I'll be in the stands and so will your parents, your brother Ricky, and your friends, and so will thousands of people who so want you to do well. But don't think about us. Just think of Uncle Carl and Uncle Jesse. And then you'll be fine. Good luck, Speedboy.'

Danny watched as Spike got up and walked away. His limp seemed more exaggerated today. Maybe that was because it was relay day.

Before they went into the stadium, Deon gathered the four of them together in a huddle. Deon had turned himself into the team captain and he was good at it. Danny respected him. Deon seemed strong, reliable and not the sort of guy to be disqualified by a false start.

'Listen, boys,' Deon said, 'when we go into that stadium in a minute, it'll be for the very last time. Our last chance. The end of our Olympics. The end of the London Olympics. This is it. So don't leave any energy in your legs. I want to see it all out there on the track. Come on, boys! This is our chance! Our last chance. Let's make this the race of our lives!'

And, with that, they marched purposefully to the stadium. Suddenly, Danny felt good and confident. He recognized that feeling – the feeling of warmth running like a warm tap through his veins. He didn't feel nervous, not like the last time he was in here, not at all. *I've got it back*, he thought to himself. *I've got it!*

The team then separated and walked to their appointed positions around the track. Danny went to the place of the third handover and he smiled when he realized who he would be up against: not only Usain Bolt but Ryan van Zyl.

Good. Danny felt ready now. Van Zyl was just the last of his doubters. His schoolmates, his dad, the media – they'd all doubted his ability. And van Zyl was the last in the queue. *Good.* Danny felt strong. He felt it was time, at last, to prove the remaining doubters wrong.

He went straight over to Bolt and shook his hand. 'It's good to see you back,' Bolt said. Danny liked that.

There were no such pleasantries with van Zyl. The South African smiled his gold-glinted, toothy grin at Danny as he walked over. But Danny was ready for him this time. 'Hey, little boy,' van Zyl snarled, 'I thought you were too scared to run in the Olympics.'

'Well, you thought wrong,' Danny replied. 'But the main reason I came back was because I was looking forward so much to kicking your butt.' And for the first time since Danny had met him, van Zyl said nothing back. Nothing at all.

The runners lined up in their lanes and waited. Danny watched Deon in the blocks. He felt his heart beating, but he felt that reassuring warmth too. *Uncle Carl and Uncle Jesse*, he said to himself. *Uncle Carl and Uncle Jesse.*

Bang!

The gun went off and Deon did too; he got a good start, a great start. As he approached Tyrone, he was behind the Jamaicans, nearly level with the South Africans and ahead of the rest of the field.

Deon passed the baton to Tyrone and the handover was clean. Tyrone took off like a bullet down the back straight, but could make no headway against the Jamaicans or the South Africans. Great Britain were third, clearly third. *Come on, Tyrone! Come on, Tyrone!*

Tyrone handed over to Max and suddenly Great Britain were second. The Jamaicans were no longer running. They had dropped the baton; they were out of the race! *Come on, Max, we're second! Come on, Max!*

When Max approached Danny, there were two races going on and the Jamaicans were in neither of them. The first race was between South Africa and

Great Britain for the gold medal. The second was between the rest of the field as they battled it out for bronze. It was Danny against van Zyl for gold. The crowd was deafening, but Danny couldn't hear it; he could only concentrate on Max. He felt more focused and more ready than he had ever felt in his entire running life.

Danny felt that flush of warmth for the last time as Max thrust the baton into his hand. Van Zyl was half a metre ahead of Danny as Danny set off, powering his way down the finishing straight. *Pump it, Dan, high legs, pump.*

20 metres gone and Danny was not cutting into van Zyl's lead.

30 metres: he could still get no closer to van Zyl. *Come on, Dan, keep your rhythm, pump and keep your rhythm.*

50 metres: still the small gap remained.

60 metres: was van Zyl tiring? Danny felt he was edging closer.

70 metres: he was almost on van Zyl's shoulder. Ahead of them on the big stadium screen, they could both see the gap closing. Van Zyl seemed to respond and get stronger, but Danny kicked again.

80 metres: *keep strong, Danny. Pump it, maintain rhythm.* Suddenly, they were side by side. Danny felt stronger, stronger than ever.

90 metres: van Zyl looked across to Danny. Big mistake. Never look, everyone knows that, because it will only slow you down. Never look. But the

expression on van Zyl's face said it all: he looked scared. Danny did not see this; he only had eyes for the line. He stretched forward his shoulders and dipped for it.

100 metres: he was the Olympic champion. He and Deon and Tyrone and Max. And he only knew this because, within seconds, the other three had joined him at the finish and were jumping all over him.

'Champions! Olympic champions!' Deon shouted. 'Danny, you made us Olympic champions!'

★ 30 ★

THE END

What do you do when your dream has just come true? What do you do when you have just won the Olympics?

The answer is you get your medal.

But first you have to talk to the people from BBC TV, and then the people from BBC radio, and then you have to talk to people from TV stations in America and Australia and China and Japan and, it seemed, pretty much every country in the world that Danny had heard of.

They all wanted to ask so many questions. 'Is it true you're still at school?' 'Is it true you live near here?' 'Is your father really a postman?' 'Do you think you'll beat Usain Bolt one day?' 'When will you beat Usain Bolt?' 'Are you going to be a postman one day too?'

Some of the questions were funny. Some were just silly. But Danny didn't mind. His dream had come true. All he wanted now was his medal.

He hugged Deon and then he hugged Max and

Tyrone. He wanted to hug his mum and dad and Ricky, and Spike too. He wanted to share this moment with them. But when you have won the Olympics, he discovered, you cannot do what you want. Olympic champions do what they are told.

All he wanted was a medal. And to show it to his family. But, after talking to all the TV reporters, he was told he had to go into a press conference to talk to more journalists.

The press conference room was under the Olympic Stadium and it was huge. It was bigger than the school hall at Newham Secondary. There was an army of cameramen at the back, and every seat in front of them was filled. There must have been about 250 people in there. *Who are they all?* Danny wondered. He felt slightly shy, slightly nervous. He recognized Pete O'Byrne, the guy from *The Times*, who had said he was too young to do well at the Olympics, Jenny Nicholas, from the *Daily Express*, who had also said he was too young. But no one else.

They started asking questions and Danny and his teammates tried to answer them.

A guy with an American accent asked: 'Is this the best day of your life?' Danny looked at Deon, Tyrone and Max and they laughed and then, exactly at the same time, they all said, 'Yes!'

And then they were asked about whether they felt proud, and they all said yes.

The next question was from Jenny Nicholas. 'Now

you've won your Olympic gold, Danny, at the age of eighteen,' she said, 'is there anyone in the world who can beat you in four years' time at the next Olympics?'

'I don't know,' he answered, 'it's impossible to say. I don't know if Usain will still be competing then.' And then he stopped and thought for a minute and came up with a much better answer. 'But there is one guy who I've raced many times and never beaten.'

'Who is that?' asked Jenny Nicholas.

'My brother. His name's Ricky. In my world, he's always been the fastest guy I know.'

The journalists went quiet momentarily and, when they could see that Danny was serious, they all scribbled fast into their notebooks.

And then, just when everyone was quiet, Danny leaned forward: 'Do you think I could ask you guys a question?'

The audience all nodded. They smiled. They seemed surprised. 'OK, thanks,' Danny said. 'When can I get my medal?'

This triggered laughter all around the room. Danny liked that, but he wanted an answer too. Eventually, Jenny Nicholas, who had been giggling loudly, told him: 'You're due up in thirty minutes!'

Half an hour later, Danny, Deon, Max and Tyrone stood waiting. The Americans, who won bronze, chatted to them happily. But the South Africans kept their distance and Danny chuckled to himself because, whenever he looked at van Zyl, the South African would look away.

There was an announcement inside the stadium: '100-metres relay, men, medal ceremony.' This was followed by a trumpet blast and then the South Africans, followed by the Britons and the Americans, were led through to the medal podium in the stadium where the crowds screamed their applause.

Danny looked around. He so wanted to see his parents and Ricky. But all he could see were 80,000 people clapping.

They were told to stand up on the podium and, at this stage, Danny could feel his heart beating fast. He had Max on his left and Deon on his right and all four of them put their arms round each other's shoulders.

They applauded as the Americans were given their bronze medals. They applauded again when the South Africans got theirs – but not quite so heartily. And finally, it was their turn. First Max, then Danny, then Deon and then Tyrone. The medal felt nice and heavy. Danny looked at it; it seemed the most beautiful thing he had seen in all his life.

'How many more of these are you going to get, Dan?' Deon said jokingly, as they stood to attention for the national anthem.

Danny felt proud; he felt amazing. He watched

the Union Jack flag being raised on the flagpole for gold medal-winners, and he sang loudly as 'God Save the Queen' was played.

He looked round the stadium and there, clearly, fifty metres to his right, he spotted them. His mum, his dad, Ricky. Only now did he feel tears welling up in his eyes. His Olympic dream had come true.

100-METRE FINAL STATISTICS

HISTORY OF THE WORLD 100-METRES RECORD

10.6 – Don Lippincott (USA) – 6 July 1912

10.4 – Charlie Paddock (USA) – 23 April 1921

10.3 – Percy Williams (Canada) – 9 August 1930

10.2 – Jesse Owens (USA) – 20 June 1936

10.1 – Willie Williams (USA) – 3 August 1956

10.0 – Armin Hary (West Germany) – 21 June 1960

9.95 – Jim Hines (USA) – 14 October 1968

9.93 – Calvin Smith (USA) – 3 July 1983

9.92 – Carl Lewis (USA) – 24 September 1988

9.90 – Leroy Burrell (USA) – 14 June 1991

9.86 – Carl Lewis (USA) – 25 August 1991

9.85 – Leroy Burrell (USA) – 6 July 1994

9.84 – Donovan Bailey (Canada) – 27 July 1996

9.79 – Maurice Greene (USA) – 16 June 1999

9.77 – Asafa Powell (Jamaica) – 14 June 2005

9.74 – Asafa Powell (Jamaica) – 9 September 2007

9.72 – Usain Bolt (Jamaica) – 31 May 2008

9.69 – Usain Bolt (Jamaica) – 16 August 2008

9.58 – Usain Bolt (Jamaica) – 16 August 2009

Ben Johnson (Canada) broke the world record twice. He improved it from 9.93 seconds to 9.83 in August 1987, and he set it even lower in the Olympic final in 1988 when he ran 9.79. However, both records were wiped from the record books when it was later discovered that he had been cheating by using drugs to help him run faster.

Tim Montgomery (USA) lowered the world record from 9.79 seconds to 9.78 on 14 September 2002. However, his time was also wiped from the record books when it was later discovered that he too had been cheating by using drugs to help him run faster.

The times in the list become more precise from Jim Hines's record in 1968 because that was when electronic timing was introduced. Before then, world records were all timed by stopwatch.

Usain Bolt's average speed when he broke the world record in Berlin in 2009 was 23.49 mph.

The fastest land animals are:

- Cheetah: 70 mph
- Pronghorn antelope: 61 mph
- Lion: 50 mph
- Wildebeest: 50 mph
- Thomson's gazelle: 50 mph

However, even these do not compare well with the fastest bird, the peregrine falcon, at 200 mph, or even the fastest fish, the swordfish, at 68 mph.

THE OLYMPIC 100-METRES WINNERS

1896 ATHENS OLYMPICS
Thomas Burke (USA) won in 12.0 seconds. This was the first 100-metre final in the modern Olympics.

1900 PARIS OLYMPICS
Frank Jarvis (USA) won in 11.0 seconds. He won when the favourite, Arthur Duffey, strained a tendon in the final.

1904 ST LOUIS OLYMPICS
Charles 'Archie' Hahn (USA) won in 11.0 seconds. Hahn was known as 'the Milwaukee Meteor'.

1906 ATHENS OLYMPICS
Charles 'Archie' Hahn (USA) won in 11.2 seconds. Hahn later wrote a book called *How to Sprint*.

1908 LONDON OLYMPICS

Reginald Walker (South Africa) won in 10.8 seconds. Walker was a nineteen-year-old clerk from Durban. He was coached by Sam Mussabini, who also coached Harold Abrahams, the 1924 winner.

1912 STOCKHOLM OLYMPICS

Ralph Craig (USA) won in 10.8 seconds. Craig would return in 1948, the next time the Olympics were held in London, as a member of the American sailing team.

1920 ANTWERP OLYMPICS

Charles Paddock (USA) won in 10.8 seconds. Before the final, Paddock was given a glass of sherry and a raw egg by his coach, supposedly to help him go faster. He died in a plane crash in the Second World War.

1924 PARIS OLYMPICS

Harold Abrahams (GB) won in 10.6 seconds. Arthur Porritt, the New Zealander who came third, later became the official surgeon of the British royal family.

1928 AMSTERDAM OLYMPICS

Percy Williams (Canada) won in 10.8 seconds. When Williams got back home to Canada, he was given a sports car as a reward for his achievement.

1932 LOS ANGELES OLYMPICS

Thomas 'Eddie' Tolan (USA) won in 10.38 seconds. One of the runners in Heat Two of this event was Liu Changchun, who was the first Chinese athlete ever to compete in the Games.

1936 BERLIN OLYMPICS

Jesse Owens won in 10.3 seconds. After becoming famous at the Olympics, to try to make some money, Owens ran in public races against horses, dogs and motorbikes.

1948 LONDON OLYMPICS

W. Harrison Dillard (USA) won in 10.3 seconds. Dillard's hero was Owens. He met Owens once, and Owens gave him his first pair of running shoes.

1952 HELSINKI OLYMPICS

Lindy Remigino (USA) won in 10.4 seconds. This race was so close that Remigino, convinced that he had been beaten, congratulated Herbert McKenley for winning. When he was told the actual result, he was astonished.

1956 MELBOURNE OLYMPICS

Bobby Joe Morrow (USA) won in 10.5 seconds. The bronze medallist, Hector Hogan, was an Australian and he died of leukaemia four years later.

1960 ROME OLYMPICS

Armin Hary (West Germany) won in 10.2 seconds. Hary was the first German ever to win gold in an Olympic track event.

1964 TOKYO OLYMPICS

Robert Hayes (USA) won in 10.0 seconds. Hayes would later become a professional American footballer and played for nine years for the Dallas Cowboys.

1968 MEXICO CITY OLYMPICS

Jim Hines (USA) won in 9.95 seconds. Hines's medal was later stolen from his house by burglars. He then placed an ad in the local newspaper asking to have it back and it was returned to him in the post.

1972 MUNICH OLYMPICS

Valeriy Borzov (Russia) won in 10.14 seconds. Borzov nearly missed his quarter-final because he fell asleep inside the stadium. He only just made it to the start-line in time.

1976 MONTREAL OLYMPICS

Hasely Crawford (Trinidad) won in 10.06 seconds. Crawford was Trinidad's first Olympic champion and had six calypso songs written in his honour.

1980 MOSCOW OLYMPICS

Allan Wells (GB) won in 10.25 seconds. Wells was coached by his wife, Margot, who has also coached rugby players, including Danny Cipriani, Paul Sackey and James Haskell.

1984 LOS ANGELES OLYMPICS

Carl Lewis (USA) won in 9.99 seconds. This was Lewis's first gold medal. He would win four in Los Angeles and nine Olympic golds altogether.

1988 SEOUL OLYMPICS

Carl Lewis (USA) won in 9.92 seconds. A very famous race. Ben Johnson, the Canadian, actually won by a very long way, in 9.79 seconds, but he was later found to have taken drugs and so was stripped of his medal and Lewis was made the winner.

1992 BARCELONA OLYMPICS

Linford Christie (GB) won in 9.96 seconds. Christie was thirty-two years old, the oldest Olympic 100-metre winner ever.

1996 ATLANTA OLYMPICS

Donovan Bailey (Canada) won in 9.84 seconds. Linford Christie, by now thirty-six years old, was in the final to defend his title, but he was disqualified for false-starting. He was absolutely furious.

2000 SYDNEY OLYMPICS
Maurice Greene (USA) won in 9.87 seconds. The silver medallist was Ato Boldon of Trinidad, who was Greene's training partner.

2004 ATHENS OLYMPICS
Justin Gatlin (USA) won in 9.85 seconds. Gatlin would later try to follow other sprinters and play professional American football. However, he never made the grade.

2008 BEIJING OLYMPICS
Usain Bolt (Jamaica) won in 9.69 seconds. This was a world record, but it was particularly amazing because he slowed down in the last 20 metres and, when he crossed the line, he was almost dancing.

WANT MORE ACTION? MORE ADVENTURE? MORE ADRENALIN?

GET INTO PUFFIN'S ADVENTURE BOOKS FOR BOYS

It all started with a Scarecrow.

Puffin is seventy years old.
Sounds ancient, doesn't it? But Puffin has never been
so lively. We're always on the lookout for the next big
idea, which is how it began all those years ago.

Penguin Books was a big idea from the mind of
a man called Allen Lane, who in 1935 invented
the quality paperback and changed the world.
**And from great Penguins, great Puffins grew,
changing the face of children's books forever.**

The first four Puffin Picture Books were hatched in 1940 and the
first Puffin story book featured a man with broomstick arms called
Worzel Gummidge. In 1967 Kaye Webb, Puffin Editor, started the
Puffin Club, promising to **'make children into readers'**.
She kept that promise and over 200,000 children became
devoted Puffineers through their quarterly instalments of
Puffin Post, which is now back for a new generation.

Many years from now, we hope you'll look back and
remember Puffin with a smile. **No matter what your age
or what you're into, there's a Puffin for everyone.**
The possibilities are endless, but one thing is for sure:
whether it's a picture book or a paperback, a sticker book
or a hardback, **if it's got that little Puffin
on it – it's bound to be good.**

PUFFIN BOOKS

RUNNING
FOR GOLD

Slot is chief sports reporter on *The Times*. He
ree times been named Sports Feature Writer of
ar and three times Sports News Reporter
Year.

9113000077675

Books by Owen Slot

Running for Gold
Cycling for Gold